BRISBANE RIVER ANTI-MEMOIR

Philosophy of An Aquaphile

by MARTIN KNOX

PUBLICATION DETAILS: PREVIOUS BOOK

First Published – 2023
This edition published 2023 by Novel Ideas
Brisbane, Qld Australia

Copyright © Martin Knox 2023

 A catalogue record for this work is available from the National Library of Australia

The National Library of Australia Cataloguing-in-Publication

Creator: Knox, Martin, author.

Title: Bribane RiverAnti-Memoir – Philosophy of an Aquaphile / Martin Knox.

ISBN: 978-0-6489930-6-3 (paperback)

Subjects: Fictional memoir.
                   Anti-memoir.

All rights reserved

No part of this publication may be reproduced, stored in a retrieval system, or transmitted in any form or by any means, electronic, mechanical, photocopying, recording or otherwise, without the prior written permission of the author.
This is a work of fiction. All names, characters, countries, provinces, cities, organisations, government positions and incidents are either the product of the author's imagination or are used fictitiously. Any resemblance to actual persons living or dead, businesses, companies, events, or locales is coincidental, or for purposes of satire and fiction narration, without fear, favour or affiliation with any organisation or cause.

DISCLAIMER
All rights reserved
No part of this book may be reproduced in any form, by photocopying or by any electronic or mechanical means, including information storage or retrieval systems, without prior permission in writing from both the copyright owner and the publisher of this book.
Names of people and places have been changed. Resemblance of characters to real people, of certain places to real places and events to real events, is unintended. Some events have been compressed and dialogue has been recreated. Several fictional characters have been introduced for interlocutory purposes.
The author asserts his moral rights.

Typeset in Times New Roman 12pt by Donna Munro Graphic Design.
Cover artwork by Donna Munro Graphic Design. Cover photo credits to Brisbane City Marketing and Yogi Purnama.
Printed and bound in Australia by Ingram Spark.
Copyright © Martin Knox 2023
htttps://www.martinknox.com
martinknx46@gmail.com

DEDICATION

This book is dedicated to my family: Zoe, Tessa, Amani, Uly and Dorian, hoping that my writing will help them to respect, understand and conserve the World they will inherit, with care for living things, especially humans, animals and environments, through philosophies of freedom, voluntary responsibility, reason and science. I appreciate their support but opinions and any errors are my own.

ACKNOWLEDGEMENTS

I am indebted to the following.

Donna Munro has looked after the formatting, cover design and publishing.

Miles Whiticker encouraged my idea to frame my investigation of river flooding within Heidegger's philosophy of phenomenology.

The University of Queensland's Student Philosophy Association's Sam Adams led reading of Guy De Bord's The Society of the Spectacle which was my background reading for understanding government of the Brisbane River.

The University of the Third Age's discussion group Matter's Arising, led by Garth Sherman and Leonard Evans, was a forum where group member's ideas were shared and opinions aired.

Dave Jones, discussed some of the ideas and philosophies with me, between songs with our guitars.

Seville Road Writers Group led by Nancy Cox-Millner and Robyn Martin. provided me with feedback on my writing.

Sunnybank Hills Writers Group read my drafts carefully and critically, exploring my ideas.

GENRE

In his book Anti-memoirs, 1967, Andre' Malraux wrote:

'What is a man? A miserable pile of secrets.'

There are certain things people expect from reading a memoir and those often are not the same things I expect when I read an anti-memoir. Memoir readers tend to expect a narrative arc, which goes more or less smoothly from A to B. On the way they expect to find something new, with a before and an after – an epiphany. My book doesn't fit that mould. Real lives are lived more messily. My book has revelations throughout, more of lived experience than of character development.

This book is an anti-memoir, with the author's recollections of living beside a river and people he could have met, with other luck, who are introduced to help him tell his story. I wrote my story not wanting to dwell on the question Who is the narrator? Because authenticity in many passages is derived from wide sources, rather than from the anti-memoirist's narrowly lived experiences.

Anti-memoirs are books that 'de-self' the writer. In some places, I have taken myself out of it, while still having my protagonist use the first-person voice to relate the physical world, with contrived characters and faked conversations, without disclosing much about myself. This anti-memoir is more about the reader than the author and his associates. When you read it, hopefully you will think to yourself 'That's something I've thought, too', or 'That's how I feel', or 'Now I know how I would feel if I had lived by that river.'

AUTHOR BIO

Martin Knox grew up on a farm in Somerset England. He graduated as a chemical engineer from Birmingham University and worked in the petroleum industry in Canada. He researched alternative systems of government at Imperial College, London. He emigrated to Australia and was employed in mining development. He became a high school teacher and wrote science textbooks published by the Queensland Department of Education.

This book is his seventh novel published. He has been writing fiction novels full-time since 2013: speculative, love, politics, crime, sport, totalitarianism and satires. He is involved in public policy-making, has proposed an underground railway for Brisbane and a new paradigm for climate science. He discusses current issues at U3A and has studied philosophy with students at the University of Queensland.

He writes letters, plays the guitar, sings badly and walks by the river.

He is divorced with children and grandchildren.

LIST OF NOVELS PUBLISHED

Available from Amazon in Australia, USA, UK and Canada

The Grass is Always Browner (2011)
Love Straddle (2014)
Presumed Dead (2018)
$hort of Love (2019)
Time is Gold (2020)
Animal Farm 2 (2021)
Turkeys not Bees (2022)
Brisbane River Anti-Memoir (2023)

GLOSSARY

( ) reference listed at the end.
AEP Annual Exceedance Probability
AEP Annual exceedance probability
AHD Australian Height Datum
Aquaphile water-loving person
BCC Brisbane City Council
CBD City Business District
Cumec Cubic metres per second
Dasein existence 'being there'
DFL Defined Flood Level
ENSO El Nino Southern Oscillation
Existential free and inherently responsible
Existentiell refers to the aspects of the world which are identifiable as particular delimited questions or issues,
Facticity the quality or condition of being fact.
Fallenness quality of being fallen or degraded.
FSL Full Supply Level
ML Megalitre
Ontical from the point of view of real existence.
Seqwater Southeast Queensland Water Authority.
Thrownness exposed to different life situations

CONTENTS

	PROLOGUE		
	PART 1 WATERSIDE LIVING		**PART 4 REDUCING FLOODING**
1	First Impressions	30	Phenomenology
2	Logan River	31	Dasein
3	Water	32	Bracketing
4	Superhero	33	Erosion
5	Island Home	34	Dredging
6	Deciding Where to Live	35	Politics
7	Geological Origins	36	Dam Storage
8	Learning the Ropes	37	Modelling
9	Living by the River		**PART 5 THE FUTURE**
10	Riverside Community	38	Alternatives
11	Southbank Hub	39	Agreement
	PART 2 BRISBANE RIVER HISTORY	40	Occupation and Affection
12	Indigenous History	41	Carry On
13	Climate	42	Flood Proofing Resilience
14	Drought	43	Planning and Preparation
15	Cyclones	44	New Bridge
16	Flooding Rains	45	River Obstruction
17	After the 1893 Flood	46	Down the Tube
18	1974 Flood	47	Climate Change
19	2011 Flood	48	Sea Level Rise
	PART 3 SCIENCE	49	Brisbane Sailing Port
20	Who was to Blame?		**PART 6 AQUAPHLIA**
21	Aftermath	50	Risks People Tolerate
22	Advantage of Being There	51	Daring
23	Double Up	52	Escape Plan
24	2022 Flood	53	Water Voles
25	Flood Victims	54	Being There
26	Dam Failure	55	What has Potential?
27	Grania	56	Sense of an Ending
28	Natural Flooding		
29	Limitations of Scientific Analysis		

FIGURES AND PHOTOS

FIGURE	TITLE	PAGE
Fig 1	Figure 1. Map of Brisbane River Catchment.	86
Fig 2	Heights of Flood Peaks in Brisbane.	188
Fig 3	Brisbane Circle underground railway proposal.	254

PHOTO	CAPTION	
1	Queen Street looking towards Petrie Bight during the 1893 floods in Brisbane.	2
2	We built a home beside the Logan River.	10
3	We bathed in our swimming hole.	12
4	We sailed our trailer sloop in Moreton Bay.	28
5	Our house on Macleay Island in Moreton Bay.	30
6	Orleigh Park.	90
7	The author pointing to black mark from the 2011 flood peak. On the balcony apron.	101
8	Orleigh Park flooded taken from Unit 2 balcony March 1st 2022	109
9	Atrium Apartments. Unit 2 is on the first floor with Unit 4 above	121
10	Dredge Woomera arrives in Gladstone, Queensland.	193
11	Orleigh Estate where homes were washed away in 1893.	245

PROLOGUE

Howard was a colleague and friend of mine, when I worked at Wattle Mines. I had kept up with him since, playing tennis weekly. Like me, he was an engineer, interested in colonial history and public policy. He had written a history of mining in Queensland and I asked him to help me find information on the history of the Brisbane River for my anti-memoir.

'When was the worst ever flood of the Brisbane River?' I asked Howard.

'There were bad floods in the 1840s,' Howard said. 'In 1891, when Brisbane had 100,000 inhabitants, the river rose to 5.33 metres. But a day of reckoning came in 1893. The Port Office gauge on January 29, 1893 reached 8.35 metres, the highest flood ever recorded, 3 metres above the 1890 levels, claiming four lives and leaving thousands homeless.'

I looked up the rainfall statistics.

'Average annual rainfall in Brisbane was 1,100 millilitres,' I said. 'The total for 25 days in February 1893 was 1,000 millimetres, the wettest month on record. The mean values for January and February were 160 millimetres.

Howard said: 'A landowner beside the upper Brisbane River recorded the impact.

> '(I) heard a tremendous roar like a train coming out of a tunnel [. . .] I looked up the river and saw a wall of water coming down 50 feet high, it struck the cliff and shook the house [. . .] fully 300 yards back from the cliff.'
> Henry Plantagenet Somerset. (1, p23)

'Two weeks later, on 15th February the river level was back up to 8.09 metres,' he said, continuing to read from his research notes. 'It was a devastating disaster. Fifty people were drowned and many thousands were homeless.'

The central business district was flooded and rowboats plied on Queen Street, the main shopping street.

Queen Street looking towards Petrie Bight during the 1893 floods in Brisbane (Sourced: John Oxley Library)

'The weather was extraordinary,' I said. 'Two separate cyclones had delivered extremely heavy rain. Brisbane endured three floods, separated by just a few weeks. At Orleigh Parade, where I now live, an estimated 30 houses were completely washed away on Saturday 4th February, complete with all their contents.

'Many of these houses, along with others being carried down the river, smashed against the pylons of Victoria Bridge, which eventually gave way with the northern half of the bridge collapsing,' Howard said. 'Many other buildings impacted the bows of ships moored along the river, with crunching heard across town.

'According to one report, the houses destroyed were 'particularly beautiful and costly residences. Just two weeks later, a further flood carried away more houses. Afterwards, not even the stumps remained. Only one house was left.'

'Could a flood of that magnitude occur again?' I asked.

'Why not?' Howard said.

'They have built two dams to prevent it,' I said defensively.

'That could be wishful thinking,' he said.

PART 1

WATERSIDE LIVING

CHAPTER 1 FIRST IMPRESSIONS

It was 1965 and I was 19 when I glimpsed a lifestyle I wanted and set a goal for my future. I was at Windermere in England's Lake District, admiring waterfront mansions, luxurious amidst tranquil beauty. They contrasted with my childhood home on a farm in Somerset, by the sea, rustic and utilitarian.

'How good it would be, after seeing the world, to retire from the fray to a place like this,' I said to a student companion.

Exclusivity was a small part of it. I wanted to live beside water surrounded by wild hills.

In the years following, I emigrated to a job in Canada, travelled in Latin America, studied at London University and lived in Australia. My interest in living near water continued and I became keen on sailing.

I left the UK partly for adventure and partly from alienation by nanny state overreach, restricting opportunity for my engineering training.

'The bureaucracy of collectivism is too limiting,' I said. 'I need freedom, competition and individualism.'

I walked ashore from the liner *Australis* in Sydney, with Carol, my Australian wife and our baby Sarah, in 1976, when I was 30. On the ship, immigration officials had indoctrinated us to get jobs, to buy a house, have barbecues, go to the beach and pay our taxes.

Carol's parents collected us from the quay. As we drove along the highway north from Sydney, I was shocked by the dry conditions. When I turned on the TV at our overnight motel in Grafton, a small town, I was appalled to see a farmer shooting his emaciated livestock. It reminded me of photos from the liberation of Auschwitz.

'The animals are starved and without water,' I said to the receptionist. 'Does this happen often?'

'Almost every year,' she said.

'. . . several times usually,' my father-in-law put in.

'How do the farmers keep going?'

'After rain, there's food,' he said. 'The animals get fat and breed like crazy. They can't be stopped.'

'Aren't there limits on numbers of farm animals?' I asked.

'Yes. Droughts cull the excess. Either that or they drown in floods.'

'Overstocking, I call it. How cruel is that?'

I knew it was rude to criticize when you are a visitor, but the condition of the animals was shocking.

'No-one likes it, but it's nature's way,' said my father-in-law. 'Don't let it bother you, er, Chance.'

Chance is my name.

'Why did they call you Chance?' asked my mother-in-law.

'My mother was sure she would have a girl. When I was born a boy, my father said it was chance. 'It's a name that will bring him good fortune,' he said.

'It's worked for me so far,' I said. I was usually optimistic and I appreciated that I had had many opportunities.

We drove on north, along the Pacific Highway.

'Why are the highway and railway bridges constructed from timber?' I asked.

'Flood water comes up over the roads. Stone bridges would block water from flowing under them.'

It was hard to believe this dry country could ever have that much water on it.

Australian conditions were unlike those on my family's farm in the UK. Within a short time of arriving in Australia, I had encountered drought, bushfires, cyclonic winds and temperatures in the 40s. But it was several years before I experienced flooding rains.

In the UK, the weather was more predictable. Farmers could usually count on raising and selling their animals and crops. The major variation was the amount of subsidy paid by the government. Returns in the UK were not large, but they were reliable.

Harsh conditions and disasters occurred in Brisbane infrequently. There had been a flood in Brisbane in 1974, but a few years later most people had forgotten it. The climate was usually congenial, allowing an outdoor lifestyle with wonderful parks, forests and the best beaches in the world.

For several years after we arrived, Queenslanders regaled us with stories of deadly snakes, poisonous insects and lethal fishes. We were hesitant to explore the bush at first, until we realised that scaring immigrants was part of the culture. Newcomers' fears entertained the locals and the spinning of unlikely yarns was an art, called 'rubbishing'.

Understandably, Australians styled their homeland as 'the lucky country'. Extreme conditions were played down and adverse conditions could be avoided with forethought and precautions.

Today, after living in Brisbane for 46 years, my first impression of a harsh land has mellowed. There are hazards but much that is good. I am fortunate to live here. I haven't suffered flooding of my home nor bushfires. My resilience has developed as I have gradually become habituated, by trial and error, facing catastrophes with a will to survive. When I arrived from England, in this dry land, I had no inkling of how riverside living would dominate the next 46 years of my journey through life, until today.

I had graduated from university as a chemical engineer. Later, I had spent four years as a research student in management science. My employers liked my curiosity and imagination and let me loose to explore whatever took my fancy so long as there was the prospect of developing a profitable project from it. My managers didn't understand my skills but I gained a reputation for strategic analysis that they used to leverage their own promotions.

My bosses asked me to investigate ideas they had and my investigations would unfold opportunities.

'If you don't have the answer yet, you need to do more work,' one said.

I explored at my own speed, until I arrived at actionable conclusions.

My analyses progressed from design of chemical plants, to coal export projects and alternative mining methods. As an analyst, I assumed freedom to investigate hallowed ground, confronting icons and promoting new ideas that were sometimes perceived as heresies. The company wanted a lackey, not a creative engineer like me. I made a break away and became a high school science teacher. I analysed teaching and learning methods, wrote student textbooks, developed online teaching and rationalised assessment methods.

My career teaching science succeeded in baffling school managers, because I wanted success for every student in my class, with lifelong learning. I liked to teach theories in the contexts of their discovery. I analysed relationships between ideas, developed hands on practical activities and set investigations that developed a love of science.

Since retirement I have been writing novels. I write stories about various fiction topics, applying a kaleidoscope of post-structural philosophical viewpoints, especially Heidegger's existential phenomenology (4).

My work as a science teacher coincided with flooding of the Brisbane River in 2011. I investigated possible causes and mitigation methods, explaining to students what had been done and possible improvements that would reduce impacts. My interest developed into systematic exploration of the question students asked: Can flooding of the Brisbane River be prevented? The question was of most concern to those who lived beside the River, as I did. My findings are reported as a narrative in this book.

After the flood in 2022, my approach morphed into existential concern with how mechanisms for controlling floods, such as dams, could be influenced by political and technical leaders. The second part of this book looks behind the science method I used in the first part, analysing the potential of the Brisbane River by phenomenology. Responsible authorities could use my conclusions to develop technologies to reduce flooding of the Brisbane River.

Waterside living in a hot climate can have a cooling effect, but it can be offset by flooding peril. The extreme conditions can be manifest at the same time of year in Brisbane. They are opposed concerns, but individual experiences vary widely. I will attempt to find a balance in advantages and disadvantages of riverside living.

Many people are tempted to buy a home near a river. My experience could advise investment in waterside real estate. My philosophy accepts a remote possibility of disastrous flooding offset by near certainty of delightful living for decades.

CHAPTER 2: LOGAN RIVER

My perspective has changed since 46 years ago, when after emigrating from England my wife Carol and I looked for a place to live near my job in Brisbane. It was too far from the coast to live by the sea. My reflex was to search for a place to live near a river or lake. Living near water would mitigate the dry conditions, even if it meant commuting a distance between the city and waterside.

I was surprised how far I had to drive to reach a river. I had learned at school in England that Australia was the driest continent and oldest land mass, but the words did not communicate the reality of a land with rocky, leached soil and scorched vegetation. I had grown up beside the sea and the dryness of Australia came as a shock.

We built a home beside the Logan River

It was forty kilometres from Brisbane City centre, out through the sprawling suburbs into the dry bush, before we reached a place where we wanted to build a house. It was a hectare of land, with a swimming hole, overlooking the Logan River.

We bought the land and with a builder planned our dream house. A year later we moved in. After living in a terraced house in northwest London, our new home in Australia was wonderfully natural, individual and private. Our house was huge and there was room for all our hobbies and projects. We had space, lots of it.

I was 32 and drove into the city to my job as an engineer, planning mines. I commuted 40 kilometres, about an hour each way, to work. To get more time with my family, I spent my weekend leisure time at home.

Carol started a speech therapy practice in the local town, leaving baby Sarah with a minder. A year later we had another baby, Michael. We led a happy family life beside the Logan River.

'She's a bonzer river,' a local told us. 'A self-cleaning swimming pool.'

We climbed down the riverbank with our children to swim together as a family. When they were older they enjoyed hours of unsupervised fun. On hot days, neighbours came and bathed in our pool, by a house-sized outcrop of sandstone in the river bed, with water sweeping over it, scouring out a swimming hole metres deep. There was a natural cave of sandstone.

Taoists liken the gentle dance of water flowing through a serene river, to learning from past mistakes, with the profound wisdom that echoes through the ages, guiding us towards harmony and enlightenment. It was timeless and wonderfully peaceful.

On hot lazy afternoons, it was a great place to cool down, relax and talk.

'I wonder what the poor people are doing,' I said, immersed with the current gently caressing me.

'This place is alright, Chance,' a neighbour said. 'People have been coming here for 50,000 years.'

'Where did they live?' I asked.

'Holes in the riverbank, in thatched shelters,' he said, 'I reckon.'

We bathed in our swimming hole.

In Australia, prehistory, flora and fauna are not widely known, as they are in the UK. Apart from rock paintings and a few artefacts, the past was unrecorded and oral traditions were disappearing. Little was known of indigenous living before Europeans arrived in 1788. Because indigenous input was unavailable, inexpert speculation served for history.

When more rain had fallen than could be absorbed by the soil, the run-off collected in freshwater habitats which enabled plants and animals to survive in moist conditions. Riverbanks, lakes, dams, lagoons, billabongs, swamps and creeks had plants and animals living more densely than away from water.

Most of the plants growing along permanent waterways needed the continual presence of moisture. On the other hand, vegetation that colonized shallow impermanent bodies of water had strategies to survive periods of dryness. Tubers and underground rhizomes provided a food store enabling long periods of dormancy, until water returned and growth recommenced.

Melaleucas along creeks and rivers grew to ten metres with weeping branches and red flower spikes like bottle brushes.

Casuarinas had male and female trees growing to twenty metres by the waterways, with slender, green to grey-green twigs bearing minute scale-like leaves in whorls. The fruit were woody cones of ten millimetres.

Wild animals living in the area were stressed from takeover of their habitats by humans, domestic animals and pets. At first, kangaroos came up to our house, but they soon disappeared.

There was stillness about the rock pool that transcended human affairs.

Here I had time to think about my job at Wattle Mines and how to meet my manager's expectations. My assignment was to compare our company's proposed coal mine for supply to a new power station, in competition with other mines. My evaluation concluded that we had an edge and should win a multibillion dollar supply contract.

'We could lose,' said Howard, a work colleague. 'They will decide it by politics. Reasoning isn't trusted in Australia.'

'Why not?'

'People believe in leaders and parties, not ideas,' he said. 'Players won't support your project unless it will win them votes and get them re-elected.'

'It's not democratic,' I said. 'The winning project should be the best, not a project promoted by a political party on the make.'

But he was right. The government decided the power station would be constructed near a mine in the Premier's electorate. I was chagrined. It seemed like political corruption. I learned that in Queensland, government favour was needed to secure contracts. I was a planning engineer and it troubled me that my skills were superfluous.

'We almost succeeded,' my manager said. 'We came close.'

'It seems like a kick in the teeth,' I said.

'In many countries they don't even have tendering.'

It was true. We had been able to tender in Queensland, whereas in the UK our farmland had been taken for a CEGB power station, without tender, or explanation.

'Our government's mantra is 'Application equals tender,' said Howard cynically. 'Resources are allocated by favour, not by competition.'

Queensland's Premier was Joh Bjelke-Peterson, who seemed intent on state development by government hegemony.

'Politics here is different to the UK,' I said. 'Here graft makes the difference. Things get done. In the UK they don't do much, except talk.'

'The corruption here is more visible,' said Howard, 'because we don't hide it.'

'Is doing of favours, advantaging politicians, an accepted practice here?' I asked.

'When it's out in the open, it is okay,' said Howard. 'Our local economy is too small to have market competition. Insider dealing can't be avoided.'

Premier Joh alienated many people who wanted the government to be less self-interested.

At home, by the river, I had time to reflect and live in harmony with nature. In the summer we bathed in the river. Our children brought their friends there, climbing down the steep riverbank, to play for halcyon hours in the shallows under the trees. When they were young they skinny-dipped unselfconsciously and we trusted their innocence.

The act of daring to live by a river possibly developed certain of my senses with extreme sharpness, in a world with different signs where I could learn to live, talk and write, as a river person. I was inspired to begin writing letters and essays, learning to play classical guitar. I painted portraits, designed stained glass windows and made things from wood and metalwork.

The Logan River was a natural corridor for water birds. There were herons, eastern koels, plovers, and ibises with their haunting cries punctuating the night. There were others no-one could name. Foxes slunk along the riverbank hunting for rats and bandicoots. Rabbits, escaped and illegal, gambolled in the hay pastures. The riverbanks grew slender grey gums in profusion, shedding grey bark streamers and exposing white bark beneath. The trees grew fast upwards to capture the light, hung with vines.

Besides seeking a place where we lived close to water, we chose our building block because we could keep horses for our children to learn to ride. Horses became a part of our lives, our friends, for many years.

We began with a Shetland pony, Jimmy, small and round, peering from under his forelock. When Sarah outgrew him, we bought Benjamin for her. Michael took over Jimmy. Michael's legs soon grew too long and I acquired Zahidi's Pride for him, an alert part-Arab mare. She was tall and Michael was at first daunted, but he got used to climbing up and was soon galloping around.

The children went to the local pony club for Saturday meets and weekend camps. They prepared their horses in the stable yard, spending hours grooming and plaiting. They learned to avoid bites when tightening the girth and kicks when scraping mud from hocks and frogs. A well-behaved pony received bread and Jimmy got some anyway.

After several years we took Zahidi to mate with a grey Arab stallion, standing at stud on a nearby property. Amid much excitement, eleven months later she produced Taj, an inquisitive and flighty colt. Michael trained him.

'Taj isn't intelligent,' he complained. 'He doesn't learn.'

'He's intelligent enough to be a horse,' I said. 'What do you expect? You have to be patient.'

I helped him train Taj not to panic when tied up firmly, a bad habit of his mother. When her lead rope pulled taut, she would jerk back, going berserk and breaking her halter. It was a dangerous fault in her training by her previous owner and she required careful handling. When Taj was 3 months old we tied his halter firmly to a tree. He went crazy for 10 minutes and then lay down, as if dead. We untied him, repeating the treatment on successive days, until he got used to firm restraint.

Michael's and Sarah's learning from their horses was profound. They treated their horses with consideration and courtesy, like loyal friends. The bond that developed between a horse and its rider was fragile, with the rider's willpower prevailing. The girls learned self-control and maturity.

Later, when Michael went to university, he discovered girls and moved out from home. He lost interest in his horses and we sold them.

The downside of living by a river was when the river was in flood, we couldn't leave home. It was more than 10 kilometres to the nearest shop. We did most of our shopping in a weekly trip.

Settling by the Logan River had initiated us in riverside living, a preference that became a habit that conditioned choice of our next home, when we moved into the city by the Brisbane River. Part of our enjoyment was country living and the substitute that we eventually accepted was living beside a city park.

CHAPTER 3 WATER

Our river swimming hole was a delightfully peaceful place to go. The water was sparkling clean, the surface glassy and the bottom was rippled sand.

The riverbank was steep and it would be difficult to carry a pump down the steep riverbank. At first we collected water for the house from the roof gutters, but they clogged with eucalyptus leaves from overhanging trees, requiring regular clearing, or they would overflow.

We stored water in a tank and used it carefully. The roof water was insufficient and we looked for additional supply. The river water was rumoured to harbour cholera. I employed a contractor to drill a 120 metre deep bore, but the water tasted brackish, okay for sheep, but maybe borderline for us.

It didn't taste like city water and Carol was wary.

'Chance, I would like you to get the water tested.'

She was forceful, as usual and not far-sighted about where this would take us.

'It hasn't done us any harm yet,' I said. 'What if we find it's marginal? What would we do then?'

'Pump from the river.'

'It's a lot of work,' I said, 'It isn't necessary.'

'I'd rather be safe,' said Carol.

Her posture on most things, after eight years of marriage, was opposite to mine and we had moved into open conflict. She wanted traditional activities and lacked flexibility to adapt to the country environment.

'Our bore water is not unsafe,' I said. 'Borderline is safe enough. We can use it as a back-up, eking out the supply from the roof.'

For eight years we drank water from the roof diluted with bore water. There was enough, even in a drought, when we pumped a trickle from the bore. But when we needed more water for the horses, I bought a pump and began pumping from the river into a large house tank. Filling it was a demanding chore. We never had any problems with cholera. We held water in reserve from the roof and when the river was low and in stagnant pools, we drank bore water.

We had planned to grow fruit trees but there wasn't enough water for them.

Townies obtain water by turning on a tap but I had to clamber down the steep riverbank with a heavy pump on my back, to provide water for two thirsty horses. One of the children would wade out with the foot valve, to attach the intake pipe to a stake driven into the sandy bed of the river. In Winter, the water was cold, but we didn't complain. The pump couldn't be left on the riverbank for more than a few hours, or it would get legs and disappear, or be washed away in a flash flood.

It was hard work to get water, conserve it and use it frugally. In our minds the river flowed generously, supporting flora and fauna. We were river people and took our moods and essential being from it. Living there had difficulties at times, but it suited us.

Grass grew well in summer and I cut it frequently, until we had horses to graze it. We divided our block into small paddocks, resting areas grazed bare. Wee Jimmy ate continually. He could have descended from pit ponies, who hauled coal wagons in underground coal mines. His kind had worked in dark tunnels for stints of a month, or more, until they were weak from starvation. Then they were brought up to the surface and turned out to grass. The best grazers put on weight fastest and survived the cycle best. Those without stamina would go to the knacker. Jimmy's genes had survived from ponies who had put on condition rapidly. He would graze all night, quickly becoming as fat as butter.

Besides having large appetites, the horses drank a lot of water and our tanks soon emptied. The land was unconsolidated sandstone and soaked up water. There was insufficient to irrigate the fruit trees and vegetable garden and they died. Our land sloped on a river terrace, with thin, leached soil. I quit trying to grow green lawns. Keeping grass alive in patches was the best I could hope for.

We gradually found out what sort of river it was, with growing respect. In a drought, the flow seeped through the sandy river bed from pool to pool. When the river bed was dry, we could walk upriver to paddocks with cattle grazing on the banks. They were surprised to see us. Our children had rehearsed climbing the nearest tree to protect themselves from dangerous bulls. One day a horned animal charged towards us and Michael shinnied up a sapling. It was thin and slowly bent over under his weight, lowering him down to the ground, watched curiously by a harmless bullock.

'Nice one Michael,' we laughed.

My job with Wattle Mines was to develop export of coal to Japan and other countries. I travelled to mines in Australia and overseas. At that time the Japanese wanted to secure their nation's oil supply and were developing technology to convert Australian coal into oil. Our team was planning to develop a coal mine at Wandoan on the Darling Downs, to supply a conversion plant at Sumitomo's steel works at Kashima, north of Tokyo.

They planned an enormous project, with coal being railed to Gladstone for export. The vast coal resource would be mined by huge draglines. Washing stone from the coal was a challenge and we planned to bring water to the mine from a dam to be built on the Dawson River near Theodore. Water was scarce and agriculturalists opposed the dam and the mine. Allocation of water was always a political process in Australia.

'Processing coal to oil takes water,' said Howard. 'It won't happen unless the government gets behind it.'

The state government was enthusiastic. Japanese visitors inspected the site of the proposed coal mine with approval.

'You have only 10 metres of rock over 20 metres of coal,' said a visitor to the open cut, viewing the outcropping seams of coal.

'That's correct,' I said.

'It's amazing. Japanese coal mines have hundreds of metres of rock over less than a metre of coal.'

I was a visitor for three months at a pilot plant near Tokyo, observing functioning of the technology. It was planned to scale up to a huge operation. Their engineering was impressive and it seemed the project could get the go ahead any day. The conversion process was expensive but with soaring prices for imported oil and a supply of cheap coal, the project seemed reasonable. The wartime blockade of Japan's oil supply had sensitised them to oil insecurity.

I felt excited by my work, which would benefit Australians with coal export taxes and Japanese energy users with a supply of oil. I was aware of only minor environmental problems, which would be overcome.

When the price of oil fell in the 1980s, Japan's energy security improved. But the process emitted greenhouse gases and attractiveness of converting coal to oil was decreasing. Attention was switching to other energy supplies, such as liquefied natural gas. Nevertheless, we continued to deliver bulk samples of coal to the Japanese, until they lost interest and the project languished.

I began planning a coal slurry pipeline project in Queensland. Coal could be pulverised and made into a paste with water and pumped from a mine at Rolleston to the coast, where the water would be removed and the coal dried for shipment to power stations overseas. It had advantages over railway transport. I flew with a Texan oilman in a light plane, along a 300 kilometres route we had chosen for the pipeline, to be constructed through the Expedition Range to Gladstone. Unfortunately, this project folded, due to concerns about environmental effects and water supply.

When there was a downturn in the coal industry, our exploration and development department was downsized. I was transferred to coal marketing, where commercial acumen took precedence over engineering accuracy.

Mark Twain put it this way: 'A mine is a hole in the ground with a liar on top.'

I was in a sales team who promoted mine products. I was unhappy and complained to Carlson, a member of the marketing team.

'I'm not going to lie to customers about our products,' I said.

Debonair and self-confident, Carlson was the very model of a modern marketing man. He was stolid, with a square honest face and customers liked him.

'You have to forget about your engineering technical honesty and go for the jugular,' he told me. 'Our job is to rip off potential buyers.'

Marketing was ethically barren work and my morale plummeted.

My employment had otherwise been fulfilling. I gained experience of a huge continent and its enterprising population. I became aware of the physical, economic, social and psychological implications of water supply for homes, mining, industry, agriculture and recreation. Water was used to clean, wash, cook, cool, refresh, lubricate, dissolve, irrigate and bathe, with many other uses. It was a precious substance and we were fortunate to have it in abundance on our doorstep.

My writing about water at this time was technical, describing properties and processes involved in capturing, transporting and using it. When my engineering reports contained imaginative and creative writing about the human implications, it was regarded as disloyal to our corporate traditions.

CHAPTER 4 SUPERHERO

On Friday afternoons, I forgot about my job until Monday and applied myself to my home and family. I built a large workshop. I made a henhouse and welded a barbecue.

I constructed a two storey A-frame stable and cubby for Sarah and Michael to spend their first nights 'away from home'. They brought their friends to sleep over in a world of their own, not far from their parents, with stabled horses below, snuffling, snorting and stamping.

When I became disenchanted with my job marketing coal, I quit Wattle Mines. I had lost confidence in the hesitant devious management. Their strategies were to minimise payment of taxes and gain government favour by sycophancy. They had no sustained interest in diversifying into the technologies and new business areas I proposed. I left to preserve my self-respect.

We continued to live by the Logan River. It was a beautiful place and we were fortunate to live there all those years. Our house saw our comings and goings, our triumphs and our failures, for 23 years from 1978 to 2001. Every room, every window, every doorway, had its own story. We lived close to nature, with indoors and outdoors merged. We didn't lock our doors.

I took a year off and retrained as a science teacher. I taught science and maths at a state high school. Effective interaction with school students needed more than the independence and technical skills I had brought from Wattle Mines. I had to develop new skills to survive. I developed classroom activities with a minimum of teacher talk and a maximum of hands-on science experiments.

My teaching salary was about half of my former earnings but teaching science was more satisfying, helping students to learn skills through which they could contribute to society and lead meaningful lives. I was excited to have the opportunity to make a difference. The workload came as a shock, except for wonderful school holidays with my children.

Carol's esteem diminished sharply with my salary, but it went up in my own. Working as an engineer, I had been out of touch with young people and the lives of ordinary people. When I started teaching at a secondary school in a nearby town, I reconnected with my own children and my community. It was an opportunity for honest endeavour, a pleasant revitalisation of my life and I was happy.

Teaching took all my time and energy, in preparing lessons for my classes and marking student work. Students perceived me as of similar age to their fathers and opposed me, from relative safety. They hadn't before encountered a science advocate and were interested in the philosophies of science I explained to them. Some parents and teachers were bigoted or cynical and wanted to limit my teaching to the desiccated curriculum. When I explained science to them, their concern was dispelled. At age 40 science was my passion. I performed exacting science demonstrations and innovative feats outside the classroom. I cultivated my prowess and was revered by some students, as a superhero with a science mission like Superman, who had said:

'WHAM! BAM! POW! WHEN YOU USE SCIENCE, YOU ARE MUCH STRONGER THAN YOU THINK YOU ARE.
'TRUTH, JUSTICE AND A BETTER TOMORROW.'

When there was a drought, the river slowed to a trickle. Beyond the river lay the dry country of Beaudesert Shire. When we came there, it was cattle country, but two decades later it was being taken over by 'weekend farmers.' Irrigation pumps hammered day and night, turning the river flats from brown to green and emptying the river.

'Why do they allow people to build weirs across the river?' Michael asked.

'They want water for irrigation.'

'Is it simply a free-for-all?'

'It would be, except that people downstream wouldn't get any.'
'How do they manage?'
'Some upstream people are kind and release a little.'
'Could we break down the weirs?' Sarah suggested. She had a deep desire to be a force for positive change, by bringing people together to fight evil. Directness was her metier.
'I don't want to make new enemies,' I said.
'Then might is right?'
'Perhaps a flood will wash away their pumps,' I said.
'That would be great,' she said. 'It would be pyrrhic justice if all irrigators drowned.'
'You sound like a grazier in the outback, before there was law.'
'There's no harm in hoping,' she said.

Our home by the river was the centre of our family's life together. We had room to spread out our hobbies and projects. We played musical instruments. The kids played piano and drums. They disliked accompanying me on my electric guitar. Even with the volume turned up and maximum distortion on my amplifier, I wasn't trendy and cool enough.
'That sounds terrible,' Sarah said.
'Sorry, that's the best I can do.'
'Stick to the Beatles, Dad.'
They made collections of stamps, figurines, rocks and insects. Our kids were friends with neighbouring children and got up to all sorts of adventures, outdoors and in. They recorded videos of detectives solving simulated murders.
There was a constant round of driving them to extra-curricular activities at school. Michael was a keen basketball player and I drove him to games and cheered from the side-line. He was a valuable team player, sharing in the hard work, defending and scoring well. Sarah played drums with the school orchestra. She had many interests, often in a leadership role. She wanted to be of service to others.
Living out in the country had its drawbacks. I spent a lot of time driving to work, to children's activities and to the shops, through our local maze of roads, laid out in a grid of two and a half acre lots,

about a half with houses. There was no through traffic. Our house was at the end of a cul-de-sac and we felt safe. The turnaround was a no-man's-land where our children met up with neighbours' children in neutral territory, performing tricks on their bicycles. Michael rode his horse to the local park, with others accompanying him on foot, or sometimes doubling up behind him.

This was a place where the light was green with leaves and the air had eucalyptus you could taste. No sooner was the winter's shower of yellow chains of Laburnum flowers finished, than the bee hum began again, from the flowering wattle. In summer, tree frogs were deafened by crickets. Autumn was when peewees attacked their reflections in our windows.

The potting shed rang with budgie whistles, with broods of nestlings in nest boxes. An empty fish tank was home to white mice. Smith, our cat, watched them, fascinated for hours, like fast food ads.

Our family parties spilled from the patio on to the lawn. Australians in the bush are sometimes perceived as rambunctious and garrulous but there may be good reason. If you didn't stamp around and make a lot of noise, you could step on a poisonous brown snake. If it detected you coming by vibrations, it would flee.

Foxes came at night and tried to break into the henhouse, or into the pigeon loft above it. Wasps forever built bottles from river clay, with larders of anaesthetised spiders for their larvae.

Our riverbank grew ragwort, annual ragweed, lantana, green cestrum and castor oil bushes, all noxious weeds that we had to destroy, by edict of the Shire Council.

'Why those plants?' I asked a local.

'They are probably on a councillor's hay-fever hit list.'

We learned at our cost, if we didn't spray them, the Council would come in with a truck and spray everything, including our plantings, leaving a hefty bill for us to pay.

'Destroying all vegetation is pretty drastic,' I said. 'It's a strange method of preventing hay fever.'

'If you were a sufferer you would think differently.'

'Spraying the riverbank might have a local effect,' I said. 'But the noxious weeds are everywhere else.'

I sneezed then, which somewhat weakened my objection.

'It gives the council something to do,' said the local.

'That could be true,' I agreed. 'In the recession in the 1930s, John Maynard Keynes had proposed employing people to dig holes in the road and fill them in again, to stimulate the economy. He would have approved of Beaudesert Shire's noxious weed programme.'

When we went away, neighbours took good care of our cat and horses. We looked after their dogs. There was a Neighbourhood Watch system, so we didn't need to lock our doors at night.

'Where are we going to go this weekend?' Sarah asked one day.

'Nowhere.'

'Good. I want to stay home.'

It was music to my ears. Our kids were learning to entertain themselves.

We rambled together as a family along the riverbank. Herons and hawks took wing. The drying up of the land would have been oppressive without the river to offer renewal and sustain a profusion of plants. Flood and drought were the two sides of the rainfall coin, always in spin. Whereas a flood could balance drought, we dreaded floods and fires more for their invasive effects. A bushfire came up to the horse paddocks, but it didn't cross them or reach the house.

The safety and permanence of habitation in European settlements was not possible here. The nomadic lifestyle of the indigenous people was more appropriate.

The river attracted water snakes. They pursued green tree frogs but fell for cane toads and many snakes died. Frogs, large green ones, lived in our house, in the toilets.

'Why do we have frogs living in the blue toilet?' Carol asked.

'It's wet and they thrive. They burrow down into the transpiration trenches and come in through the sewerage pipes.'

'What do they eat?'

'Don't ask.'

I became a writer of science teaching materials. They provided students with practical experiences, especially projects in the real world. I developed skills in selection of information and in design of instructions that students could relate to and succeed with.

Several times I rejected employers' proposals that, to gain experience, I should transfer to country Queensland or interstate. I was committed to living at our home by the river near Brisbane until the children finished university. We stayed longer, 22 years. I explored our locality by the Logan River as a science teacher, to find learnings for children and students. In those days, I didn't look beyond science for meanings.

Living there meant that our kids grew up in one house, in one neighbourhood and stayed at their school for the duration of an entire course. My employers regarded my stubborn intransigence in rejecting transfers as self-indulgent and arrogant treachery. For our children, it was a narrow upbringing, but they diversified later. Now they have their own children, they value continuity.

CHAPTER 5 ISLAND HOME

Carol and I had bought, many years earlier, land to build a house on Macleay Island in Moreton Bay, our sailing playground. The Brisbane and Logan Rivers discharged into the Bay, ringed by islands offshore. When in flood, the rivers disgorged, from their mouths, tree debris from agricultural clearing inland in the dry season, accumulated sometimes over several years.

Tides distributed rafts of stumps, trunks and branches along the coast. The floating tree material clogged beaches and threatened to entangle the propeller and keel of our sail boat. For several months after a flood, flotsam made sailing, fishing and bathing hazardous.

We sailed our trailer sloop in Moreton Bay

When we sailed, we went for long weekends, or even for a week exploring the islands. We towed our trailer sloop 40 kilometres from home and launched it at the Redland Bay boat ramp. Our boat's cabin had four comfy berths, an ice box and a gas camping barbeque. When the weather was foul, we were dry and warm inside at anchor, stuffing ourselves with tea, baked beans and sausages.

Sundown was the best part of the day aboard. We relaxed in the cockpit with drinks, enjoying spectacular sunsets. We turned in early and listened to the radio waves beamed across the Bay to our stereo headphones, also to the soft sounds of water lapping the transom and fish kissing the keel, as they fed on algae with smacking lips.

We usually began our sailing excursions with a visit to our land. We ran the boat up on to our beach and boiled the kettle for tea. While we waited for the tide to lift us off, we called in to see neighbours and began planning the house we would build there some day.

When the weather turned rough, we took our boat home to its safe berth, in our shed.

After delaying for over a decade, we decided to build our dream house on our land.

'Don't rush into it, will you!' Howard jeered. 'Are you sure the location is right?'

The 15 square kilometres of Macleay Island had about 2700 residents, a primary school and a small supermarket. Our house overlooked its own beach, with sweeping views over Moreton Bay and the northern islands. As teenagers our children lost interest in sailing because it was 'uncool'. There wasn't enough privacy for them in the cabin. They preferred to go to our apartment we rented out at the north coast, where they could roam in the shopping centre.

We kept our island home for weekends and holidays, because commuting to my city job was too far. It took us an hour to drive from home to the ferry terminal, half an hour to cross with our car, then 10 minutes to drive to the house.

The new house kept alive my association with the Bay now that my crew had deserted. We sold our trailer sailer. Carol chose the furniture and enjoyed going there, at first, but was uninterested in rugged island living. Waterside living on the island was for me a pleasant change of scene and different from living by the Logan River.

Our house on Macleay Island in Moreton Bay

We could paddle with bare feet in rock pools at low tide. The island beach had more wild life than the river, with crabs, pippies and yabbies. I fished and caught bream or whiting. Visitors to our beach included pelicans, herons, whistling kites, Brahminy kites, curlews and lapwings. Breezes from the sea were briny and fresh, with ozone or salt in the air. The foreshore had mangroves, creating a fertile environment for small sea creatures. The mangrove smell was organic, with a hint of sulphur.

'What did the sea say to the river?' asked Howard, joking, on a visit for a weekend. 'You can run but you can't tide!'

It was one of the few times Carol laughed there. The lifestyle was too solitary for her.

The beachfront apartments we had owned, first at the north coast and then at the south coast, were urban. We had rented them out, but it wasn't remunerative, because by booking for our own use in school holidays, we lost the best rental opportunities. We sold these properties to fund building on the island.

Our island home met my deep need to be close to water. The sheltered waters of the bay were on our doorstep and I could walk along the beach in either direction. We swam at a community beach two minutes away. The islanders only slowly accepted us, viewing our interest as casual and temporary. Many of the houses stood empty most of the time, insulting permanent residency, as if it was a default option.

After graduating from university with doctorates, our children moved away from home. When they left home, Carol and I went to the island alone. Apart from preparing food, eating and maintaining the gardens, we pursued our own interests. I loved it there and hoped to live there in ten years' time when I would retire. My writing hobby was undistracted. I did a writing course by correspondence, obtaining validation of my responses to set tasks that encouraged me to start writing novels.

I wrote five draft novels, about mining, water, genetic modification, factory farming and nuclear power. Those manuscripts repose in my on-line archives and are rarely consulted.

Carol didn't find enough to occupy her. Not able to go shopping or visit her family, she fretted to go home early. She said if we had a tinny and outboard, we could launch it from our garden and go visiting friends on other islands. When I bought one, she went for a jaunt around the island and didn't want to go again.

'You haven't given it a chance,' I said to her.

'It's too noisy and bumpy for me,' she said.

I didn't reply because I was annoyed. She had been in dinghies before. I couldn't see why she had wanted one and then changed her mind.

Whereas I loved being on the island, Carol was unhappy there. Her experience was of many present-at-hand negatives rather than enjoying the many ready-to-hand positives. Our Macleay Island experiment was a disaster and destabilized our living in our house by the Logan River. Carol wanted to move into the city. Regretfully, I agreed. Living by the Logan River had been wonderful and we were fortunate to have lived there for 23 years.

Our island home enabled me to understand what happened upriver from the Logan River outfall. By going to our Macleay place at regular intervals, we discovered differences from our experiences of flooding and droughts inland. This brought understanding, respect and appreciation for our river environment.

CHAPTER 6 DECIDING WHERE TO LIVE

We advertised our house for sale by auction.

'I'm sad to be leaving,' I said.

'What will you miss most?' Carol asked.

'The River,' I said. 'It was a good friend.'

'Sarah and Michael have grown up here. Leaving is a break with their past.'

The two had their own cars and when they left home, the place seemed empty without them. There was no-one to ride their horses and we sold them.

We wanted to live closer to the city and began looking for a new home. People often find a new home by driving around until they see a place for sale they like. We searched along both banks of the Brisbane River for a waterfront building site. We knew nothing about identifying, interpreting and regulating of flood-risk. River flooding was far from my mind.

We didn't know what information about flooding to ask for. We were fair game for unscrupulous real estate salesmen and land developers.

The rule for developers was new homes had to be constructed above the council's Defined Flood Level. The Council certified flood-prone sites uninhabitable. The sites were sold cheaply for development. People trusted the Council's approval system would keep them safe and the Council had collaborated with developers in duping the public. The regulations merely obfuscated flood risk. It was a profitable game.

The possibility of a much higher flood level, 8.35m experienced in 1893, was never brought to our attention, in the same way that a comet or an asteroid, on a collision course with Earth, would be forgotten.

Carol and I seldom agreed on aesthetic merits of properties. When we argued, there was insufficient goodwill for compromise. We tried to solve impasses by discussion but negotiation was zero sum. Resistance was overcome when one of us surrendered to the other's despotism..

When Carol found a waterside apartment in Brisbane I was sceptical at first.

'I've found us a place to live, by the river,' she said. 'C'mon have a look.'

I wasn't hopeful. We went together to a prestigious address overlooking a park by the river in West End, a bohemian suburb close to the city centre.

'Atrium' was a 3-storey, 6-apartment block, well–constructed and tastefully finished. I liked it immediately, but it seemed expensive. When Carol told me the asking price, I was pleasantly surprised: it was affordable. It was close to the ferry and bus terminal and the location seemed excellent. Years later that assessment appears deficient.

'It's not far above the level of the river,' I said. 'Could it flood?'

'The real estate agent says it was built in 1996, and the living room would have been above the 1974 flood level, which was 5.45 metres.'

'Above the Defined Flood Level (DFL)?' I asked.

'Yes. The ground floor is just above it, at 5.8 metres.'

Years later I found that the apartment had been built well below the minimum habitable floor level of 8.0 metres.

I couldn't imagine the extent of a Brisbane River flood, never having experienced one.

'The Wivenhoe Dam was built 13 years ago to mitigate flooding,' Carol said. 'The agent says this place will never flood.'

It was a lie. I know now a dam cannot eliminate flooding. When the dam fills, water has to be released causing flooding. I didn't know that then and like a fool, accepted it would never flood.

I wanted to believe it and my assessment of flood risk was cursory. The building site had flooded 25 years earlier. The DFL was designed by the Council from historical flood levels. Memories had faded and few could recall the effects of the flooding. The possibility of higher floods wasn't mentioned by the seller's agent, nor queried by our friends and relatives.

'It has never flooded and probably won't,' I concluded. 'Anywhere else it would cost a lot more.'

It seemed like a reasonable investment.

'I like it,' I said to Carol, surrendering.

It was one of very few times we agreed.

The main attraction was West End's location near the city centre. My writing had led me to groups of writers and readers who I met with locally to discuss books. Other writers' views and ideas could be valuable. The city had sources of information I needed, such as libraries, bookshops and lectures, complementing Internet resources.

Wivenhoe Dam had been officially opened in 1984. We drove to view it when its construction was nearing completion. It was a huge structure but if we had known the history of Brisbane River flooding we would have had less confidence in its ability to protect us.

'The dam is assumed to hold back water that would cause flooding in Brisbane,' Carol said.

'If the dam is kept full, it wouldn't prevent flooding,' I said. 'It would be useless except for supplying towns water. It could be dangerous.'

'They are planning to keep it 30% full.'

'Heavy rainfall could fill it in a day or two,' I said. 'Then river flooding could follow.'

'People believe it will stop all flooding forever,' she said.

I asked my colleague Howard if the Wivenhoe Dam would prevent flooding. He was cautious, choosing his words carefully. I knew that we would be taking a risk.

'Wivenhoe Syndrome is the popular belief that a dam will protect city homes from flooding,' said Howard sceptically. 'More than half the river catchment is downstream of the dam.'

'Does that mean that a half or more of heavy rain might not be held back by the dam, even if it was empty?'

'Yes.'

'Would you buy a place just above the flood level?' I asked Howard. He hesitated, then pronounced his verdict.

'If I did, I would keep my fingers crossed,' he said.

Despite warnings, we never seriously considered that the apartment was flood-prone. We trusted it would be safely above levels possible for future floods. We found out, after signing the contract, that flood insurance for the building was not available.

Howard told me a story.

'A lawyer and an engineer were discussing insurance,' he said.

'You need fire insurance, burglary insurance and flood insurance,' said the engineer.

'The fire and theft and burglary I can understand,' said the lawyer, 'but the flood insurance? How do you start a flood?'

I laughed, but realised the issue for us was not criminality in faking of insurance claims, but about flood insurance not being offered. Insurance wasn't available for the apartment we wanted to buy. Insurance companies declined to risk paying out for regular natural events and wouldn't indemnify flood risk, however infrequent. We asked people how this affected the value of the property.

'If you are high and dry, you don't need flood insurance,' said a cynic.

Others had a different view of our need for insurance.

'You would pay a premium, year after year, adding up to more than your losses in a flood. Insurance is not worth having,' said one.

'It could be difficult to fund repair of flood damage,' said another. 'Insurance is a way of saving up. If you can save up yourself, you don't need it.'

'You could afford the cost of fixing damage to your apartment building,' was a more optimistic view.

'Insurance would be expensive and it would delay fixing the damage and moving back in,' was least favourable.

We regretted having to take on risk, but apartments in dry locations were more expensive and we were unwilling to move away from the river. Everything I knew about the Brisbane River at this location was good.

'Flooding is unlikely,' I said. 'It is a small risk, more than offset by the advantages of location by the river.'

The location had the compensating attractions of the river and park. Our new place was only a few minutes' walk from my workplace. I could trade-off my loss on the swings for the gain on the roundabouts.

We offered less money, but it was refused. We were hooked and paid the asking price.

For our move into the city we had acquired an apartment beside the Brisbane River, built in 1996, above the defined flood level. At that time we hardly gave flooding a second thought.

CHAPTER 7 GEOLOGICAL ORIGINS

After teaching at Beaudesert State High School, south of Brisbane, for 6 years, the Education Department transferred me to a support group, to write a series of science textbooks. For the next 5 years I drove into Brisbane City every day. The journey took an hour, becoming longer as the city spread out and traffic worsened. Then we moved into the city.

'How do you like living in the city?' Howard asked. We had remained friends since working together at Wattle Mines.

'We should have moved here a long time ago,' I said. 'I have been driving back and forth to North Maclean, wasting my time, risking my life and others'.'

We didn't move until we found a place we liked by a river. Being near water made my life more enjoyable. I call my attraction to water *aquaphilia*. Others can be drawn instead to mountains, wide skies, grass lands, beaches or open spaces.

My work was at West End, quite near the city centre, where the Brisbane River meanders across its floodplain, through a channel averaging 250 metres wide, fed by its catchment in the interior, stretching from the Great Dividing Range to the Darling Downs.

'I like the Brisbane River,' I said to Howard. 'It's not too large. China's Yangtze is massive and would be frightening.'

'Although the Brisbane River is small, you'll find its floods pack a heavy punch,' Howard said.

An observer's view of the Brisbane River, as it winds through the city, would include the unpredictable rainfall and modest tides. The river is unlike the River Ganges in Bangladesh, where monsoonal rains cause many people to live on the river delta, suffering flooding annually. Brisbane rain is not enough for a monsoon season, nor for annual flooding. Rainfall is irregular, but can be torrential.

Brisbane City is situated 15 kilometres from Moreton Bay, with the tidal range reaching 80 kilometres inland. Unlike many other rivers that flood regularly, the Brisbane River does not have a delta with multiple channels and coastal lagoons. It is bordered by mangroves, which widen into marshy areas and swamps.

Carlson, a work colleague, was amused by my affinity for rivers.

'Rivers are so lazy they only get out of their beds to flood,' he quipped.

Carlson was a coal marketer who knew the area's fossil fuel resources and geological history. I told him of my conversation with a mechanic servicing my car.

'It is time you had an oil change,' he said.

'Why?' I asked.

'Your oil is old,' he said. 'It's been two years.'

'That engine oil has been around for much longer than that,' I said. 'It was formed from plant and microscopic animal remains buried in sediments from rivers flooding between 145 and 200 million years ago, in the Jurassic era. Bacteria and other microorganisms converted them to petroleum and the oil was trapped in Upper Cretaceous rock, until it flowed out into oil wells. It has been in my car for about two years, but it's hundreds of millions of years old. A couple more years won't do any harm.'

'WHAM. BAM. POW' thought my Superman.
'TRUTH, JUSTICE AND A BETTER TOMORROW.'

Carlson laughed.

'Did the garage man believe you?'

'He wasn't happy for me to ignore the oil's use-by-date,' I said. 'His livelihood depended on oil deteriorating.'

'Use by dates are a scam!' Carlson said. 'Another scam is the building of this city on the river flood plain, despite flooding being assured.'

'The pioneers settled Brisbane close to deep water, for docking of supply ships and building houses near well-drained stable streets, above the level of riverine flooding,' he said. 'Later, settlers filled in lagoons, swamps and marshes, where floodwater had taken a shortcut across a meander, leaving oxbow lakes and billabongs. They straightened and trained the river course to keep to a single channel. They built on the former wetlands and erected buildings along the riverbanks. They blocked the flood spreading out, raising flood heights and prolonging flood durations. This has worsened flooding.'

'Flood water falls as rain in the high country and runs together into the river,' Carlson said. 'Water flows from the Somerset Dam at 113 metres above sea level, into the Wivenhoe Dam at 86 metres. From there if flows long a course that descends steadily to sea level. As the river fills, it becomes wider, deeper and slower, spilling over its banks. In Brisbane, the average width is 250 metres and closer to 500 metres towards the mouth.

'Rocks in the river source country breakdown physically and chemically and are worn by wind and rain into sand. The riverbank may erode releasing pebbles, gravel and sand. When flow is slow, smooth and laminar, flow is in parallel layers. Sediments sink to the river bed and flow is blocked by deposits. Backwater from the obstruction raises the water level. The flood flows faster, causing turbulence, mobilising and churning the sediments, carrying them downstream. Currents eddy around obstructions and swirl perpendicularly, mixing the layers.'

'Where the river deepens and widens, the flood water slows down, becomes laminar again and the larger particles settle, forming deposits.

'Flooding is caused by deposits blocking the channel and by earthworks and buildings blocking flow across the floodplain.'

'We don't hear about these aspects. Flooding is usually attributed to bad weather, not obstruction.'

A few days later, I was sitting with my grandson Amir, 12, on the Riverbank beside a sandy beach in Orleigh Park. He heaped up sand at the water's edge and watched wavelets wash it away.

'The sand is moved by the water,' I said. 'It's called a sediment.'

'What does a sediment do?' Amir asked.

'It settles on the bottom. The water gets deeper to flow over it and then there is flooding.'

'Can the sediment be cleaned out?'

'That's a great question. Yes, it can be dredged out.'

'What is dredging?' he asked.

'A dredge is like a vacuum cleaner that sucks up sand and mud on to a barge. They sometimes drag buckets with chains to scoop it up.'

'What do they do with the sand and mud?'

'They dump it out in the bay, at Mud Island.

We watched the sand slip down into the water, slumping in.

'Does dredging make a difference?'

'Ships can go up the river and flood water can flow away faster. The hole gradually fills up with more sediment from up the river.'

'Do they dredge again?' asked Amir.

'They should do, but they stopped years ago.'

'Why.'

'I don't know.'

'What will happen?'

'The river can become blocked. Fast flowing water can carry boulders, rocks, large pebbles, gravel, sand and silt,' I said. 'They can sink forming deposits, building up and causing the water level to spill over the banks on to the flood plain.'

'Why doesn't flood water sweep the sediment along and clear out the channel?' Amir asked.

'Good question, Amir! The channel would clear when flow is too fast to allow settling and deposition,' I said. 'At other times sediment would build up and flow would be held back, in a channel partly blocked, with shallows and sand bars. A channel can become clogged with tree stumps and branches. Sediment eventually pours into Moreton Bay, where a plume of fine material spreads out, discolouring the water for hundreds of kilometres, until it spills off the continental shelf, into the ocean.'

'Are you sure this happens in the Brisbane River?' Amir asked. 'How can you tell? I can't see what is going on. The water is too muddy to see the movement of sediments.'

'When I studied hydrology,' I said, 'we experimented with models of water channels carrying sand and gravel. We watched particles bouncing through a long rectangular perspex channel and being entrained, or lifted up, from the bottom. When we increased the water flow rate, in a steeper channel, the turbulent conditions held up all the sediment. We also had computer models of river flow, that could predict effects of rainfall on river and sediment flow. It would be good to find out how sediment will affect future flooding of this river.'

'Did you learn this when you worked for the mining company?' asked Amir.

'No. I studied hydrology at university.'

'What's hydrology?'

'It's the science of water movement on the surface, underground and in the air.'

'Why did you study that?' asked Amir.

'To find out how to stop the River flooding.'

'By dredging?' he asked.

'That's one way' I said. 'Another is to reduce erosion on farms, preventing sediment getting into the river.'

While we had been talking, we were joined by Carlson, who had been walking in the Park.

'Tell us Carlson, how does sediment from farms cause flooding?'

'Farming can cause flooding in cities,' he said. 'Country and City folk blame each other for flooding. Farmers are blamed for clearing of trees, grazing of European animals and cropping with monocultures, degrading soils, causing surface water run-off and flash flooding. Agriculture takes water for irrigation, killing waterways by fertilisers and causing erosion of millions of tonnes of topsoil.'

'What's a monoculture?' Amir asked.

'A crop, with all the plants of the same type.

'What's wrong with monocultures?' asked Amir.

'When the plants vary, there can be layers of vegetation and different animals, like worms, to increase water penetration and prevent erosion. Farmers can prevent erosion and reduce flooding by growing a variety of plants.'

'How do city folk cause flooding?'

'Country folk blame river flooding on urban development, such as clearing of flood plains, filling of natural water storages and obstruction of river channels,' Carlson said. 'They also blame city folks for the water storage dams that release water causing flooding.'

In my new job as a science teacher, I felt drawn to geology by my job earlier in mining. It wasn't as interesting to students as 'sexy' topics like forensic science, but geology explained environments and job opportunities and many students were interested when they had practical assignments.

'When you have learned about the land where you live and how to conserve its resources, you will realise this is a land of opportunity,' I told students.

Geological understanding was largely theoretical. Having their own view of the unknown could give students self-respect when they realised their position within the ancient history of the Brisbane River.

Although I had learned a lot about the Brisbane River, I didn't yet have a critical appreciation of policies affecting it as a waterway, source of water, transport route and effluent disposal facility. To find them out it was difficult to observe the river and its environs as an object because it was 344 kilometres in length and moved. I had observed it at the Wivenhoe dam and sailed in the estuary where it flowed into Moreton Bay. I sailed on the River in West End and became involved in the riverside community.

CHAPTER 8 LEARNING THE ROPES

Our trailer sailer was too large for the Brisbane River and there was nowhere to park it at our West End apartment, so we sold it. We joined Kurilpa Sailing Club nearby in Orleigh Park. A club member sold us an ancient Gibson P5 sailing dinghy. On Saturdays in the sailing season, we rigged it on the grass beside the ramp and launched it for races.

'It's sociable,' said Carol. 'The people are friendly and helpful.'

We sailed in club races but soon discovered our sailing in Moreton Bay had not skilled us for dinghy sailing. We were used to relaxing between setting the sails for the next tack, with time to look around and talk. But our dinghy tacks on the River were frequent and fast. Our boat was barely self-righting and to prevent capsizing, we had to balance it by changing seats from side to side, while ducking under the boom, which swung across dangerously overhead.

'I don't enjoy crawling under the boom on my knees,' I said. 'It's undignified.'

Although our success was limited, it was good fun trying. We enjoyed jousting for position at race starts, beating upwind, standing out on the gunwales when hard over and running around marker buoys, without infringing competitors' water. We had to steer to avoid collision with faster river traffic, such as CityCats and jet skis. We were too small to have right of way over ferries. Unlike the torpor of sailing on the Bay, we had to stay alert on the river.

River sailing led me closer to hermeneutic understanding, interpretation of the Brisbane River, but not as far as systematic philosophical explanation of the river phenomenon. There were many embedded 'existentiell' particulars and they prevented synthesis of general 'existential' understanding.

'There is a lot going on in a river, too much to take in at a glance,' I said.

Sailing on the river was unpredictable. Large buildings were arrayed along the riverbank and every time we sailed behind one, or under a bridge, the wind changed in strength and direction, with destabilising gusts that could cause us to capsize. The river flowed in large loops called meanders. Water depth varied across the channel too. On the outside of each bend, the water was deeper and the current faster. On the inside, it was shallower and we went aground.

My writing of this part would be more inspiring if I could tell you we had sailed well and had cut a fine dash on the river. Instead it was the biggest come down of my sporting career.

It is convenient to blame the unstable design of our dinghy.

'Why are we floundering again?' asked Carol.

'Because we are recovering from the last flounder,' I said.

When we capsized, our life jackets kept us afloat, as we clung to the hull of our recumbent craft. Righting her and clambering back in were challenging. When I tried to pull myself inboard my upper body strength was tested. It was found wanting when I pulled Carol in. Fortunately, the club's motorised dinghy came to support us.

River sailing was precarious.

'Have they spotted us?' Carol asked, as we were being swept downriver towards the next bend, clinging to the upturned hull, with the sails underwater.

'They're coming now,' I said.

It was a relief when they towed us back to the clubhouse. There was a loss of face and we hoped we would become more adept.

We capsized many times, until we had had enough. Our last voyage was when our mainsail was buried underwater and we were swept by the current behind a jetty, where our dinghy lodged inverted, the sail ballooning in the river current. We could hear wood breaking. We untangled ourselves from the rigging and trod water. It was a traumatic experience. Carol went to hospital with a visual aura, like a migraine. Fortunately, the condition soon disappeared, but she never sailed again.

'I could have drowned,' she said.

It was my fault and I felt very bad. We retrieved the dinghy almost undamaged, but our pride was injured and we practically gave the boat away. Sailing on the Brisbane River is much more difficult than sailing in Moreton Bay. They say it takes a couple of years to learn the ropes in river sailing, but we had had enough well within that time.

My sailing experience in Moreton Bay was of little value on the River at West End. I learned about effects of river bends, channels, rainfall, winds and tides. Sailors exploit the opportunities offered by the river, instead of regarding them as obstacles, as landlubbers do.

I met sailing people who had gained a detailed knowledge of the River locally, over several decades. They understood the underwater part of the river and how flooding could change conditions. I was looking for effects having causes that could be changed for the better. I hadn't known exactly what I was looking for. I had to keep on turning over stones, hoping something would crawl out.

CHAPTER 9 LIVING BY THE RIVER

Our apartment was a stone's throw from the West End ferry terminal. From there we could drive, ferry, bus or walk to most places with convenience. City Cat ferries connected with Council buses. I enjoyed being close to the river, able to catch a ferry to the University of Queensland, one stop upriver, or to the City Business District four stops down. The sleek catamarans glided sedately and quietly, nosing in to take me to the university swimming pool, or to public lectures, or to a reading group.

My work changed, from classroom teaching, to a 5 year assignment writing textbooks for use by Queensland's distance education students. I was the writer in a publication team able to draw on the skills of a cartoonist, an artist, an editor, a proof reader, a playwriter, a keyboard operator, a copyright officer, an audio producer, a video producer and a publication officer. During 4 years, I wrote 32 published science booklets.

When I had completed the writing task, for fifteen years I taught in the Brisbane School of Distance Education, a few minutes' walk away from my apartment. Students learned remotely, by online delivery. It was enjoyable to teach with my own teaching materials and plans.

'How is discipline with the distance students?' asked Carol.

'I don't have any problems,' I said. 'I can put them in solitary study spaces or disconnect them if they play up.'

The lesson material I had written was often based on personal experiences. The students respected my efforts to present material that interested them and their achievement rewarded me amply.

I walked by the river every day, usually at dusk, enjoying nature. I learned to prepare lessons in my head. Walks in the park inspired my creativity.

The river took its moods from winds and tides, sometimes with stillness, sometimes with waves swirling angrily. The river's tidal range was within 1.3 metres of mean sea level, with king tides of 2.2 metres. Sometimes the walking path through Orleigh Park had water lapping the riverbank's rock facing a metre below the footpath, a reminder that flooding wasn't far away. The river course was fringed with mangroves, with places for young fish and other water creatures to live and breed, having a distinct organic smell.

Walking along the pathway by the ferry, the water shone like a David Hockney painting of a swimming pool, with light reflected in patterns, at times a lacelike web, an intricate embroidered veil that obscured the depths with a curtain of filigrees of light. Always the river surface was textured at the interface between currents below and air movement above, an endless source of gleaming tranquillity and fascination.

'The water seldom looks the same twice,' I said to Carol. 'On some days, the surface is glossy, reflecting glare. On other days it glints and sparkles, dappled in patches when there is a breeze.'

We compared our impressions of how the patches of river surface differed from each other.

'After a boat passes, the water is marked by a flattened stream,' she said.

'The wake is a procession of oblique waves, rolling in lockstep, with the leader surging in over the mangroved riverbanks and crashing onto the rock cladding of the embankment,' I replied.

'When the wind blows, small waves from passing boats break noisily, with a crash and gurgle,' Carol said.

'Sometimes the water seems heavy, oily and viscous,' I added. 'At others, it is light and glassy or fizzy. The surface swells with tiny mounds of water, as if it is boiling with eddies circulating from churning and upwelling of currents below.'

It was a placid scene, with fish jumping at dusk. How I loved to walk beside that river! There was so much to see, hear and smell, all around.

The river water lay obediently in its channel, without any sign it could flow up over the riverbank and into the houses. I imagined flooding as water coming from a place higher upriver, where heavy rain would raise the water level, into a wave rolling down the river. The water flowed down the channel when it could and overflowed when it couldn't.

'It always seems to be cooler by the river,' Carol observed.

'The water reflects away solar radiation,' I said. 'The cold water cools the air.'

'On hot days there can be cool breezes.'

'Cool air from above can sink down, because it is cooler near the water.'

'Then it must be true that it is cooler here,' she said. 'That settles it.'

Magpies and kookaburras sang to us and ibises searched the rubbish bins. Whether it was the bracing river breeze, the gentle lapping of waves, or sunshine sparkling, or ripples on the surface, there was something deeply restorative about being in or near water. It wasn't as pristine as the beach at our Macleay home, but it had other attractions.'

Orleigh Park had been planted in 1918 with an avenue of majestic weeping fig trees, interspersed with eucalypts, tulip trees, hoop pine and ponga oil trees. Walking along the footpath between the fluted trunks, reminded me of walking down the nave of Salisbury Cathedral in the UK, with skylights above and fronds dangling down.

The fig trees were sedate, inhibiting facile conversation.

'This space belongs to the trees,' said my daughter Sarah. 'We have to respect them.'

Our chatter was hushed and our glances caressed them. Sarah photographed the trees carefully.

Brush turkeys inhabited pockets of remnant vegetation, shaded by fast-growing Tipuana trees, with magpie families searching for insects on the grass beneath. Residents were wary of their swooping attacks, which could injure eyes. Possums were seen mainly at night, climbing in suburban trees, on fences and along overhead cables. Herons visited the waterside unobtrusively. Crows and ibises frequented rubbish bins.

The wild animals had been compromised but were holding their own.

At dusk, fruit bats winged past in thousands, along their flyway over the water, spread out hundreds of metres wide, arriving from over the horizon, going past and out of sight, down river, like silent bombers on a raid. The gaps between them were wide, some carrying heavy young clasped to their bodies. Silent and unhurried, they laboured through the balmy air, going around and over fig trees along the riverbank.

On other days, the bats came in procession, in a line skimming the tree tops. Some of them crash landed in the trees, to feed on fig flowers, fruit and nectar, clambering around in the upper branches, squeaking querulously with their helium voices, until they flapped away, merging into the tide of passing bats.

We watched the bat parade at dusk from our balcony. I was humbled by the bats' determination. By comparison, the humans in the park seemed easily distracted and tentative.

'The bats' group purpose transcends individuality,' remarked Howard. 'Human sorties are more haphazard, or follow-my-leader. These animals are heading for a common destination.'

When they did not appear for several consecutive evenings, I was alarmed. I asked Howard what could have happened to them.

'The authorities could have had them destroyed,' he said.

'Why would they do that?'

'To prevent them spreading infectious diseases, like Hendra virus,' said Howard. 'They could blame them for the Covid outbreak.'

'Is it true?'

'I doubt it. It seems a bit too convenient to me, putting the blame on wild animals.'

'They are lovely animals,' I said. 'They were here first. Those bastards!'

A few nights later, they were flying past again, but in reduced numbers. I never did find out what had happened. I trusted there were enough good people to prevent genocide.

I had learned that bats flew smoothly in air above and near the river, declining more direct routes over buildings. Nature takes the path of least resistance. But water in the river did not run smoothly, circulating within the stream. I wondered what caused river turbulence and to what extent river flow was being slowed, with flooding worsened by sediment deposition and flow obstructed by bridge pillar islands.

CHAPTER 10 RIVERSIDE COMMUNITY

What could the future hold for Orleigh Park where I lived?

Orleigh Park belonged to the river. It attracted visitors bruised by the hustle and bustle of living and working in the metropolis, who came there to salve egos and emotions. Residents like me reluctantly shared our territory with visitors from further afield, who crowded in at weekends.

The river was a hive of human activity, with CityCats arriving or leaving every few minutes, carrying up to 170 passengers when full to 18 terminals along the river. The catamarans were sleek, quiet and fast, up to 25 knots, threading their way between private boats and rowing shells, slowing down under bridges as they neared North Quay in the CBD.

Many students commuted upriver one stop from West End, to the University of Queensland. In the evenings, the red portside lights of the ferries regularly hove into view from my lounge, with their white masthead lights at a jaunty angle. Rowing club shells plied on the river at weekends, with sailing dinghies engaged in tacking duels and fishers casting their lines, over the wakes of roaring jet skis.

There was so much activity on and around the river, the phenomenon was too rich with embedded particulars for a single hermeneutical narrative to reveal the river's Dasein. Each uncovering deflected attention away from something else. My perceptual field was restricted, as was the field of my thought processes. I had too many interests, biases and prejudices to describe my experiences coherently and I could only make lists.

Orleigh Park hosted walking, dog walking, picnics, jogging, fun runs, cycling, roller skating, scooters, playground, swings, quoits, boules, swarming up ropes, seesaw, pole climbing, slides, tight rope walking, fire twirling and juggling.

The hive of activity in the park seemed energised by the crowd there, as if the activity level was contagious. Part of participants' enjoyment was in being watched by others. I was from the UK and viewed with suspicion the indolent local males, beer stubbies in hand, ogling girls, or the easy camaraderie of women without men.

There was space in the park for informal soccer and cricket games. Frisbees were thrown and there was sunbathing on the grass. A fig tree festooned in lights lit up at dusk, illuminating cascades of electronic foliage. There were: barbecues, tables, toilets, bicycles for hire and skateboards. It was a favourite place for: family reunions, weddings, religious services, celebration lunches, and visits by Santa.

I liked to promenade through the park with my family at dusk on a weekend evening, when the park was filled with a colourful crowd, people of all ages playing or just sitting around on the grass with their friends, chatting. Those on their own relaxed and watched the sights, feeling the breeze and thinking their lonely thoughts. We stopped to talk with other families along the way.

'When people see the river moving freely, they express themselves openly in favourite activities,' I said to Carol, as we sat on the grass. 'The river does what it wants and they do too.'

'Are you doing what you want?' asked Carol.

'Yes. This place does it for me. There's enough space for everyone to feel they own a special piece of privacy.'

In West End, shopping streets previously dominated by roads and by vehicles had been planted with trees and converted into shady boulevards, for commuters and for active transport. Magnolias and jacarandas boasted their vivid colours.

The park had family picnics at weekends. People squatted in a circle on the grass, or on chairs they had brought. No-one stood up for long at a gathering of social equals. The positions they adopted levelled the company, possibly a custom of Aborigines in the outback. The park was narrow and picnic groups occupied much of the space, with informal ball games in the remainder.

Our daughter and son visited sometimes; Sarah was researching for a PhD in humanities in Sydney and seldom came home. I read through her thesis and was amazed by the complexity of her language.

'Could you increase readability by putting in some full stops and easier words?' I asked.

'No. This is what is expected. They would take full stops out,' she said.

Michael, the younger one, had nominally lived with us, while he studied science for a PhD at the university, spending most of his time in Vietnam. I read his thesis too. His language had shorter sentences and fewer polysyllabic words. His statistical analysis amazed me. He developed a thesis of practical importance.

Carol and I continued in our jobs, easily accessible from our new home. Carol became principal of a school for children with special needs. When my job as a writer of science textbooks finished, I went back to teaching and began writing a speculative fiction novel as a hobby.

I had long been a passionate believer in empirical science, for discovering and controlling technologies in our lives. I wanted objective knowledge to be generated from hypotheses that could be falsified, the Karl Popper way. It was a severe discipline, demanding objective evidence.

My trust was in empirical science to regulate technologies, but younger people wanted control by governments and media. I was disenchanted by scientists who declined objectivity and responsibility, as they scrambled for government funds. I withdrew from public policy forums and expressed my views in my novels.

I was somewhat reclusive and inadvertently I abandoned Carol to her own interests. Our marriage began to fail.

'Why don't you come on our trip to Hong Kong?' she asked me.

'It's not a place I want to go,' I said. 'I'd rather finish my book.'

She was a few years older than me and her psychological type was 'silent generation,' whereas I was a 'Boomer'. Her generation had cultural and social forces that emphasized hard work, loyalty and thrift, whereas I was self-absorbed and anti-establishment. Her values were traditional and pre-war. She was an ardent women's libber, a bully and disagreeable, unable to reason or compromise. In her company I felt trapped.

When Carol proposed going to a restaurant or theatre with her group, I would say 'You go with your friends.' I disliked activities in informal groups.

It was difficult for us to discuss anything without it becoming a clash of opinions. Carol enjoyed talking about politics whereas I was more interested in ideas, trends and theories. Carol was frustrated by my lack of interest in household tasks and that I was always 'up in my head', pondering about the deep things of life while she was the one taking care of the duties of the household. I would have welcomed her help with my writing, but she had lost interest in me and was always negative. We had little chemistry. When Michael and Sarah left home, her life was empty.

Since coming to live in our apartment in 1998, I had led a charmed existence, unencumbered by illness, disability, accident, disaster, death or war. By 2006, Carol wasn't so charmed. The attention from me was frequent disagreement. She deserted me and went to live with an old male friend from her university days.

Separation seemed necessary, a tragic ending to our marriage.

'We have been pulling each other down,' she said, as if our intents were symmetrical. Her misandry prevented reciprocity.

My son Michael continued to live with me until he completed a PhD and went to a job in Africa. My social activities were few but enough. I discussed current issues at U3A, read philosophy with UQ students, went to meetings with writers, reading groups, discussants and community activists. I played guitar and sang with an old friend. Alone I enjoyed reading and watching movies.

I had a few good friends who I could discuss my writing with. When I was following a theory, I liked to articulate it as part of understanding it.

I missed sharing bottles of wine with Carol, on our balcony overlooking the river. I quit drinking alcohol. I didn't miss the family meetings she called with our children, to discuss her agenda. We were both opinionated and our arguments and quarrels had been intense.

I had never expected to live alone. Inner-city living could be lonely without a partner having interests in common. When I retired from teaching, I contributed to a community group campaigning for better development of West End.

When we divorced, Carol got our island house and I sold it for her, bringing her a good profit. I was sad to lose it. I remained in the riverside apartment where I am still living.

'Waterside properties increase in value faster than others,' I said, as an article of my faith. 'They can't create waterfront properties and demand for the few there are always increases.'

Divorced and without a job, I spent most of my time writing.

'You wanted to be alone to write,' said Michael. 'Now you can do that, Dad.'

'I never wanted to be alone all the time,' I said, because I didn't see as much of him as I would like. I wanted to be in contact with him and Sarah every week. I often resorted to writing to them, getting a reply sometimes.

Michael had lived at home for a couple of years, until he went to a job overseas. He was a talented salesman and entrepreneur, able to sell anyone on any idea, finding employment easily. Sarah loved living in Sydney but then went to a university lecturing position in Canada. Contact with my family in England had broken off, after a dispute about residential care of my father.

'You can't treat him so badly,' I complained.

'You don't do anything for him,' a sibling said.

'You have him locked up in an awful place. It is cruel.'

'He has dementia.'

'That's no excuse for cruelty.'

'He's unaware most of the time.'

I regret now not quitting my job earlier and should have gone back to the UK to look after him. I didn't, because caring for an old person with dementia was beyond my experience. I had come through my life so far without taking care of anyone, except the children when they were small. The call of duty wasn't strong enough, so I worked on. I was a poor filial carer.

Following divorce, I have lived alone in my apartment overlooking the River for 16 years. My children and their families sometimes stay with me when they visit Australia. The four members of our small family operate singly, with independence despite children. We have kept in touch with emails and meetings on Zoom during Covid.

Living by the Brisbane River has had new aspects and advantages. The popularity of Orleigh Park, on my doorstep, had made me aware of our riverside community and its vulnerability to flooding.

When, the park is inaccessible, through bad weather or flooding, it is evident that we have no alternative place to go and need the park for our welfare.

Our local community has preserved and nurtured biodiversity of the flora and fauna along the riverside and in adjacent areas. There has been opposition to large tall buildings that would block the floodplain. The riverside has been developed for recreation instead of car parking. The river has been preserved for ferries, crew rowing and kayaking. There is other traffic mid-river, such as jet skis and private party vessels.

Despite our best efforts, development of the community on the river floodplain would worsen river flooding. The nature of the river was not being respected.

CHAPTER 11 SOUTHBANK HUB

Southbank had become a transport hub without it being planned. It was near the centre of a city that had grown outwards on both sides of the river, connected by bridges used by vehicular, rail and pedestrian traffic. River flooding had in the past threatened transport across the river. In 1893, river flooding cut the Victoria Bridge and they had made do with ferries, until the bridge was replaced after four years.

Several other bridges had been built, with a recent spate of pedestrian bridges.

'We are going to have bridges close together, like in Venice,' someone said.

'I am not sure Brisbane will have enough cross river interaction to resemble Venice,' I said. 'A stroll across a canal for a drink in Venice would be more like a hike across the river in Brisbane.'

Cross-river traffic of all kinds has steadily increased in Brisbane. Buses, cars, railways, ferries, cyclists and pedestrians converge at Southbank on a few bridges, tunnels and ferries. When the river is in flood, access by these routes is cut and the city comes almost to a standstill.

City planners wanted to tame the river 'beast', but major floods have disrupted the city for weeks at a time. With bridges blocked and public transport services cancelled or clashing with private cars for road space, gridlock developed in the city centre. West End was used for street parking by commuters to the CBD. The situation was precarious even without river flooding and I campaigned with a local group for release of Kurilpa Peninsula from the stranglehold of cars.

I was indignant about the population influx, congested streets and shortage of parking spaces. Pedestrian and cyclist safety was threatened and I took part in a campaign to get the speed limit reduced from 60 to 40 kilometres per hour.

Pollution of the river had been a problem but strict control of effluent discharges had cleaned up the river water. Rod fishing had resumed. River water quality was improving and fishers lined the bank at Orleigh Park. Sharks were seen regularly in the tidal reaches of the river.

Visitors to Brisbane, accustomed to the clear blue water flowing in their countries' rivers, remark the brown colour of the river water, due to the presence of tiny colloidal clay particles, released by weathering of headwater rock. 'Would it be possible to purify the water by mixing in truckloads of flocculent, to aggregate the clay particles from suspension?' a water treatment engineer asked me.

'No,' I said. 'Flocculation requires still water. In any case, to 'purify' a river by chemical treatment is an oxymoron.'

The City Council planned for the South Brisbane suburb to have the city's fastest growing population, as a dormitory for city workers able to access their employment by public or active transport, crossing one of several pedestrian bridges. The plan had stimulated construction of residential apartment blocks and shopping precincts on the Kurilpa Peninsula.

'The CBD population density is planned to equal Hong Kong's,' said Howard.

'Would development be commercial or residential?' I asked.

'Both,' he said. 'The CBD could develop as a street level commercial centre for state-wide organisations and their employees, with residential apartments above.'

'It makes sense to connect with state-wide transport,' I said, 'except for the Queens Wharf Casino development, with its out-of-state visitors. Their customers may not need ready connection with state transport. Why do they have to be in the CBD?'

'Good point,' said Howard. 'The casino could be somewhere else, like near the airport, instead of crammed into the city centre.'

'If the casino was at the airport, transporting workers to it would be a headache,' I said. 'Better that thousands of casino workers live in the CBD or the Kurilpa Peninsula.'

'The casino is better located in the city centre.'
'The government wants a BrisVegas.'
'Without crime?'
'They hope.'

Development of the city centre was planned in tall buildings. Our group had been effective in campaigning to hold down heights, but developers were not much deterred by Council regulations.

'What is the limit on heights of buildings?' I asked Howard.

'In South Brisbane it is set at 12 storeys,' he said. 'The Council wants to increase it to 90 storeys. We are opposing it. We don't want a concrete jungle without recreation areas and without sunlight. Tall buildings become inaccessible in power outages. In floods, people are trapped or shut out. Homes are box-like cells, isolated, dangerous and dehumanising. These buildings could become centres for slum living and crime.'

'Without regulations more sensitive to people's needs, West End could become unpleasant to live in.'

'The outlook is bad,' said Howard. 'Without control, the future is grim.'

North and South Brisbane connected across the Victoria Bridge, where a Southbank hub had become congested. Development strengthened existing links rather than providing new public transport routes.

The city and its hub, the river flood plain, bridges and dams have problems of proximity. 'Brisbane River flooding inhibits the efficient functioning of the City,' he said. 'Construction of bridges and buildings in the City is worsening riverine flooding.'

It had been disconcerting for me to live on the Kurilpa Peninsula, a promontory into the river near the city centre, with tall blocks of apartments constructed densely. Urban growth has proceeded by entitlement to intrude, dwarf and subtract, rather than by careful reasoning. Developments clustered on the riverbanks have lacked amenity and diversity. It is easy to be critical of the intense development at the hub of Southbank, hosted by the River, because the suburb seems to have been overtaken by ugliness without redeeming features.

PART 2

BRISBANE RIVER HISTORY

CHAPTER 12 INDIGENOUS HISTORY

Europeans' experience of the Brisbane River is recent, after a convict settlement was founded in Brisbane about 200 years ago. Information from earlier could have been recorded and passed on from Indigenous people.

My story of living beside the Brisbane River will now go back in history as far as there are objective records, reviewing experience of Indigenous people and the local climate, free from personal biases and subjective interpretations, if possible.

It took almost 200 years of settlement by Europeans for the Brisbane River and its floodplain to be transformed into a waterway that in recent times has flooded intermittently. An historical perspective could reveal the earlier natural form of the River and flooding before there was mitigation. Before about 1820 there were no written accounts. Reports from earlier were orally transmitted and of questionable authenticity. I have pieced together the following impression from several sources, without scholarly rigour, a tentative description of pre-settlement conditions.

Aboriginal people lived in and around Meannjin, or Brisbane and Moreton Bay for at least 22,000 years. In the 2016 Census of Brisbane, there were 70,735 Aboriginal and Torres Strait Islander people.

Plains of grassy forests – ironbark, bloodwood, apple, stringy bark – dominated the region, where kangaroos, wallabies and possums grazed. Many parts of the southside were reserved by Aboriginal people as hunting grounds. Intrusion of scrub bushes into the open woodlands and grasslands was suppressed by fire-stick farming.

Creek drainage basins dissected the forests with marshy waterholes, where fish, crayfish, waterfowl and edible aquatic plants were harvested. Vine forests and rainforests grew in small pockets close to the Brisbane River, adding stores of medicines and fibres. Apart from extensive hunting grounds, the country provided wood, bark, reeds and rushes. Spears, baskets and necklaces were crafted.

The indigenous people have sometimes been depicted as suffering hungry and desperate lives. An opposing view is that they could easily gather and hunt enough food in a short time to have leisure time for social and cultural activities. Little time was spent in internecine strife. Although they had territories, neighbours had traditional rights of ingress and passage.

I wanted, but didn't obtain, any description of the river and floods before 1820.

The Brisbane River and its flood plain are an ancient highway, its length explored for thousands of years. The Turrbal and Jagera people had long been accustomed to play the role of tolerant hosts. Europeans settled on land, along the banks of the Brisbane River, utilised as a natural 'highway' by adjacent Aboriginal groups and more distant visitors.

The entire Brisbane valley saw much concourse of peoples using the river and its surrounding flats to travel between gatherings and ceremonies on the coast and in the highlands. The River has always been a common ground, a territory of first contact. This continual flux, and the nature of Aboriginal society with clan, language, totemic, group and social traditions, meant that the association of Indigenous groups within Brisbane's south side was complex.

In 1825, the lower reaches of the Brisbane River were described (40) by European discoverers as dense, vine-clad jungles festooned with blue and purple convolvulus, adorning both banks, with perfumed salt-water lilies floating on the tidal edges. Around the site of the future Brisbane, primeval forests of gums, bloodwood and ironbark clothed the ridges, and the flats nurtured patches of thick pine and fig tree. Fish, reptiles, birdlife and mammals abounded.

Ian Lipke's novel 'Nargun' (39) is a fictional story about early contact between Aborigines and European settlers. It is a tale with violence and suffering on both sides.

His fiction describes the lifestyle in an Aboriginal encampment before Europeans arrived. It was mostly peaceful, as the people went about their routines. Lipke's story focuses on the infrequent fights with neighbouring tribes, or with itinerants trespassing on their traditional territory. White settlers coming from the south occupied lands taken from the indigenous people by force.

Nargun, a legendary local warrior, had unhealed scars from his manhood ceremony. He meets a family displaced by white settlers. His tribe takes them in. Nargun learns superb tracking and fighting skills. He also learns how to fight with honour and knows the harsh punishments when the clan's rules are broken.

Nargun learns tracking that includes how not to leave a trail that others can follow, with many clever deceptions. He learns how to make and use weapons: the spear; the club; a shield; and a breathing tube for hiding underwater. He learns how to prepare to ambush and attack others, defending against large and small groups, both at home and in others' territory.

Lipke's story is imaginative, with an Aboriginal clan preoccupied with guarding its territory and its resources. Lipke provides important details of idyllic camp life for these nomadic Australian Aborigines. They depended on a wide range of foods they hunted and gathered in the natural environment before moving on.

Battles with adjoining tribes killed many warriors and stole their women, while their children and old folk hid away in fear of their lives. There was collaboration between tribes in resisting white controllers of convicts and settlers in their country. It is a tale that celebrates a resilient culture and fighting spirit that contemporary Aborigines could have preserved, accounting for their higher incarceration rate today.

Bruce Pascoe's book 'Dark Emu' (18) contradicts some of the nomadism in Lipke's story, especially the 'hunter-gatherer' label. He presents evidence that pre-colonial Aboriginal Australians were domesticating plants, sowing, harvesting, irrigating and storing foods. The 'nomads' label has been convenient for settlers to use when denying them land rights. Aborigines fought for their land against the invaders, just as they had against neighbouring tribes. It was winner-takes-all guerrilla warfare with pitched battles.

It could be deduced from Pascoe's information that Aboriginal Australians would have been fish-farming in creek pens adjoining the Brisbane River. They could also have been growing plants in cultivated areas on the river flood plain, possibly irrigating them. Further away from the river, more of their food would be obtained by hunting.

'The explorers and early settlers didn't make much mention of Aborigines farming on the scale narrated by Pascoe,' said Howard. 'His information is conjectural and lacking corroboration by other historians.'

'They may not have come across it, or didn't recognise the fish traps and cultivation as farming,' I said. 'I don't think we can totally dismiss Pascoe's account. It's possible he exaggerated the extent of farming.'

Albert Holt's book *Forcibly Removed,* (37), suggests that later, when the colonists herded survivors into concentration camps, such as at Cherbourg in Queensland, they suffered privations but clung to their separate tribal identities and rarely united in opposition against their oppressors.

Tom Lawson (36) argued that The British colonial policy towards the indigenous people of Tasmania, in the first part of the 19th century, amounted to ethnic cleansing. Massacres of Aborigines have been recorded in Queensland, but not genocide on the scale he reported in Tasmania.

Keith Windschuttle's book (35) has likened fighting between Aborigines and settlers as similar to the skirmishes in North America between indigenous Indian peoples, settlers and military. Windschuttle's book is scholarly and dismissed supposed total genocide in Tasmania, consistent with Lipke's portrayal of a warrior race engaged in guerrilla warfare, beaten by diseases and superior arms. Critics have said Windschuttle never visited Tasmania and wrote the book in London.

Settlement by Europeans occupied land traditionally used by indigenous people for their encampments, restricting access and movements.

Indigenous people raided South Brisbane crops in 1827. A purpose could have been to starve out the fledgling colony. From then till the 1870s, former Aboriginal pathways between South Brisbane and Logan River, and South Brisbane and Cleveland, became roads pivotal to most Indigenous-settler contact, whether for trade, transport or armed attack.

From the 1850s, local Aboriginal people took up selling fish or bark to settlers, or worked for the district's early timber-getters. Others found jobs assisting with stock or domestic duties on emerging farms, for instance, at Cooper's Plains and Holland Park.

Indigenous people lived by the Brisbane River under trees at several major camping grounds. When settlers had first arrived, the Indigenous people were accustomed to walking across the South Brisbane river shallows at low tide. The river bed averaged 1.5 metres deep, until dredged to 6 metres at their crossing point in 1900, when it was navigable as far as College's Crossing near Ipswich, over 80 km upstream from the river's mouth.

Boundary Street in West End was a racial southern border to segregate the indigenous Jagera and Turrbal people from British settlers. Boundary posts marked the edge of town where 'non-whites' and 'indigenous people' were not allowed to cross after 4:00 pm on weekdays and Saturdays, but not at all on Sundays. In South Africa such separation of the races was known as apartheid. It began in Brisbane in 1859 and continued in the 1890s to 1950s, ending after 300,000 black American servicemen stationed in Brisbane, almost half the population, went home.

The city had been founded on the north side of the river because the south side was lower lying and flood-prone. The land was zoned for factories and commercial developments, such as warehouses and milk processing. Homes on the southside were cheaper and the northside was preferred by affluent people who could afford better quality homes. Private schools and professional employment were predominantly on the north side. There was a disparity in residential development on the south side, but the south gradually caught up. Factory sites were sold to build apartments and office blocks. West End became an attractive residential address. An apartment construction boom was underway near where Indigenous people had used to cross the river.

The traditional Aboriginal lifestyle was disappearing. Aboriginal people were attracted to the commercial precinct of Brisbane, as a place where European commodities could be obtained and they could be paid by photographers to pose.

About 60,000 years after humans arrived in Australia, it has been only 200 years since settlement of people from overseas commenced. Pre-colonisation history has been lost with disappearance of valuable experience of the land and indigenous people. History of the Turrbal and Jagera Aborigines who lived here for so long is largely absent.

Australian prisons with higher than proportional incarceration of Aboriginals, could indicate lingering resistance to European hegemony. This thesis is more consistent with Windschuttle's narrative of guerrilla warfare than Lawson's depiction of genocide of a passive native people. Pascoe's thesis of Aboriginal farming would be consistent with more resistance to Europeans than for a nomadic people. It could be reasonable to suppose that the Brisbane River had Aboriginal fish farming and cultivation and dispossession was fiercely resisted.

Modern experience may not be enough to understand the ways of the River people. Before extrapolating to forecasting the next 200 years, it may be possible to infill variations of Aboriginal experience during the previous 59,800 years, by joining the dots from contemporary culture, art, language, or some other way.

This historical perspective has mentioned occurrences and traditions that could resonate today. It has revealed absence of recorded information about the past of the Brisbane River, before European settlement. I have identified some points of supposition. They do not much overlap with or contradict the history of the river recorded by the colonial administration and its settlers. The cultural heritage and oral traditions of Indigenous people need to be consulted and respected, before any change to the operation and uses of the river are considered.

CHAPTER 13 CLIMATE

I have traversed the geology, indigenous history, drought, climate, cyclones and flooding of the Brisbane River catchment in my work as an engineer. I have surveyed main events by Cartesian analysis and looked for ways to improve riverside living conditions.

Brisbane River is the largest river draining a southern portion of the north-east coast of Australia. It's reach inland is tiny, compared with the long intermittently flowing rivers that interlace the interior of the continent. From the other side of the watershed, the Murray-Darling basin carries water inland, to the South Australian Gulf near Adelaide. Rainfall is infrequent, but such is the vastness of the catchment, there is often flooding at confluences. The absence of rainfall for long periods and the high temperatures kill most plants, except perennials growing along watercourses. Further inland the landscapes are generally deserts, shaped by wind and water erosion, with little vegetation (41). In the vicinity of the coast, the catchment of the Brisbane River is better vegetated, because this area receives a little more rainfall.

The interior of the continent experiences, in winter, large dry anticyclones moving predominantly from the southwest to the northeast. In summer, the Brisbane River is affected by wind circulation from cyclonic systems offshore in the equatorial north, or in the Pacific, moving south and affecting the east of the continent. Cyclonic winds, circulating clockwise, drive onshore, bringing rainfall of various intensities irregularly. The ground near the coast is less absorbent than the sands of the interior and sizeable surface flows can occur, with erosion of land unprotected by vegetation. Flash floods convey much of the water away into modest temporary rivers, meandering through flood plains, that hold the water, until the part not evaporated reaches the ocean.

Flooding of the Brisbane River is commonly attributed to the vagaries of Brisbane's climate. It has become usual to blame it on aspects assumed to be deteriorating due to climate change.

Although Brisbane has a mostly pleasant climate, hot summer weather is a feature of the area. High temperatures, high humidity and cyclones with high winds and heavy rainfall are routinely associated with the greenhouse theory of global warming. Trends in temperatures and rainfall have been claimed and conversion of electricity production from fossil fuels to renewable energy is being attempted, to avert climate change, despite controversy. Perhaps because the climate can be insufferably hot, there is more concern about climate change in Australia than in many other countries.

Significance of possible climate change will be considered in a later chapter. Here I discuss issues in climate measurement that have confounded me, my family, scientists and governments.

Sarah, my daughter, found the summer heat in Brisbane oppressive, preferring Sydney's climate. Michael stayed in Brisbane, working at night at the university research centre, evading the heat of the day.

I sat with Sarah and Michael on the veranda at my apartment, gazing down on the people in the park and the boats on the river.

'It's getting hotter and hotter,' Sarah said.

She always had strong opinions.

'The temperature change isn't sudden, unidirectional or continuous,' I said. 'The media cherry-pick the hottest days, claiming trends as sensational evidence of climate change. A balanced view would find there is cooling as well as warming, with change gradual, on average.'

'The government must stop the warming,' said Sarah.

'They don't have much say in it,' I said. 'About 98% of our warming is supposed to be contributed by emissions from other countries and only a few of them are doing anything to prevent it. Should we have to produce electricity at greater expense to mitigate a change that most foreigners are unconcerned about?'

'Hmph,' said Michael doubtfully. 'If we in Australia stop using fossil fuels, others may do so.'

'They may not. Why would they be led by us?'

'Are you denying global collaboration?'

'I am sceptical, as you know,' I said. 'I am not convinced there is a climate crisis or that we know what is causing one. I want evidence that fossil fuel combustion gases trap infrared radiation, causing global warming.'

'There's lots of evidence,' Sarah said. 'Climate change could cause the El Nino Southern Oscillation (ENSO).'

'I thought it was the other way around: there is evidence of ENSO causing climate change.'

'The climate may oscillate, but wholesale climate change is not predictable.'

'It's not rocket science,' said Sarah. 'Rain and droughts in Australia are predicted to be effects of movement of heat globally.'

'The theory doesn't have a predictable force swinging climate between El Nino and La Nina phases, in the same way that a force of gravity swings pendulums.'

'I heard air temperature and pressure in the equatorial Pacific oscillate every 2-7 years,' Michael said.

Sarah was quiet. She was mulling over the complexity of the problem.

'That's hardly a regular pattern,' I said. 'The change process could be chaotic, triggered by something small, like the beating of a butterfly's wings in Paraguay, or some such. Hot and cold sea currents do bring different weather, but the oscillation is less predictable than some commentators have pretended. My view is that ENSO is a retrospective rationalisation of weather variations, without much capability for useful prediction. It seems to have a confirmatory bias, amplifying recent weather trends.'

'It helps me, that bad weather won't go on forever,' Michael said. As usual, his interest was practical.

'What good is that?' I said. 'Do you know the availability heuristic? It is a psychological error, causing us to recall more examples of an event that is familiar, rather than those more numerous, as we should do.' (18)

'Is it recency bias?' asked Michael.

'Yes, we remember more of recent events. There is also an effect bias. Cyclones and droughts are infrequent and have dramatic effects, taking attention away from more frequent mundane weather.'

'Why do bad effects get most attention?' he asked.

'They are more noticeable,' I said. 'Like ENSO explains dry and wet weather in cycles.'

'It's little better than nothing,' I said. 'A truly scientific theory has three qualities: it explains what has happened in the past; it has a hypothesis that can be tested; and it can make useful predictions about the future. The ENSO theory is not scientific on two of the three counts. It only explains the past.

'Is it a statistical theory?' Michael asked

'How do you mean?'

'It explains chance.'

'It doesn't even do that,' I said.

'ENSO doesn't have the usual stamp of scientific approval by empirical evidence,' I said. 'But not many so-called scientific theories do. It is an elaborate theory. Like many other scientific theories, ENSO is impossible to falsify. What we have is a truism. ENSO weather is always true, either El Nino or La Nina. We only find out which we have after the weather is wet or dry.'

'Get with it, Dad! Everyone believes in ENSO,' said Michael. 'You really are a dinosaur about climate. What's your problem?'

'I don't have a problem,' I said. 'Running with the herd is all some people want, but like lemmings they could rush over a cliff. In case you think I am part of the problem, I am probably doing more to prevent climate change than you are. I behave as though climate is being changed by human overconsumption of all types of energy. I minimise my consumption of energy, including food, washing, heating and vehicular transport. Do you?'

I didn't want to quarrel with Michael. Like me he was a thinker but unlike me he accepted others' opinions of unexplained matters. He accepted when I didn't. That was his problem, but I wouldn't press him on it. I longed to confront him with details of the faked part of climate science, but this wasn't the time to do it. I had found very few people who could discuss climate science without getting emotional.

'I do what is agreed by a consensus of scientists,' Michael said. 'I try to minimise emissions.'

'True science does not require consensus and is capable of being falsified,' I said. Greenhouse warming cannot possibly be untrue by this method. The Greenhouse Theory is deceitful and promoted by scoundrels, among others.'

'Do you believe it?' Sarah asked.

'No, I am sceptical,' I said. 'It's unsound. A sound theory has to be testable and irrefutable.'

'Perhaps there is a way to test the Greenhouse Theory,' she said.

'I have proposed a test (8).' I said. 'I want someone to conduct the experiment and send me a report.'

I explained to them my proposed test (8) comparing warming of air with and without greenhouse gases. But my partisan polemic fell on deaf ears.

'Could you test it yourself?' Michael asked.

'I don't have the equipment,' I said. 'If I did, I wouldn't do it, because results achieved by me would be regarded as biased.'

'Hasn't anyone done a test?'

'I haven't heard of it. Not a controlled test, anyway,' I said. 'I infer they won't do a fair test because it would refute the Greenhouse Theory. Important people are profiting by assuming the Greenhouse Theory is correct. There is a climate change industry selling alternatives to fossil fuel technologies. Installing solar panels, wind turbines, batteries and electric cars is only the beginning. Climate change solutions are promoted by the media and governments with an appearance of certainty, as part of a capitalist Spectacle described by Debord (34). The Greenhouse Theory is a matter of belief akin to religion.'

The above notwithstanding, some readers may believe enough is known about the effects of climate change on the Brisbane River for mitigating technologies to be selected and implemented immediately. Without better understanding, such action would be rash and possibly harmful. More measurement of climate is needed.

Cutting fossil fuel use could do more harm than good considering possible effects. The adage attributed to an experienced carpenter is 'Measure twice, cut once.'

Caution is needed.

CHAPTER 14 DROUGHT

Europeans settled in the southeast of Queensland for its cooler climate. The hot north, with greater humidity, had relied on the labour of dark skinned people, both indigenous Australians and kanakas from South Pacific islands, forcibly recruited and able to work hard in the hot sun. In recent times, Australian fruit growers have brought pickers from Pacific islands, especially Vanuatu. Others laboured on sugar plantations, laid railway tracks, worked on cattle stations, or as domestic servants. Early in the 20th century, many from South Pacific islands were deported in an act of unjust and cruel racial discrimination. Many had lived in Australia all their lives, where they had been exploited. They did not have homes in the islands to return to.

Italians and Mediterranean peoples replaced the deportees in the cane fields. From December to March, heat and humidity kept people with air conditioning indoors on many days. The south of Queensland climate is sub-tropical, with summer rain and comparatively dry winters, when drought is likely.

The longest drought since British settlement occurred between 2001 and 2009. Wivenhoe Dam dried to its lowest level, at 15 per cent, in 2007. Brisbane residents became frugal users of water, exercising restraint that reduced water consumption by more than half, to 130 litres per person per day. Watering of gardens with mains water was banned. Hosing was prohibited and water-saving shower heads were fitted. Grey water was recycled from sinks, washing machines and showers into toilet tanks, or used to water plants and lawns.

As Wivenhoe Dam neared empty, regulation of usage, rationing and sharing of water supplies commenced, also conservation, storage, recycling, desalination and importation of water by truck or pipeline to eke out supply. When rain replenished the dam, consumption soon returned to previous levels.

One day I was buying a shower rose in the plumbing section of my local hardware store, when a young woman spoke to me.

'Excuse me, can you help me? Do you know which of these shower heads would use the least water?' she asked.

Since Carol and I had separated, I had become aware that there were many single women around, at work, in the community and at events I attended. I was 47 and this 30-year old woman was within my range of interest.

'I heard somewhere that a rose with many jets to wet you all over quickly uses least water,' I said. 'Like this one.'

I showed her the one I was considering buying. She looked at it.

'How do you wash yourself?' I asked her.

It was a risqué personal question, but she was not embarrassed.

'First I take my clothes off,' she said. 'Is that what you mean?'

She turned around under an imaginary shower.

'I turn around once, soaping as I go,' she said.

She completed it quickly.

'There,' she said. 'How do you wash yourself?'

'I play the spray on my face and down my front, then I turn around several times, wetting my back and sides. Then I soap all over and repeat to wash it off.'

'I think you use more water than I do,' she said.

'I'm impressed,' I said laughing. 'I might try your method. My name is Chance.'

'I'm Rachel.'

'I'm going to buy this shower head,' I said. 'Would you like me to show you how well it works, at my place, before you decide?'

'Yes, but I don't want you to wet yourself,' she said.

'Haha. Do you live around here?'

'Yes, on Devon Street,' she said. 'And you?'

'Orleigh Street. I'll install it and you can see it. Can you come to number 35 this evening, about 7 pm. Would you like to go for a drink after? There's a bar on Bathurst Street.'

The shower was a success and we had a pleasant chat over a drink. She was gorgeous. It took a careful person to want to see a shower rose working before buying it. She impressed me.

Rachel and I were soon in a loving relationship. She had a lively mind, her own ideas and we connected intellectually. We both had a passion for understanding how the world worked. At first she was an enthusiast who found beauty and fascination in nearly everything and explored new ideas, experiences and adventures. When we came across heavy topics that could have turned into arguments, we sidestepped away.

My feelings for her grew and we met outside work, at restaurants and movies. I made an effort to look younger with clothes and beard. Rachel was delightful company. She was an emancipated woman, widely respected locally for her many accomplishments. After being together for six months, we started sleeping together.

'What do you do?'

'I am a librarian,' Rachel said. 'What about you?'

'I am a science teacher.'

'Why did you separate from your wife?' she asked.

'Our kids left home and there was nothing holding us together. What do you want to do with your life now?' I asked her.

'Serve,' she said.

'Who?'

'That's enough about me,' she said. 'What do you want to do?'

'Write. Writing novels is my hobby.'

'What is your aim?'

'I want to sell books that are respected,' I said.

'You want to be famous?'

'A little, in narrow circles.'

'It sounds like you are on an ego trip,' Rachel said.

'My ego has been taken over by my id. I operate on instinct.'

Long before electric scooters became popular, Rachel rode around the city on an electric bicycle. She was original, wearing saris and kimonos, rotating bright colours on a daily schedule. Her critical viewpoint was useful to me for researching Brisbane River living. She had a wide experience of living close to the Brisbane River.

The Brisbane River dried to a trickle in the drought between 2001 and 2009. Artesian water continued to surface and there was a little rain in a few places. Water storages depleted and supply of townswater became uncertain. When it rained, river water would pour into artesian reservoirs in aquifer rocks subcropping in river beds, before replenishing surface flows and refilling dams. The situation for humans and livestock was often desperate and they had to turn to expensive alternative sources of water.

Water stored to mitigate flooding can also prevent drought. Water released to save a dam could possibly have prevented drought. Floods and droughts are opposite sides of water supply, which is as uncertain as the arrival of cyclones. My search for Brisbane River improvement would focus on water storage operations, which depended on technology and weather forecasts.

CHAPTER 15 CYCLONES

'Since 1858, there have been 207 tropical cyclones along the east coast of Queensland with the majority in North Queensland,' I told my science students. 'There have been 46 tropical cyclones near Brisbane and the Gold Coast.'

'Several times annually, cyclones capable of causing flooding in Brisbane track into the river catchment area.'

'Every cyclone crossing the catchment has the potential to flood Brisbane,' I continued, showing statistics on an overhead projector. 'The Brisbane River catchment area is 13,600 km^2. A cyclone is a whirling vortex maybe 20 kilometres in diameter, with an area of 300 km^2. It would take 50 vortexes to cover the catchment. One vortex wouldn't be enough to cause a flood, but a moving cyclone can affect a much wider area, with heavy rain for days on end.'

'What happens?' a student would ask.

'As a cyclone approaches from over the sea, the wind and rain gradually increase for several hours. Winds are powerful enough to break large trees, roll over vehicles and remove roofs from buildings. The moisture cools as it rises and condenses into heavy rain.'

'Are cyclones the same as tornados?'

'No. Tornados occur in the USA and are narrow, violently rotating columns of air, in contact with both the surface and storm clouds. They are called twisters. The only tornados we have are tiny willy-willies.'

'Are cyclones larger than tornados?'

'Yes.' I said. 'Cyclones have localised effects with varying rainfall intensity and duration. They are extensive, with winds circulating clockwise, as viewed from above in the Southern Hemisphere.'

'Why clockwise?' a student would ask.

'In Australia, the spin of a cyclone is clockwise, caused by the Earth rotating. Friction between air and Earth drag the air mass from west to east,' I said. 'The air also circulates from high pressure at the cold poles towards low pressure at the hot equator.'

'So the air has two forces pushing it to rotate clockwise: friction and pressure?'

'Correct.'

'Would a cyclone rotate clockwise in the USA?' another student would ask.

'No. They call it a hurricane and the net forces act in directions opposite to here: anticlockwise.'

'What happens in a cyclone?'

'The centre sucks in hot air, spins it and lofts it, with winds reaching 400 kilometres per hour or more,' I would say, waving my arms dramatically. 'As the spinning centre, or eye, passes overhead, the wind stops and reverses direction. A cyclone often crosses the coast and moves inland, losing wind speed and changing direction erratically, causing flooding that can continue for days, or even weeks, until it slows and disappears.

'How does the air reach 400 kilometres per hour?'

'Hot air rises in thermals. Glider pilots get a free ride going from thermal to thermal, even for 2,000 kilometres, from Brisbane to Adelaide. They search for upward flows of air above dark cultivated land, that absorbs and emits solar radiation. The next field may have a reflective, pale coloured crop of grain, not absorbing radiation, with cool air sinking downward. In a small plane, flying low over country alternating from dark to pale, the different land colours give a bumpy ride.'

'Why do thermals occur over the ocean?'

'At the equator the ocean has intense infrared radiation warming the air above the water,' I would tell them. 'Warm air expands, it rises, cools and the pressure lowers, causing condensation into water droplets in a tall dark cloud.

'Has anyone seen a cumulonimbus cloud, shaped like an anvil, with a ledge at the top?' I asked.

The arms of most of the class would go up.

'When you see a very large one of those, you probably have a cyclone coming. You should lie down under a table, so large things can't fall on you.

'Who can tell me why a cyclone can be dangerous?'

'Strong winds,' someone said.

'Correct. At the centre of a cyclone the air is spinning around in a vortex. This builds up as the centre of a tropical cyclone, with heavy rainfall, hail, thunder and lightning.'

'I don't get it why the air spins in a vortex,' a student said.

'There is a low pressure aloft and at ground level, air is sucked in quickly from all around, conserving momentum as circular motion, creating a vortex, going inwards and up the way water goes down a plug hole. That's the Coriolis Effect.'

I ended my lesson by asking them to imagine what it would have been like 200 years ago, to see a tall dark cloud coming.

'It would have been mysterious and frightening.' said a student. 'You wouldn't know what to expect.'

'Good answer. In the 19th Century humans sought land and minerals, pitting themselves at remote frontiers: against weather, climate hardships, natural disasters, hostile peoples, lawlessness and diseases,' I said. 'Conquering of the Brisbane River 'Beast' was hoped to be a triumph for science over superstition. It was a story of survival, made respectable in 1859 by Charles Darwin's book The Origin of the Species. The rigours of surviving in Brisbane were for the good of Queen Victoria and the Empire.'

'Jolly good,' said a student with an English accent.

'Science could not hold flooding of the Brisbane River under its thumb,' I said. 'Cyclones threatened the city regularly and several times dumped huge volumes of water in the Brisbane River catchment area, causing floods.

'In those days they wouldn't have had measurements of wind speed or cloud photographs to know what was happening. The best they could do was to predict their strengths and tracks and prepare early. It is difficult even today. Here's a true story about running from a hurricane.

'My daughter and family were living in Houston Texas in September 2005, when warnings were given for Hurricane Rita. We would call it a cyclone. Three weeks before they had escaped Hurricane Katrina, the most devastating hurricane in U.S. history up to that point, causing damage of $125 billions (August 2005).

'The radio advised citizens to evacuate because the hurricane was predicted to land south of Houston. My daughter drove north with her family, along with 15 million people moving inland from coastal Texas. They spent 24 hours jammed in freeway traffic, running out of petrol. Eventually they reached the home of a friend at Lake Livingstone in east Texas. Within a few hours, the hurricane passed over them, raging around for a day, with moderate destruction. They had fled into its path, which had missed Houston and tracked to east Texas. They would have been safer to have stayed at home in Houston, which was spared. The moral of the story is that hurricanes can be unpredictable. In Australia, cyclone paths are unpredictable too.'

Students liked my cyclones lesson for its drama. Images of cars lofted into trees were entertaining. It rated better than dinosaurs, but less well than wine-making. Wine-making had to be cancelled after other teachers complained that their students were staggering and shouting. After that, cyclones rated best.

My analysis of the Brisbane River attributes the worst flooding to cyclones. Next I will explain the water cycle, how a cyclone is manifest and what was done before and after the four worst floods of the Brisbane River surged into the city.

CHAPTER 16 FLOODING RAINS

I had described a cyclone as a mass of moving air, under control of pressure. I explained to my grandson Amir, 12, how a mass of water also moved, under control of gravity.

'Where does water come from?' I asked him as we sat in the park, overlooking the River.

'Why does flood water have to come from somewhere?' he asked. 'Can't it just be there?'

'Water moves around, so it has to come from somewhere. I will start with water condensing in an updraught of air in a cyclone, forming rain, which falls to the ground and becomes a flood.'

'Why not start in the air before that?'

'Good question, Amir. I could start anywhere in the huge circle called the water cycle. I don't have to start with it condensing.'

'Does water go away and around, then come back again?'

'Yes, when it evaporates it becomes invisible. When it condenses it becomes rain which you can see in clouds and puddles. It falls from the sky, runs away and then eventually comes back again in clouds, in a different place.'

'Is there any way to stop it raining, Grandad?' asked Amir.

'You would have to stop the water particles in the air combining into droplets and falling, inside the tall dark cloud,' I said.

'How?' he asked.

'You would have to stop them becoming large and heavy, or freezing into hail and falling to the ground,' I said. 'Can you think of a way to keep the water up in the clouds?'

'With a parachute?' said Amir.

'Good idea. Like an umbrella blocking the droplets from falling?' I said. 'It would have to be large and very strong, because the upwind could be violent.'

83

'Could water falling on top collapse it?' asked Amir.

'Yes, it could. A better way to keep the rain and hail aloft would be to assist the updraught.'

'With a fan?' said Amir. 'Or a heater? Or an explosion?'

'I'm not sure a heater would help us,' I said, 'nor an explosion. Maybe a wind turbine could be mounted, with the generator operating as a motor and turning the blades, blowing air vertically.'

It was far-fetched but technological innovations sometimes resulted from asking What If?'

'Could it use electricity instead of generating it?' asked Amir.

'When there's a cyclone they have to stop a wind turbine from spinning to stop it over-speeding and being damaged,' I said. 'You could write to the electricity company's wind turbine people and ask them when there's a cyclone, to spin it to blow upwards.'

'Could it work?' asked Amir.

'It would need to spin fast to hold rain up in the sky,' I replied.

'Perhaps the updraught from the fan could boost the natural updraught and hold up hailstones the size of a basketball,' Amir said.

'That would stop rain falling,' I said.

'When the hail falls, people could be hurt,' Amir said.

'Yes. Then flooding would be the least of your worries,' I said. 'We are going to have to think of a better way of keeping the water aloft.'

'It might be easier to stop flooding after the water has landed,' said Amir.

'On the ground, rain and melted hail would run together and into a stream or river, flowing by gravity from a high place to a low place,' I said. 'What could be done to stop the rain running into a stream?'

'The ground could soak it up,' said Amir, excited. 'Farmers could dig up the surface with ploughs.'

'Yes,' I said. 'Flash flooding can occur because the ground is unabsorbent and there is no infiltration. Permeation of water can be stopped by compaction by the hooves of cattle and sheep, or pores can be blocked by fine clay particles.'

'Kangaroos have large footprints,' said Amir. 'They would compact the soil less and the rain would be absorbed, with less surface run off.'

'To prevent flooding, graziers could change from cattle to kangaroos,' I said.

'How would they hold a kangaroo in a crush?' Amir asked. 'It would try to jump out.'

'Why would they put a kangaroo in a crush?'

'To treat them for parasites,' he said. He had been to a station and worked cattle. 'The crush could have a roof, with a hole for its head to stick out, to put the medicine in.'

'That's enough,' I said. 'You can work on that idea by yourself later.'

I felt bad stopping his creativity, but it would be good if he discovered he could do it independently.

'The other way to increase infiltration is planting crops with roots that open up the soil,' I said. 'Contour ploughing slows surface water from running downhill. It prevents erosion and flash flooding. What are the two ways we have found to stop flooding?'

'Ploughing and kangaroos.'

I told Amir about the flood which occurred several years before he was born.

'On 10th January 2011, during 24 hours up to 9 am, there was a deluge of 300 mm spread over most of the Brisbane River catchment of 13,600 km^{2}.'

'Did any rain fall before or after?' Amir asked.

'Good question,' I said. 'Yes, lots, before. Why did you ask?'

'The soil would fill up and water would stay on the surface, causing flooding.'

'Correct,' I said. 'The ground was saturated and there was flash flooding. The dams filled quickly. Wivenhoe Dam and Somerset Dam could together receive half of rainfall from the Brisbane River catchment. A 300mm deluge could, in 36 hours, have filled the 3 million megalitre dam completely full. But Lockyer Creek and Bremer River join the Brisbane River below Wivenhoe Dam.

Brisbane could be flooded. Here, I'll show you on this map where the rain fell.'

I showed him *Figure 1*.

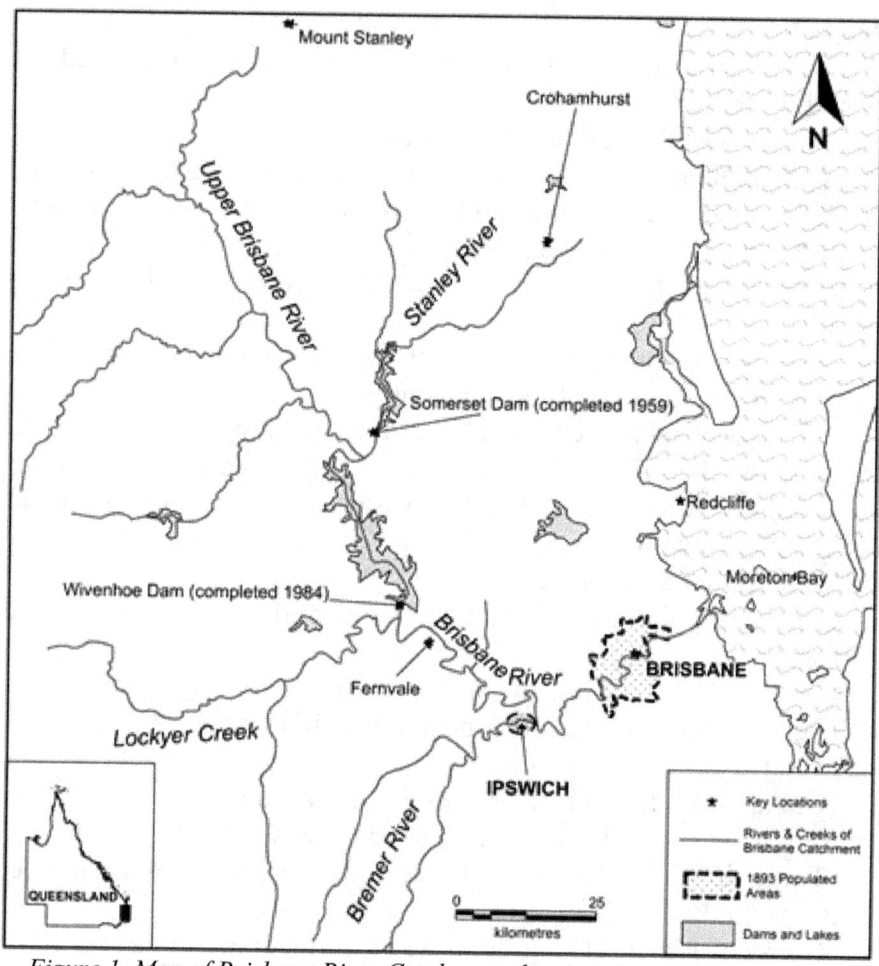

Figure 1. Map of Brisbane River Catchment showing rivers, Somerset Dam, Wivenhoe Dam. Drafted by Nick Cook.

We went back to my place for lunch and discussed the map together.

'Would the Brisbane River water be caught in the dams?' Amir asked.

'Only about a third, in the flood this year,' I said. 'Two thirds of the rain fell downstream of the dams. But the Wivenhoe dam almost filled and they had to release water. It flowed down the river channel, becoming progressively less steep, wider and slower flowing, with water able to build up across the flood plain.'

'Did the river have floods before the dams were built?' Amir asked.

'After the great flood in 1893, for 66 years they straightened and deepened the river, training it to run in its channel. They made space for floodwater to overflow. They preserved the flood plain and low lying land, lakes and swamps, to store water. That would hold back flash flooding, delaying flooding and preventing torrents in the city. They kept vegetation and storage areas for absorbing flood water.'

'Wanting to hold back water is the opposite of helping the flood water get away down a channel.,' he said. 'How weird was that?'

'Correct. Well done Amir. The balance between freeing the flow and holding it back gradually changed towards damming, instead of clearing the river channel. Creating additional space to hold back flood water started interest in the damming of the Brisbane River. The Somerset Dam, commenced in 1934, opened in 1959 and the Wivenhoe Dam, in 1984. After their construction, freeing the river of obstructions and absorbing flood water were neglected.'

'How can a river be prevented from flooding?' asked Amir.

'Brisbane City Council nominated a defined flood level, a height on a peg, as the lower limit for development and it was applied to most building approvals, but factories could be built lower,' I said. 'When flooding occurred above the defined flood level, the Council approved homes that could be flooded.'

'Why?' asked Amir.

'Why not?' I said. 'It is usual in Australia that people can do what they want so long as it doesn't do anyone harm. If the house they build floods, they are responsible. Do you know what responsible means?'

'It would be their own fault.'

'What if no-one knew it would flood?
'Too bad.'
'Yes. Should the government try to reduce flooding of homes?'
'Yes.'
'I agree. The main ways are to withhold building approvals, to increase infiltration, to construct flood plain storage and to prevent obstruction of waterways.

'Buildings constructed on the flood plain block flow. The government doesn't allow developments in the lowest lying positions, because buildings can be a barrier to flood water getting away, even if the developer accepts the flooding risk.'

'Can anything else be done?' asked Amir.

'Yes,' I said. 'Flooding is exacerbated by soil compaction, deforestation, land clearing, obstruction of waterways, high volume releases from dams and high tides. During the first 100 of 130 years since the 1893 flood, there was more attention to flood mitigation than reducing these exacerbating factors. They could have prevented obstruction of the river channel. Flow of water away is held up by obstacles such as deposition of sediments; construction of bridge support pillar islands in channels; and private jetties that break away and jam against the pillars.

'During a raging flood, backwater from these obstacles could raise flood height for kilometres upstream, possibly by several metres. The amount can be calculated.'

'Have you calculated it?' asked Amir.

'No. I would need to have measurements from many river stations,' I said. 'Adding up all the bridge backwaters, the increased water level would flood many homes.'

'What is backwater?' Amir asked.

'It's the river level upstream being raised by something blocking it, like the bow wave and wake of a ship being raised above the sea surface level.'

'What happens to the flood water when the river level goes down?' Amir asked.

'What do you imagine?' I said.

'It flows into the ocean.'

'Yes,' I said. 'There it gets evaporated into the sky, forms clouds, turns into rain and goes around again. The river is the part of the water cycle that collects rain from the land.'

'How does the water know what to do?' Amir asked.

'It obeys laws of condensation and gravity,' I said.

'Is that all?'

'They're enough,' I said. 'Would it be better if humans were in control?'

'Yes.'

I explained to Amir the scope is limited for humans to intervene in the water cycle because of the large sizes of climate, clouds, rainfall, land, river, ocean and winds.

'Where in the cycle could they try to stop river flooding?' I asked.

'Flooding is caused by climate and weather.'

'That's true,' I said. 'Could they change the climate and weather?'

'A little, perhaps,' he said.

'It would be difficult, because they are large and other countries could be affected,' I said. 'The system is too vast for humans to tinker with the whole world. But it may be possible to make small changes that would stop the Brisbane River flooding.'

Amir was interested and when he visited later I briefly reviewed with him the four worst floods in Brisbane, in 1893, 1974, 2011 and 2022. I told him about the floods, encouraging him to ask more questions.

I had enjoyed his questions, unlike media whose questions, as part of their propaganda, often assumed controversial theories were correct. In my opinion it was irresponsible to expose youngsters to exaggeration, fake science and dystopian predictions.

CHAPTER 17 AFTER THE 1893 FLOOD

The flood had been the worst in recorded history. It was four years before the Victoria Bridge re-opened to traffic.

Orleigh Park

The Council purchased a sliver of land beside the river and created Orleigh Park. In June of 1917 they planted fig trees, many of which have survived, providing the Park with much of its character and beauty.

'The flood was caused by record rainfall, before the Somerset and Wivenhoe Dams were constructed,' I said. 'The rainfall was unprecedented. There were two cyclones close together. It could happen again.'

'To prevent further flooding they gave most attention to deepening and straightening the river channel,' said Howard.

'It was a less costly method to reduce flood heights than dam building,' I said.

'It would have been better to relocate the city off the floodplain, at a site upriver, or downriver, or inland,' Howard said.

'Then why didn't they do it?' I asked him.

'If you tell people Brisbane is in the wrong place, they will say 'it is too late now to move it', Howard said. 'Property owners have preferred to restore the value of their existing properties, rather than beginning anew somewhere else. It would have been as true in 1893 as it is today.'

'Maybe they were devastated by the flood and lacked courage to make a new start,' I said. 'The flood submerged a large part of the city. But a dam would not remedy it. It took them 41 years until 1934 to start the Somerset Dam and 25 years to build it. There cannot have been much faith in it.'

'It catches only 11% of the Brisbane River water,' said Howard. 'It was hopeful.'

'They let the opportunity to rebuild the city slip away,' I said.

'Intuitively they may have realised relocation was needed, but they lacked precedents, analysis was difficult and they had no champion to persuade the majority,' I said. 'There was some support for relocating the growing city upriver to Ipswich. However, it was also flood-prone. The river was feared as a 'beast to be tamed'. The Somerset Dam Syndrome was borne. It was a supposed panacea that only slowly surrendered to more objective views.'

'Development of houses on the river floodplain soon resumed,' Howard said.

'The city had been located around the port, at Hamilton, but as sailing ships and steamers became larger, they stayed outside the river mouth, discharging passengers and goods to lighters, which plied up the river,' I said.

'The port had effectively moved downriver for berthing larger ships,' said Howard. 'There was a glaring city location error. It should have been built either upriver, or downriver, to avoid flooding. The site they chose was floodable.'

'I would like to know how they selected the location.'

'Me too,' said Howard. 'A more sinister interpretation is that this location benefited the rich and disadvantaged the poor.'

'Did they have conspiracy theories in those days?' I asked.

'No, but there was a class divide,' he said. 'A commentator wrote in 1885 (1, p19): *Elevation segregated the classes, with the heights overlooking the river occupied by the elite, the middle classes on the slopes, and the lower classes in the valleys and flats.*' It was market economics, not a conspiracy theory.'

'Could the elite, middle and lower classes have had the same information about building near the river?' I asked.

Howard said: 'The people choosing flood-prone locations could possibly have been unaware of flooding, or aware but reckless, or simply choosing riverside living because it was more affordable.'

'People could have been duped,' I said. 'From earliest settlement, flooding risks have been deliberately obscured by developers. A report blamed dishonest developers.

'*. . . all over this colony are townships created by 'vested interests', unscrupulous speculators, or criminal foolishness, laid out in the bottom of valleys, the flats of rivers, and low-lying plains, within short distances of magnificent situations free from the remotest danger of floods. All this is storing up trouble 'gainst the day of wrath, for assuredly Nature's laws know no mercy.*' Archibald Meston, The Queenslander, 29 March 1890.

'Flooding affected more workers' homes than gentry homes,' I said. 'By distancing themselves from lower class struggles with flooding, the upper classes may have established exclusive neighbourhoods which prevented community.'

When I considered social conditions, it seemed likely that the people worst affected by flooding would be the poor. Flooded people are a minority, time-poor, preoccupied with work, unable to afford time-saving technologies, unable to afford good education and cultural experiences. They may not have the time or wherewithal to claim for welfare support and fair treatment, such as for access to public transport, reasonable schools, sports facilities and health services. They probably did not obtain flood relief and help with restoration of their homes. Unless they had a community organisation interested in their plight, they lacked access to a voice in government.

Sailing ships at first anchored in Moreton Bay with immigrants from the UK, who were rowed up to Yungaba Migrant Depot at Kangaroo Point. Dredging enabled steam ships to dock at Hamilton. Immigrants were often single or young families and stayed in Brisbane for a few days or weeks, before travelling on to employment, often at stations in the country. Flood victims were more likely to be local people, who without social support would be devastated.

'Would deepening the river channel reduce flood height?' asked Howard.

'Yes,' I said, harking back to my training in chemical engineering. 'The water would have less friction, could flow faster, would back-up less and take less vertical space. A deeper channel could flow without overflowing.

'River overflow had previously been stored in swamps and lakes,' said Howard. 'These were being drained and filled in to build on. Floods flowing along the floodplain were blocked by buildings. Unlike the ideal of a deep canyon, the river flowed in a narrow and shallow channel, more susceptible to flooding. Historically, the Brisbane River contained upstream bars and shallows, with a natural tidal limit of only 16 km. Due to continual channel dredging, the tidal and navigation limits had extended as far as College's Crossing. When dredging ceased, sediment could have redeposited in bars and shallows.'

'Would the water also be held back by the tides coming up the river?' I asked.

'It is the height of the tide that holds back the flood,' said Howard. 'A high tide can raise the outfall water level several metres above low water level and slow the river discharge rate depending on the hydraulic conditions.'

'We don't know catchment rainfall data in 1893 sufficiently to know the areal extent of the cyclone or where the surge of 8.53 metres at the Port Office came from. It is possible that it could have been modulated by the two dams and a moderate flood would be experienced if the rainfall event were repeated,' I said. 'This is wishful thinking and opinions are needed from those familiar with catchment flows.

My investigation has led me to believe that a similar event could happen again with very low probability, perhaps 0.5% or once in 200 years. Not having the resources to calculate, I have guessed it.

CHAPTER 18 1974 FLOOD

For the next 100 years, the river authority had bucketed up and sucked away sediment, cutting, straightening, deepening and dredging the river channel. This process was referred to as 'training' the river, as if it would respond to treatment and be brought under control.

Resisting the river was in the romantic spirit of epic empire conquests, told in literature by Joseph Conrad, D H Lawrence and Ernest Hemingway, with noble heroes defending outposts of the British empire, combatting native forces and making virtuous sacrifices. A weakness of the romantic tendency was to overlook mundane solutions, like dredging.

The Brisbane River authority concluded that the floodplain needed more water storage capacity to reduce the height of flash flood 'spikes'. They considered positions and sizes of possible storages and the best position for a dam. There was much talk and little action, until a Somerset dam was started in 1934 and finally completed in 1959.

I have not seen any record of opposition, for environmental reasons, to the Somerset Dam. The Green movement commenced later at Lake Pedder in south west Tasmania in 1967, stopping proposed damming of the Franklin River, a site of natural grandeur.

The Somerset Dam was near the source of the river at Mount Stanley, 344 kilometres from its discharge into Moreton Bay. It was trusted to avert severe flooding, an elaboration spun within a romantic fantasy: 'taming the beast'. It was a belief that came to be known as the Somerset Dam Syndrome.

Trust in the Somerset Dam to relieve the capricious Brisbane River from flooding defied the facts. Three tributaries shared in the 13,600 km^2 catchment area of the Brisbane River: Stanley River

(11)%, Bremer River (15%) and Lockyer Creek (22%). Smaller tributaries contributed the other 52%.

Cyclone Wanda crossed the coast near Maryborough in early January 1974 and moved inland. It was a relatively weak tropical cyclone. Continual, heavy rain for three weeks led up to the flood, which occurred on Sunday, 27 January. Torrential rain followed and in the 5 days to 9am 29 January, falls reached 900 mm in Brisbane and the flood waters peaked at 5.45 metres. The ensuing disaster impacted tens of thousands of homes, left 8000 people homeless, caused 16 deaths and was thought to be a one in 100 year event. It was the worst flood of the Brisbane River since 1893.

My review of the 1974 flood is mainly to recall that this major flood was not much reduced by the Somerset Dam, surprising many people.

'Most of the rainfall from Cyclone Wanda fell downstream of the Somerset Dam,' said Howard. 'It was unexpected, but it was predictable. The Somerset Dam was a small and much-delayed dam on a distant tributary. Assessment of this first dam's effectiveness in the 1974 flood was uncertain, lacking a control experiment. Despite the worst flood since 1893 and a peak flood height not lowered much, the Somerset Dam effect was perceived to be positive. Only 11% of the river catchment area flowed into the dam. Instead of 'taming' the Brisbane River, the Somerset Dam was estimated to have reduced the peak height of the 1974 flood by 2 metres.

'After the flood, there was some rethinking,' I said. 'It was hoped that a larger more effective dam could be constructed downstream. The Somerset Dam had performed dismally and it took courage to consider another. It was the first dam constructed on the Brisbane River and there was lack of confidence and commitment, as indicated by taking 25 years to complete it. If there was a better site, why hadn't a dam been built there already?'

'A dam at Wivenhoe would have cost heaps more to construct, but it would store six times more water than Somerset Dam. It was attractive but perhaps the government couldn't afford it.'

CHAPTER 19 2011 FLOOD

Development of the city on the river flood plain continued apace after the 1974 flood had encouraged construction of a large dam at Wivenhoe. This second and larger dam, which could hold water from half the catchment area, was completed in 1984. In Tasmania there was vigorous opposition, on environmental grounds, to the Franklin River dam, but the Wivenhoe dam was relatively unprotested, possibly because it was wanted for both water supply and flood mitigation, without jobs being lost.

There was a property boom, confident that the new dam at Wivenhoe would prevent flooding. Citizens in flood-prone suburbs were encouraged to believe it. They said it was not unreasonable for residential suburbs to be exposed to a 50-year flood, like in 1974.

'Did this make you think twice about living beside the Brisbane River?' asked Howard.

'When we inspected our apartment in 1998, the 1974 flood was forgotten. Everyone said: 'Because another dam has been built at Wivenhoe, there will never be another flood.' We believed the dams would protect us.'

'The Council approved residential development along the river, as if there could never be another flood. They constructed river walks, ferry terminals and redeveloped 120 hectares of waterfront land. It constricted flow, slowed flood drainage and increased future flood height. Buildings along the riverbanks blocked flood ways, filling in spaces that had stored water and sealing porous ground with impermeable surfaces, all reducing the land's capacity to absorb, hold, dissipate and carry away flood water.'

'The cavalier disregard of flooding risk led to reckless change in dam operation,' said Howard. 'After an awful drought, the dam's empty flood mitigation compartment was eyed jealously. It was instinctive to want to increase water stored against further drought.

'By 2011 Wivenhoe dam's flood mitigation compartment had been partly filled,' Howard said.

'Why was it partly filled?' asked Gerry, a member of our community group. 'It should have been kept empty.'

'To make money,' I said. 'But they were caught out. When there was heavy rain, the mood of dam storage switched instantly from town supply to flood mitigation, but water stored in the mitigation compartment had to be emptied without making releases that would cause flooding in Brisbane, at a time when the River was already full. Wivenhoe Dam was soon nearly full and little flood mitigation was possible.'

'They were too clever by half,' said Gerry.

'They won't try changing the dam from flood mitigation to supply again,' I said.

'Not for a few years, anyway.'

'Not until people have forgotten.'

The heavy rainfall in 2011 caught dam management napping. There was rainfall over a wide area. By January 5th 2011, 78% of Queensland was flooded and over 2.5 million people were affected. Houses were washed away, bridges collapsed and ships were stranded.

There had been a series of rainfall events which threatened to fill the dams' flood storage compartments. Although Wivenhoe could take rainfall from 52% of the catchment area of the Brisbane River, possibly two thirds of the January 2011 rains fell into Bremer and Lockyer tributaries and joined the Brisbane River downstream from Wivenhoe. They waited until the flood peak had passed the Lockyer Creek tributary junction, so Wivenhoe releases would not be considered to have caused the flooding.

When the water in Wivenhoe dam neared full, before the fuse plugs of erodible gravel in the spillway could wash out to preserve the integrity of the dam, its flood gates were opened, causing flooding in Brisbane 24 hours later. The water had risen to within a couple of metres of the spillway when they opened the flood gates to stop the dam being overtopped and destroyed. Releases from the flood gates built into a wave, as the river channel filled and used the higher elevation to get away to the estuary and into the sea.

Faith in the new dam to protect the city against flooding, called the 'Wivenhoe Dam Syndrome', went the same way as the earlier 'Somerset Dam Syndrome'. As in 1974, the new dam was a disappointment. Up to this time Brisbane people had pinned their hopes for flood mitigation on the Wivenhoe Dam. But Cyclone Wanda dropped two thirds of its rainfall downstream from the dam. Critics blamed the dam for causing flooding which might have been avoided if the dam had never been built.

The flood in Brisbane in January 2011 was the worst since 1893, with 35 confirmed deaths and more than 200,000 people affected state-wide. The river peaked at 4.46m on 13 January, flooding more than 28,000 homes and leaving 100,000 without power. Cyclone Yasi, which hit on February 3rd, rained on a sodden river catchment.

My lived experience of the 2011 flood was traumatic.

On January 12th 2011 it had been raining heavily for several days. I was absorbed in writing when the phone rang.

It was my partner Rachel.

'How's the flood?' she asked.

'What flood?' I was puzzled.

'Look out the window.'

'Oh, shit!'

Flood warnings had been broadcast for a couple of days but I had been negligent. Water was coming across the narrow strip of grass in the park, almost as far as my street and driveway. Now there were regular forecasts, with flood heights varying widely.

Then began the natural disaster that turned me out of my home, disrupted my life and left me with a phobia of heavy rainfall, that is still with me today.

I opened the electric garage door, put a suitcase full of clothes and my computer into my car and drove out of the garage to several metres higher up the hill on the next street, where I parked. Then I scrambled to save property stored in my garage. It was difficult to know how to protect my things.

I carried about 20 boxes of my belongings from my garage up to my apartment. I took some higher up to my neighbour's apartment above mine, where she kindly made room for them. Many were heavy, filled with books and papers. Within a couple of hours, water was rising in the garages, too deep to rescue anything more.

A dog in a neighbouring apartment began barking hysterically to alert its owner, who quieted it to a catatonic whimper.

The radio said the flood was expected to be 7.5 metres, which I calculated would be half a metre deep in my apartment. I moved some valuable belongings on to tables and beds, stopping when my back hurt too much to continue.

While I was trying frantically to save items I valued most, the doorbell rang. A youngish woman was there.

'Is there anything you want rid of?' she asked.

She could have been a neighbour.

'No, I want to keep everything I can. Sorry.'

'What about that?' she pointed to a silk prayer mat hanging on the wall.

'No. That's a favourite,' I said.

'Good luck,' she said and went away.

Later that evening, the power went off. The water reached to 10 cm below my balcony. The habitable areas in our building were above water level, but the basement car park, storage rooms and electrical switch boxes were submerged. Without power, the building was uninhabitable. The water was still rising, so I decided to evacuate. Rachel kindly let me stay at her house a kilometre away. I took perishable foods from the fridge, leaving the frozen items, hoping they would stay chilled until electricity would be restored.

I stayed at Rachel's place for a week and a half, going to work every day, checking on the flood scene every morning and evening. The power was off and lights were out. There was nothing I could do except collect a few necessities to take with me.

I passed those days of evacuation in a state of anxiety. Although I went to work every day, my vision had a film of unreality. When I went back to my apartment my adrenalin pumped and I went into freeze, fight or flight mode, passive and unable. A feeling of doom loomed large in my life, as if disaster was near and I would be its victim. The ominous dread I felt was awful. Fear threatened to overflow into panic as if I was losing my mind. I scrolled through my memories of recent events in my life to find any which had turned out badly and might have triggered retribution.

Extent of the flood in 2011 could be interpreted as the dam having failed dismally to relieve flooding in Brisbane. The dam succeeded in stopping or holding back about one third of the surface run off.

The author pointing to black mark from the 2011 flood peak on the balcony apron.

The flood water took several days to recede, leaving a thick mantle of brown sludge draped over every horizontal surface and inside my mailbox. The mud smelled of hydrogen sulphide gas, like sewage. The large quantity deposited indicated it had been suspended in turbulent water, as if sediment had been mobilised by the flood. Small sand bars had been dumped from water flowing through the Park.

The flood was unexpected. It was difficult to cope with. I wanted to crawl into a hole and hide. Somehow I found the strength to join other residents cleaning up the mess in the forecourt and garages.

It was a nasty shock. 27 years after construction of Wivenhoe Dam was completed, the river in 2011 flooded my garage to the ceiling, rising to within a few centimetres of my lounge floor above. The flood level was 4.46 metres, a metre below 1974, causing 28 deaths and flooding 28,000 homes. It was the worst flood since 1893, falling ridiculously short of the boast that Wivenhoe Dam would prevent all further flooding of Brisbane City homes. It was Australia's most devastating flood in terms of damage to infrastructure, with a cost estimated at $2.38 billions, but possibly higher.

Brisbane City is, and continues to be, exposed to cyclonic rainfall. An obvious solution could be to construct another dam closer to Brisbane, or on a River tributary. Another dam would be smaller and an outcome is to recognise the limited contribution to mitigation of any one dam. At the time of writing, no such proposal has Council commitment.

PART 3

SCIENCE

CHAPTER 20 WHO WAS TO BLAME?

The flood in 2011 came as a shock. Water submerged my garage and came up to ten centimetres below my living room floor, with little warning. The peak height was 6.9 metres, a metre above the Defined Flood Level of 5.8 metres which was the construction limit. My situation had changed to a probability of 1%, of a flood level exceeding 7.5 metres, at least once in any year.

Finding that my apartment was flood-prone was of great concern to me. People unfamiliar with flooding sometimes remind flood victims of the ethic: *caveat emptor*, with a buyer having all the responsibility for checking on flooding potential. In my view, the seller, real estate agent and our solicitor, who had all unethically beguiled us with the Wivenhoe Dam syndrome and taken our money. The solicitor's search did not reveal any prospect of flooding, when it should have. Council property reports and the Floodwise Statistical Model became available to me too late for me to check the situation.

It is a common experience for people to be led up the garden path in a property purchase, but seldom does the victim admit it. The usual response is to take the first opportunity to pass the dud property to a gullible buyer, who could fall for the same ruse. We were young players in a dirty real estate game. This unloading of risk onto naïve market entrants was dishonest.

I wanted to apply Kant's categorical imperative, of treating others as I wanted them to treat me, with honesty. Instead there was a landslide of selfishness, favouring the seller.

There were many people who could be blamed. I joined in idle talk with neighbours, citing evidence of inauthenticity of dam management, with storing and releasing of water exacerbating flooding, with effects completely opposite to those wanted. The media surveyed opinions, but there was no central authority appointed to collect and analyse information.

'The Wivenhoe Dam has been misused,' I complained to a newspaper reporter, in a street interview, as the water subsided. 'The politicians made money selling dammed water, incapacitating a dam designed for flood mitigation.'

My complaint was not published and no-one accepted blame for the flood. A news story questioned effectiveness of the dam. If a dam had never been built, flooding would have been quite different. Given the irreversibility of dam building, 'scientific truth' was inaccessible. Liability applied within a certain cultural and historical context. Science's view of the self was as a disembodied intellect, situated in an abstract world of defined meaning. Descartes' method of observation, deduction and rational thought could not explain the height of the flood.

'I speculate that the engineers had calculated the flood height they would cause, varying the planned release rate until they obtained the 1974 DFL height of 5.8 m,' I said to Rachel, as she helped me rescue photos submerged by the flood.

'But they achieved 6.9 m, well above the DFL,' said Rachel.

'I suspect their prediction was in error, because their method wasn't accurate,' I said. 'Their flood height predictions had fluctuated wildly, preventing effective protection of possessions. It could have been modelling error, but it could also have been experimentation.'

'Residents who would be flooded wouldn't accept a release if it would cause a flood height above DFL,' said Rachel. 'That would be deliberate flooding.'

'Their predictions shot low, in the dark, as if that would minimise danger,' I said.

Besides property damage and loss, many residents, including me, were traumatised. When the flood subsided, values of our properties temporarily fell. The flood might have been an experiment, but my trauma continued. I was indignant, because my garage had flooded to the ceiling, destroying my possessions, wiping out precious memories.

In all, about 23,000 homes and businesses were swamped by the huge water releases. It took several years for criticisms like mine to build into a class action by flood victims, against Seqwater, for their failure to properly operate the Wivenhoe and Somerset dams, making flooding worse. My apartment building joined with others, in a crowd-funded claim conducted by Maurice Blackburn, lawyers. The case proceeded for a decade.

In 2019, the New South Wales supreme court found Seqwater was one of three parties to have failed Brisbane and Ipswich residents during the floods. In that decision, it was found engineers exacerbated flooding by failing to properly operate the dams, their actions making downstream flooding even worse. The Court dismissed half the claim and in December 2021 ruled that the Queensland government and Sun Water had to pay $440 millions in compensation for damages to 7000 home and business owners. We seemed to have won, but an appeal overturned it. The appeal withdrew the earlier award of damages. The court seemed to find that the engineers had, after all, followed an operating manual.

Our building's owners received $1,300 in compensation, a pittance compared with our claim of $20,000 for damage to our basement ventilation fans.

It was an expensive court case and did not seem to obtain justice for us. Nor did any of those responsible seem to lose their jobs. Like the Somerset Dam in 1974, the Wivenhoe Dam's performance in 2011 seemed to disappoint people, explained by rainfall that fell largely on the catchment below the dam.

The benefit of the court case was that the dam operator had been found remiss and dam operators in future could be more aware of their liability to prevent flooding. New procedures were put in place for the release of water in future. The best result could be future reduction in flooding from tightening up of the dams' operating protocols.

I was shocked by the conflicting views of the causes of the 2011 flood. In my work as an engineer, engineering reports pursued agreement, excluding emotional arguments. Popperian falsification, 'true science', was appropriate for considering hypotheses by experimenting in laboratories, but was difficult to apply to large systems like rivers. Some of the great ideas in science, such as evolution, plate tectonics and relativity, involved complex systems and those theories could not possibly be falsified either. This was the ferment within which ideas of the true causes of the 2011 flood grew, without resolution.

Events were interpreted by leaders and media, not by public debate, by opinion and rhetoric. The earlier concept of testable 'scientific truth' was replaced by eclectic post-truth arguments which could be won by publicity campaigns, media support and emotion.

Margaret Cook (1) adopted the perspective that Brisbane City Council's laissez faire development approvals had contradicted natural flow of the river. She proposed further development should only be possible above flood levels. Her retake gave respect to natural systems, such as the river floodplain.

Analysis of the flood had produced voluminous association of event variables, such as water height in dams, with operator actions. Understanding lacked integrity to the extent that blame for flooding could not be apportioned and no-one was held responsible. This outcome was unsatisfactory for flood victims, who wanted compensation and assurance that similar events could not happen again.

Residents were disappointed by the extent of flooding in 2011. Public criticism could have attributed it to many causes, including Government inaction approving construction of residences on the flood plain over many years. Media attention was focussed on the possibility of incompetent dam management. In a long and vigorously defended court battle, dam operators became scapegoats, or possibly red herrings. Their fault was not sustained and in the end the Queensland Government was exonerated from wrongdoing.

CHAPTER 21 AFTERMATH

Flash flooding can kill, whereas prolonged partial immersion of a home can be emotional and stressful for relationships. The floods had repercussions even after the water subsided.

After the flood in 2011, communities pulled together to restore common property, but there was a shortage of tradesmen skilled in flood damage repair. Until property was restored, victims' lives were blighted. The problems of present-at-hand damage and scarcity of ready-to-hand solutions were stressful.

I took part helping the others to clean up our apartment building. My anxiety made me feel unwell. I didn't feel competent to deal with problems that arose. There could be disagreement about property to be moved and how to restore it resiliently. Physical exertion tired me. I depended on others to decide what needed to be done.

With my neighbours in a line side by side, we pushed mud out of the forecourt entrance using brooms and scrapers. We shoved a wave of liquid mud out into the road, where others pushed it across the park, down the bank and into the river. When the forecourt was clear, we opened up the garages. In the gloom were heaps of devastated personal property.

The Australian Prime Minister, Kevin Rudd, wearing a Stetson, dropped by at Atrium Apartments to inspect damage, flanked by his minders and a cameraman. It was his electorate. He reminded us to disinfect any cuts on our hands and legs because contagion bred vigorously in the filth. I caught an infection that took an antibiotic to shift.

The next morning after the water receded, several coaches pulled up outside carrying 'mud army' volunteers. Dressed in bikini tops and shorts, they separated items to be washed from those to be jettisoned, creating a large heap along the roadside verge. They threw out items that I had set aside to be salvaged, including my rock collection. When I tried to retrieve it, I was accosted.

'Oi! You can't take that!'

'It's mine.'

'Not now it isn't it. It's waste to be removed.'

'It's not waste. I want it!'

'You can't take stuff from here. That would be looting.'

The jaundiced morality of this self-appointed guardian of the waste pile prevailed. The volunteers were marching in unison to a beat of property removal from our garages. I didn't want any more trouble, so I left my rock collection where it was, on the waste pile.

The mud army inspired my own-most potentiality for survival, overcoming my fallen-ness and dissension, with deference to the group. In good humour, I cleared away the damage and threw out my muddied possessions.

The Council's loader and trucks took the heaps of damaged property away.

Orleigh Park flooded taken from Unit 2 balcony March 1st, 2022.

Two utes arrived carrying water blasters. Volunteer operators washed down the garages from top to bottom and cleaned my remaining things. It was generous of them to undertake the dirty and difficult task, at little cost to us.

When power and the internet were restored, my life returned to normal. I hadn't realised how dependent I was on electricity for everyday living. Rachel and I washed and dried water-damaged photographs. I subsequently put in a claim on my contents insurance for the items I had lost in the flood, not certain if it would be paid.

The items I lost included electrical workshop equipment, tools, books and art supplies. Although I could have claimed 'new for old', it was difficult to know what to replace and my claim included amounts based on notional depreciated values. I claimed for food I discarded from my refrigerator. Many other items lost were obsolete or worn out. I made no claim at all for defunct items, such as floppy discs, audiocassettes, videocassettes and disused household items.

My claim was for only $5,000, a fraction of what had been lost. Suncorp paid my claim in full.

After submitting the claim, I relaxed, but by the end of the school term, I was too emotionally exhausted to teach. I resumed work after the Easter break. Despite seeming to have recovered, in the next flood in 2022, my anxiety returned. Small events caused me to become stressed and dysfunctional. Whereas stress can improve brain performance and help to improve memory and attention span, I had become easily flustered and forgetful. My emotional functioning and metabolism could have been affected, possibly permanently.

Besides material damage and health effects, evacuation brought relationship difficulties. A few months after the flood, Rachel and I broke up. Parting was sad. We had been good together for several years and I had a great affection for her and her family. I am eternally grateful for her material and psychological support during the flood and unstinting help in cleaning up the mess.

When I returned to work at the beginning of term 2, I chatted with a woman friend, Simone, who was a senior teacher at the school and a friend. She was empathetic and interested that I was without a partner.

'I am run down,' I said to Simone. 'I have to get back on top of things. Hopefully my willpower can recover.'

'Willpower does little for me,' Simone said. 'The physical world controls almost everything I do. You just have to be patient.'

She urged me to be tolerant and accepting.

'Willpower can add a dimension of intention to my every action,' I said. 'It is the part I can control.'

'Do you mean you can add as much free will as you want?' she asked. 'I doubt it. I've never tried. Your mind must be strong.'

It was untrue, for I was under her spell. I was attracted to her at work and became dependent on her in a relationship in which she took advantage of me. At first I enjoyed her company. She was younger and attuned to cultural and social events we went to together. At work she used our relationship to further her job interests.

Simone was a generation 'X', the group who do not wish to concern themselves with societal pressures, money and status. Many Gen Xers had been 'latchkey kids', with parents working late, without adult supervision when they got home from school. They were resourceful, independent and keen on maintaining work-life balance. Gen Xers were the first generation to grow up with personal computers, becoming tech-savvy like Simone, who taught computer subjects.

I had been attracted by her outstanding ability to present technical change to groups of teachers she in-serviced, including me. Her grasp of computers and the internet was creative. She could 'wing it' unscathed dealing with contentious issues. She was a charismatic mediator, nondirective and didn't intrude into my personal space. She had skills at work that made me proud to be associated with her.

She came to my place and we spent several evenings recording Youtube videos promoting my books. She was a natural actor, whereas on camera I could do little beyond reading from a script.

I realised too late we had little in common and I knew it was a mistake during the wedding. We parted during the honeymoon and divorced as soon afterwards as we could. It was an episode I want to forget. Having a romantic relationship with a boss at my work had been a disaster when she tried to bully me, as if I was her servant. I never went back to work. I had accumulated a year of long service leave and when I took it, I found my life was a lot better without doing work I had lost faith in, having loss of confidence in management like the one I had experienced when I left Wattle Mines. Leaders there were too fearful of losing their jobs to strategically take control of their future. After I quit, I occupied myself by writing novels.

My relationship with Simone had blossomed in the shadow of the flood and if there had been no flood our relationship would probably have remained platonic, which would have been more appropriate and avoided a painful involvement.

The effects of flooding are commonly measured as being the cost of property loss. The psychological and social costs are personal. They cannot be measured in dollars nor added up nor claimed on insurance. There was a stigma to being flooded, with relationships with others altered. My loss was partial, so the ostracism was minor and faded after a few years. The trauma of flooding can be difficult to recover from, with human costs of greater significance for well-being than property loss, which can be replaced.

CHAPTER 22 ADVANTAGES OF BEING THERE

I rebounded from the 2011 flood feeling positive about my home. I liked living there, because of the river, the park and closeness to the City. I felt 'in the swim' of city life. The people in the park seemed to be my people. My apartment was real and the facticity of my living space was boldly part of the local culture. Being there had a multitude of present-at-hand associations.

My apartment balcony overlooked a sliver of grass and trees, then across a couple of hundred metres of the Brisbane River, with a panoramic view over the water to tall buildings opposite. I could watch the water slip past silkily and silently. Rowing shells toiled past, with crews syncopating in 4s and 8s, exhorted by coxes and coaches, shouting instructions through megaphones from following motorised dinghies, above the outboard noise. Light twinkled from wavelets rippled by breezes. CityCat ferries plied every 20 minutes, to and from the university, disembarking passengers at the West End terminal, with a crash of walkways and revving engines, the catamaran's engine revving to skew around, crossing over to Guyatt Park, on the bank opposite.

I had met Karen at the University of the Third Age, a non-vocational organisation with students mostly retired. She worked as a bookkeeper for a small company in which she was a director. Her hobby was her garden, which was a riot of colour.

She was compulsive, leading a carefully organized life. Unlike me, she preferred to be conventional and was at pains not to rock the boat. Karen was a polite, reliable and principled person, who watched carefully over her children and grandchildren, screening them from my boomer anti-authority ideas.

She tried to help me with my writing, but was under-confident and too polite to be a beta reader, a critic. After a couple of years, I felt shut out from her social circle. When they recognised themselves in print, my stories antagonised them. Karen's orientation was Silent Generation, her traditional values clashing with mine.

Karen stayed at my place sometimes and we would walk by the river. Party boats, bursting with passengers, bullied their way upriver with music thumping. Jet skis roared by, bouncing over wakes.

'The river muffles all sorts of bad behaviour,' I said.

'Some people let themselves go in boats on the river,' Karen said. 'For them, it is a space without rules.'

Joggers and walkers paraded past, along the pathway through the park, lithe and trim, with bare tattooed legs, rippling abs and tanned midriffs. In the off-leash dog area, dog owners unleashed their social skills.

Some activities brought loud behaviour. Cyclists sped down the hill to the River and turned sharply along beside it, shouting to their macho friends, relaxing confidently with hands off. Skateboard riders tried to rotate their boards in the air, showing off their bravado to each other, clattering down on the concrete dangerously.

Residents and visitors enjoyed the river from paved footpaths, ferries, sailboats and kayaks. The Park had spaces for families to picnic, barbecue and play games. In the evenings, musicians, fire twirlers and tight-rope walkers performed solos, or in ensembles. There were activities such as Tai Chi, foot races, skateboarding, scooter riding and exercises supervised by personal trainers.

The view of the river from my place was framed beneath a canopy of fronds dangling from majestic fig trees. Crows called out their success at scavenging, in harsh language. Magpies paused to warble as they searched the ground for worms and titbits.

Cars cruised past, looking for somewhere to park. They disgorged children, strollers, scooters and bicycles. Families set off to walk along the riverbank through the park. There were family picnics under the trees, with beer cans handed out from eskies at barbecues cooking with mouth-watering aromas.

Karen and I took visitors for walks in the Park. Sometimes we looked down from my balcony over the action. There was pleasure in watching people being active.

Living by the river is distinguished by the unique environment. By comparison, living in a landlocked suburb with houses cheek-by-jowl is dominated by roads, with too many cars, lawn mowers and Hills hoists. Orleigh Park compares favourably with recreation areas set aside elsewhere by property developers: small, low-lying, steep and barren.

There were many practical advantages of being there. I valued being able to walk to buses, CityCats, supermarkets, the city and the cultural precinct at Southbank. Everything I could want was nearby.

Many of the people who live on the Kurilpa Peninsula value its easy access to the City Business District. City workers can walk, cycle, bus, ferry or train into the CBD.

The types of home vary. There are wood and tin workers' cottages, renovated and built under. Modernised homes have often been raised above flood level. Large apartment buildings are taking over.

The Peninsula has bridges for many of the 40,000 students at Queensland University to commute over. The river loops around three sides of the campus. Riverfront apartments at West End have been taken up by students. Access for students and staff has created demand for ferries and bridges to cross the river on foot, by car or by public transport. The suburb has become a throughway and parking lot for commuters.

I discussed with Gerry and others in our community group, the transformation of West End.

'Brisbane CBD's urban planners envisage population density growing, becoming equal with Hong Kong's,' I said. 'Offices and residential towers poke up, in clusters. New apartment buildings are limited to 12 storeys but exemptions are granted by the Council, sometimes undeservedly. Building heights could increase to 90 storeys if our protest action fails. West End's population has doubled since 2010 and is expected to double again by 2030.'

'Hong Kong is too dense,' said Gerry.

'Our traditional lifestyle would disappear,' I said. 'Many West-Enders' lifestyles are traditional, in backyards with barbeques and street cricket, while others occupy large apartments having gardens and swimming pools. There are restaurants but many meals are prepared at home. West End has three supermarkets, two of them in a duopoly. with identical goods and identical prices. The high street preserves traditional store frontages and quaint shopping from a past era. For other items, the city is conveniently close, with frequent buses.'

'What will the lifestyle here be like in future?' asked Karen.

'Some of us hope cars will be squeezed out and people will use public transport to get around,' I said. 'Present activities will continue. Walking and cycling paths lead all along the Peninsula and into the city, with access to the cultural precinct museums, art galleries and performance theatres and a swimming beach at Southbank Gardens.

'What else will people do?' she asked.

'In the short term, the Queensland Performing Arts Centre (QPAC) will have more entertainments of international calibre, drawing crowds from the suburbs and state-wide,' I said. 'Festivals at Southbank Gardens and other venues will continue to present music, dance and fountain light shows on the river. QPAC is at the hub of Brisbane's arts and entertainment industry, attracting visitors from all parts of the city and interstate.'

'Would you want to continue living here?' Karen asked.

'West End will hopefully retain elements of the traditional olde-worlde community, despite a rapid pace of development. With this wide range of interests available from my apartment, I haven't wanted to live anywhere else.'

'Where are your family?' asked Karen.

'They live overseas. I want to develop family roots here by bringing my children and grandchildren to spend time with me or even to live nearby. I want to be closer to them. The river could bring our family closer together.'

Despite having been partly flooded, I loved my home and wanted to share it with my family. The effect of the River flooding was to heighten my appreciation of the location rather than to diminish it. I supposed that a flood could reduce the value of impacted properties, but could increase the value of those that escaped flooding.

CHAPTER 23 DOUBLE UP

I considered moving to a higher place. But I loved having the river on my doorstep. In the bright sunlight of daytime, the fig trees obscured glare from the water. In the evening shade, the appearance of the river was balmy and magical. Around sunset, the water sparkled reflecting light from the other side, a rich tapestry of shimmering reflections, giving an impression of unreality.

'The light from across the river reflects from the surface many times,' I told a visitor. 'It's like a fairground with strings of lights glowing.'

An outlook with a vista of water adjacent to vegetation, has been reported to be conducive to mental and physical good health (26). I liked living there and didn't want to live anywhere else. A weakness of the scientific method was that a property which had been flooded once, could be presumed to flood again and would be stigmatised forever, as if every flood was the same, allowing buyers to chisel a low price, rejecting benefits from flood mitigation projects. If I was to sell, negotiation could be unduly protracted and the prospect was a deterrent which prevented me from moving.

It had been an unpleasant surprise when my garage flooded in 2011. It took me a long time to forget the flood menace.

'Do you still like being here?' Michael asked me.

As usual, his questioning was incisive. He was a problem solver.

He was probably hinting at something I was concerned about, that the potentiality of my place had fallen, could be losing deeper possibilities and gaining a certain inauthenticity, a temporariness of going through the motions until the next flood, however unlikely that was.

'Yes, I do like being here, very much,' I said.

People living in disaster zones learn from necessity to live in the moment. I knew a flood could come at anytime, even into my apartment's living area, never flooded before. The consequences would be dire, but I would face them as well as I could. I had to be patient and resolute.

I neglected to renew furnishings and accepted second rate repairs. It would be unwise to invest in new things when replacement could be required within a short time.

'You don't have a lot of stuff,' Michael said. 'Wouldn't you like a new lounge suite and table?'

'No. I like these,' I said.

I imagined when a flood came through I would claim furniture on insurance.

There wasn't much possibility of avoiding being flooded, because rainfall in the Stanley Range and the Brisbane River catchment area occurred irregularly with a certain frequency. But the dams could reduce the height of flooding. The authorities had preferred public investment in dams as a more practical, humanitarian and politically expedient solution than confining construction of homes to sites above a defined flood level and buying back flood-prone homes. The clincher was that constructing a dam would be cheaper compensating for flooding. The other hope, that rainfall would be lighter, was counteracted by pessimism that climate change could bring heavier rainfall.

Karen was a wonderful person. Her house was in a suburb half-an-hour away from my apartment. It was not far from the river, but set high, without any risk of flooding. It was a lovely home and I stayed with her at weekends. For several years I enjoyed a change of scene weekly and enjoyed social events with her family and friends. I went away travelling a couple of times with her family.

I was sad when relations with her stalled and we parted.

My investigation of the Brisbane River had led me to feel positive about my apartment.

Despite being flood-prone, it had a high standard of amenities holding me there. It was too small to host visits from my children and grandchildren when they all came at once from overseas. I could squeeze them into the master bedroom, with one other bedroom for them, at a pinch. I could sleep on the floor in the study. As the children got older, it was becoming more difficult to fit everyone in and I considered alternative ways to accommodate everybody.

I looked for a larger apartment, one that wouldn't flood. But I couldn't find one with equal access to the river. Flood free apartments were fetching prices up to 50% more. Public transport from my place was excellent and my daily walk under the fig trees in Orleigh Park seemed irreplaceable. The prospect of moving away from the river was daunting and I began considering what I could do to improve accommodation at my place.

I looked for an opportunity to buy another apartment in our building.

When Unit 4, directly above Unit 2, was advertised for sale, I thought of hedging my bets by buying it as a refuge to go to, when Unit 2 flooded. Together the two units would give the amenity of a large family home. My daughter and son and their families would be able to stay there, when they visited, or perhaps could live there permanently. Unit 4 could be a base for them to live in, with their children going to local schools.

Some people would be reluctant to put two eggs in the same basket, but I figured I was happy with my apartment and would be twice as happy owning two. A commodity trader might figure that when the value of one has gone steadily up, a second one would go up too.

The prospect of my family living above me was attractive. I wanted a place near mine where they could put down roots, when their travelling days were over.

I floated the idea at a family meeting on zoom.

'Unit 4 is for sale. Would you stay there if I bought it?' I asked Michael and Sarah.

Their response was immediate.

'Fantastic,' said Michael. 'It's a great place to stay.'

'It's a very good idea,' said Sarah.

'I'll consider it,' I said. 'I might make an offer for it.'

Atrium Apartments. Unit 2 is on the first floor, with Unit 4 above.

The buying price of an apartment has usually increased annually when it is young, until in middle age it becomes unfashionable and in need of repair, then its price declines. Appreciation in value of Atrium apartments had slowed, but they still offered many years of pleasant occupation with modest maintenance costs.

Having a second unit to consolidate family roots was attractive. I evaluated Unit 4 for bringing our family closer. I made an offer and after a couple of price iterations, contracted to buy it.

Sarah and Michael congratulated me.

'I want it to be a home away from home for you and your children to use,' I said. 'It is a place you can visit in privacy.

I was uneasy that the 2011 flood had been forgotten. It was as if there would never be another flood, because it had been the result of mismanagement of the dam, which was unlikely to happen again.

I had narrowly escaped from flooding of my apartment. Many people thought that flooding had been exacerbated by incompetent dam operators. I believed there could be improvement and that higher flooding of my place was improbable. There was even less likelihood of flooding of the higher apartment. It was a good investment and could develop family roots.

When it began raining in February 2022, we wondered if the dams would prevent flooding this time.

CHAPTER 24 2022 FLOOD

In 2022, heavy rainfall fell on the lower part of the Brisbane River catchment, below the dams, impacting more homes than any flood since 1893.

The BoM tried to predict flooding from weather and river data using a 'classical' scientific model tweaked to carefully match data observed at hundreds of river gauging stations. With the flood level rising, they tried to predict maximum flood height, but were caught off guard and overwhelmed by the rapidity of events. After the flood peak had passed Lockyer Creek and the other tributaries downriver, Wivenhoe Dam floodgates were opened, reducing the spike and prolonging the flood. The model ran too slowly to produce useful forecasts. The BoM flood forecasting system in Brisbane failed to produce a useful forecast.

The gaze of statistics was baleful. Some religious people prayed and made sacrifices to divine providence to obtain relief from flooding. I was agnostic, wanting more evidence of supernatural agency that could protect me. Others believed they were lucky and it was their turn to escape flooding. Fatalism, with belief in a binding, or decreeing agent, was without evidence. My view was that a flood could repeat immediately, many times, or possibly not again for many years.

Water flowed into the Brisbane River, from the brown snakes of the Bremer River and Lockyer Creek tributaries. In Brisbane it rained 677 mm over 3 days. The Council halted the CityCat ferry service when debris floating in the river threatened to foul the ferry propellers or pierce the hulls of the ferry boats. We could see trees carried past and others were submerged. The river level rose and started to come across Orleigh Park towards our building.

There were no flood height warnings and we feared the worst. We wanted the authority to take the lead with an authentic response we could follow, but we lacked information about the state of the river. We waited in vain for the BoM to issue flood height warnings, as it had eleven years previously.

There was a King Tide at about 6 pm. The river was over its banks and had reached the barbecue grill in the park. I propped open the electric door of our basement garage and drove my car out to the street behind. Michael moved his car further up the street.

The dim light did not enable us to watch closely the surrender of everything to the water. I saw enough loss of possessions for it to be painful. It was like having an interminable tooth extraction without an anaesthetic, or not knowing how soon the pain would stop.

It continued to rain all evening on Monday.

I woke at 5am on Tuesday March 1st 2022, with the power off. Water was ankle deep in the garage, flowing in uninvited, silently, in small surges and swirls, under doors, floating up plastic boxes and furniture, collapsing cardboard boxes of stored possessions and leaving an oily black mark on walls, at the highest point reached. A bookcase made of particle board collapsed and hundreds of books disintegrated into a soup of paper. There was nothing we could do to keep the water out.

The water slid in as if entitled, with no visible propulsion. Gravity had been there all along, but it took the brown flood to show what it could do.

I took a flashlight and splashed across the garage and up to Unit 4 where Michael, Amir and a school friend were staying. I hated paddling through floodwater contaminated with sewage.

'Let's take the kids to John's,' Michael said.

By evacuating we were playing it safe. The radio had no instructions about when to evacuate. Michael prompted the children to gather their things. Hats off to them for facing this calamity quietly and calmly. I gathered my things into a bag. At about 6 am we walked as a group down the stairway, into the flood for the last few steps and across the building forecourt with calf deep water streaming into the garage. The river outside had swollen and tore past determinedly. There were no boats on the river, only debris hurrying past. We paddled out the front entrance and walked along the pavement to a side street where Michael's car was parked. He drove us to John's, who welcomed us to stay there. We dried off and changed into dry clothes.

I had been fortunate in 2011 to have Rachel take me in and now in 2022, I was lucky to have John provide for us when we fled. Our evacuation was hurried, in darkness. Later trips were needed to bring away other things.

About 10.30 am I went back to Atrium with Michael. The water was too deep in the forecourt to get in and the basement garage door was closed. In the neighbour's garden, I knocked three palings off the fence and we climbed through and opened my side door into Unit 2. To reach Unit 4 we had to wade through the garage with muddy water up to our thighs. Our footing would have been insecure if we had left it any later. Michael and I gathered some things and we returned to John's. That morning the water level increased to 1.6 metres in my garage, a metre down from 2011, but more Brisbane homes were impacted, because the city had been flooded from local creeks, whereas in 2011 most of the flood water came from the river.

My perception of the river changed, from benign neighbour, to malign superpower. The river was a ticking bomb that could explode at almost any time. The flood jolted me with the realisation I could be flooded repeatedly. Flooding oscillated in my thoughts like Schrodinger's cat in a closed box, beyond perception, possibly alive or dead. Existentially, I was both flooded and not flooded at the same time.

I stayed at John's place for about a week, until our power supply was reconnected.

It stopped raining on Wednesday, March 2nd and the flood gradually receded. The height of this flood was 3.85 m AHD, 0.6 m below 2011.

Next day I joined our local mud army and began clearing damaged property and removing mud, continuing over the weekend. It was a huge task and neighbours pitched in. Robert, from an apartment higher in the building, brought a cooked chicken and Coca Cola, which boosted morale.

A week later, when the power was reconnected, we could see what we were doing and could finish cleaning. I despaired when I saw the damage to my possessions immersed in the garage. Our Body Corporate Chairman dragged out onto the verge items to go to the dump. Later I realised that my loss of precious books too voluminous to store in my apartment. They were on bookshelves destroyed by immersion. I saved some other items but later regretted keeping junk I would never use. It took weeks to settle my insurance claim, but my real loss was moderate. The main effect was the inconvenience and anxiety induced.

This lived experience of the 2022 flood was traumatic. I had been stressed when I waded through the basement garage to go with Michael and children to safety. We had to evacuate and had nowhere to go until Michael's friend John took us in. A residue of anxiety lingered from 2011 and more came in waves, especially in the early morning, when it was raining. It incapacitated me: I was fearful, overly cautious, indecisive and inclined to panic. I didn't seek medical help because I had been like this before, after the flood in 2011. I seemed to recover then without medical help and I would try it again.

Friends suggested that I move my home to a flood-free location, but a difficulty was that the price I would get for my property wouldn't afford a place I would like. By continuing to live in my apartment, I was sipping from a poisoned chalice. I would sell when I could get a good price. But anxiety nagged that I should get out while I could.

It was not a choice I wanted to make. Would the consequences of staying be as bad as moving? Inertia was against going and the disruption could be similar or worse. Moving would be inauthentic, not living my best life. I decided to brave it out.

'Will you move into Unit 4, Dad?' Michael asked.

'I'm not sure. For the moment, you and Sarah can stay there.'

Michael's work was in government of overseas trade. He was a superb negotiator, meaning he usually got what he wanted. When we talked, he was several steps ahead always, seeming to know what I was going to say, from my facial expressions. It was uncanny and effective.

Whereas Michael stayed in Unit 4, Sarah was delayed in coming from Canada until 2022. She stayed with her children for six weeks. It wasn't certain how much visitors would use the apartment. Michael had furnished it and was paying the bills, with Sarah owing him her share, playing her poker hand of awaiting what would eventuate.

If I continued to live in Unit 2, my apartment would inevitably be submerged in some future flood. It would be sensible to leave before that happened, but it might not be for a long time. I tried to reduce my anxiety by living in the moment, bravely accepting the possibility of flooding inconvenience, as the cost of enjoying living with the river on my doorstep. On the other hand, by continuing there I would be cringing and compromising my happiness. It would be better if I moved away as soon as convenient. In any case, in ten years from now, I could want to move into aged care. Wouldn't it be best to move away from the river now, if I could get a fair price? But prices were falling and I postponed finding another home.

Inquiry into the flood in 2011 had proceeded for several years in a legal action, to determine who was to blame for the floods. Liability was obfuscated by the experience of the 2022 flood, which was worse. Competencies of Seqwater and BoM were questioned. There was much emotion and little analysis of the flood data.

The possibility of future flooding depended on mitigation capabilities of the Somerset and Wivenhoe Dams and whether a future flood would exceed the 2011 height and come into my apartment. A flood of that height was reckoned as a 1 in 80 years event. There was no way of knowing if I could be flooded later this year or anytime soon, or possibly not for hundreds of years, or even never. I hoped that proper operation of the dams would prevent flooding of my apartment.

The flood in 2022 distressed me more than in 2011, finally bursting the bubble of hope of flood mitigation by dams. It was the worst flood since 1893, impacting 23,400 homes. It came without warning, a trauma that I wouldn't want repeated.

Damage in the 2022 flood was estimated at $2 billions, somewhat below the $2.68 billions for the 2011 flood, even though more homes had been impacted. In both these disasters, the dams constructed to catch rainfall accomplished little. In 2022, most of the rain fell downriver from the Wivenhoe dam.

I hoped that future rainfall events would have more than one third of their rainfall caught by the dams, with height lower than the 6.9 metres reached by the flood in my garage in 2011, or 5.9 m in 2022. Rainfall location above the dams was a gamble.

CHAPTER 25 FLOOD VICTIMS

I have described the four worst floods in Brisbane, in 1893, 1974, 2011 and 2022. Now I will focus on the human effects and how these could have been prevented.

Besides drownings, the flood's victims would have been people who were old, disabled, ill, susceptible to infections, with nowhere to take refuge and those whose homes and possessions were lost to the water. Some with water in their homes stayed, with no electricity. Some who evacuated had to pay for their accommodation and for food, sometimes for months while their homes were being repaired. When business premises were flooded, employees and suppliers' people could be off work indefinitely.

There were many situations in which the flooding disrupted people's lives. Being flooded was like having your losing number come up in a conscription lottery, threatening your safety. Bad luck of being flooded could be repeated within hours, weeks, even years later, or possibly never again.

Sometimes there was recovery from flooding without much damage. Flood-proneness didn't linger like incurable cancer, or a fatal medical condition. But the experience of being flooded could be traumatising, with waking up at night, imagining your home filling with water and fear of being unable to move to safety. Flooding has often been on my mind. Moments when I could forget the stealthy intrusion of flood water have appeared with increasing frequency.

I went to work at my school every day during the flood in 2011, but stress caught up with me and two weeks before Easter, I burned out. By 2022, I had retired and worked on my book at John's place. He kindly provided internet access. My writing helped me to relax.

It was 10 days until Energex restored the power supply to our street and I could go home. I had been fortunate to be able to evacuate.

For years afterwards, heavy rainfall possibly induced in me mild Post Traumatic Stress Disorder (PTSD). I never sought medical help and diagnosed myself from the Internet. Some victims do not heal, because their identity is centred around the trauma they've experienced. I felt my Being had been violated and for years afterwards my adrenalin would pump ready to freeze, fight or flee at the slightest provocation, such as heavy rainfall. It was like agoraphobia, a fear of unfamiliar conditions.

I was fortunate to be able to alleviate my anxiety without turning to alcohol, prescription drugs or psychiatry. It took several months, but eventually I forgot about it. Writing this book has been therapeutic, my days passing timelessly in flow.

An hour before the water came into my garage, I drove my car out. I heard of people who drove cars *into* their garages as the water rose, to be able to claim a new car on insurance. I don't know if they succeeded.

Recovering my property from the mud in the garage was unpleasant. Lost to the flood were books, gardening equipment, clothes, toys, and furniture. I carried up to the living area household items. Volunteers carried obsolescent PCs, stereo speakers, audio and video cassettes outside to the junk pile

Items I claimed under contents insurance came to $6000. Suncorp paid within a few weeks, with deduction of an excess of $600.

Owners in our building toiled for days in mud and heat, dragging out destroyed clothes and furniture, fittings and appliances. Without electricity and light, the task was difficult. It would take months before our lives would return to normal.

Our building structure was relatively unscathed. Greater loss was suffered by people living nearby, whose homes were inundated. Floors, walls and ceilings sometimes had to be renewed and unless owners had building insurance, the cost of this work could be difficult to afford. Unable to pay for repairs, some people had to leave.

Further afield were businesses that had to close down. Several retail warehouses had been built on low-lying land and were badly flooded in 2011, then again in 2022. Tonnes of stock were destroyed and they were closed for months. People who had been employed casually may have lost their jobs. Although employment stayed high, the community was still reeling from Covid and businesses were struggling.

I received small one-off flood compensation payments from the Federal and State Governments, also discounts from several government agencies and utilities. This help was appreciated at a difficult time.

'Chance, you should move to somewhere else!' said Howard.

'I have lived here a long time and built my life around this place,' I said. 'Moving would be a wrench, a vanquishment, a trauma adding to PTSD. I want to continue here. It is getting easier.'

When we had bought the apartment by the Brisbane River, a small risk had seemed reasonable. Now the risk of flooding seemed larger.

'It is not getting easier to sleep at night.'

The risk of flooding had seemed small in 1998, when I was a 52, but it had gradually magnified with the passing years until, until after the flood in 2022, when I was 76, it was a threat that I lost sleep over. The change was partly in my increased experience of river flooding and partly from risk aversion with increasing age.

'I have become more aware of all types of risk,' I told Howard. 'The possibility of disaster is becoming an obsession with me. It's like Obsessive Compulsive Disorder,Z characterised by unreasonable thoughts and obsessive fears that lead to compulsive behaviours. My compulsive behaviour is to constantly watch the river level, rainfall and weather forecasts on my phone, to find out any flooding situation. I am unable to step away from possible risk.'

'Could you sell your apartment?' Howard asked me.

'I don't know how much I could get. Some potential buyers could be like the princess and the pea, uncomfortable with one small flaw. Perhaps there are apartment buyers who are sensitive to flooding and will not accept any amount of flood-proneness, reported by hearsay because official records are unavailable. A buyer could get a bee in his bonnet about flooding. I hoped to sell to someone who hadn't noticed this location was marginally vulnerable, or who would accept a small risk.'

'Are property buyers prepared to accept some risk?' Howard asked.

'Risk is a part of everyday living,' I said. 'Flooding risk is no different from risks on the roads, from bushfires, or from diseases. Soldiers, police and airline pilots live with danger and get used to it. When they are killed, or injured, the community honours them and provides care for their families. Flood victims get attention too, but it is difficult to compensate for extensive property damage and loss of income. Victims' well-being may be injured for a long time afterwards. Callous people could regard victims' hardship as a just consequence of their living on a river floodplain.'

'Few people would consciously choose a risk of flooding,' said Howard. 'When people gamble for high stakes, they bet with money and property they can afford to lose. No-one bets against losing their home, as some flood victims have done. Unwittingly, they may take a risk they cannot afford.'

Retirement homes were built on cheap flood-prone land, a racket that exploited trusting and vulnerable people. Only a few have a trajectory that takes on risk authentically, riding the wild stallion of their lives, pursuing the deepest potentialities of their being, as they are entitled to.

Others have been deceived. The uncertainty associated with river flooding is exploited by unscrupulous dealers and racketeers. Home ownership on a river floodplain is a gamble. The winners are the wealthy stayers and the losers are those who have to quit because they are unable to afford to stay in the game. If they are gullible, it could be because they have been ripped off by a seller with criminal intent.

Those developers who have acted with malice afore-thought could be branded criminals.

'Come on!' said Howard. 'Opportunistic trading is not criminal; it's how capitalism is done.'

'Home buyers get more protection when buying a dangerous old car, than for a new house that could be submerged,' I said, indignantly. 'The buyer can have his solicitor do a search of public records for disclosure of external impacts, such as flood-proneness. I have never heard of a flood victim who has sued a solicitor whose search failed to warn him.

'The injustice of the situation is a fault in legal responsibility that allows the seller of a home to conceal evidence that it is flood-prone. The principal of *caveat emptor*, buyer beware, supposes the buyer can know the pitfalls. Foreigners like me are at a disadvantage. The builder of a new house takes no responsibility for it being flood-prone, beyond getting Council approval for the position being above the defined flood level. This is an ethical inconsistency that allows dishonest dealing and exploitation. It rewards fraud.'

'Developers have another lurk,' said Howard. 'When the Council raises the level of defined flooding, a developer can claim compensation for 'Injurious affection' if approval is refused for development previously approved at a lower level. It is a law in Queensland that protects developers. The effect of this provision is that there has not been much prevention of building of flood-prone homes on river floodplains. Approvals are not often rescinded.'

'My aversion to deception in risk taking is like my dislike for gambling,' I said. 'I used to bet when I was younger and was an admirer of writers like Hemingway, Twain and Runyon, whose characters wagered prolifically. As I matured, I learned to avoid gambling promoted by bookies, shills and sharpsters. I have almost as much zeal in opposing gambling as a Baptist, although I like dancing and quietness on Sundays. Australians are reputed to be the World's highest spending gamblers.'

'This is a grand place to live,' said Victor, when I walked with him by the River.

He was an old university friend visiting from the UK. He had worked for many years with a British airline and had an employee ticket concession. He was staying with me for a couple of weeks and I was showing him Brisbane.

When I told him about our floods earlier in the year, he was unsympathetic.

'When you bought, you were taken,' said Victor.

He was an artist and wore clothes he had sewn himself. Today he had on a white suit, with a Paisley silk cravat and a mauve orchid buttonhole.

'You may be right, but it's not a view I can act on now,' I said to him.

So far I have allowed in little subjectivity. Transient emotional responses of flood victims are normally left out when flooding is reported, despite these being the most salient information in evaluation of a disaster, either from an absolute humane viewpoint, or relative to another disaster competing for relief funding, such as a drought.

Victor had been impressionable when we studied together. He was dashing, rather reckless. His was an ethos lampooned in Fellini's movie Amarcord, with a Cyclopsian motorbike rider wearing goggles, roaring myopically at high speed through the centre of every film set. The rider was swathed in a heavy leather overcoat, insulating him from the World. His flamboyance, high speed and garb lacked sensitivity to environment and the plight of impoverished people.

But Victor had changed.

'If flood victims were compensated fairly, the government would find it expedient to reduce the number of homes that could be flooded,' he said.

'It would be good but it won't happen here,' I said. 'Only 2.5% of homes were impacted. Many of the 97.5% would oppose paying compensation to the unfortunates.'

'It's a paradoxxzzx of unkindness,' Victor said. 'Is it the same here with droughts and fires?'

'Yes. Government doesn't pay compensation, but encourages buying of insurance. The people who need it can't afford the premiums.'

I took Victor on a tour by bus of historic Brisbane. By English standards, it wasn't old but I realised my strong affection for my city, despite the flooding.

Floods can inspire feelings of awe and wonder at the power and unpredictability of nature, reminding people of a connection to the divine and the impermanence of life. They can also inspire fearfulness and feelings of defeat. I began to take note of victims' fear and anxiety, loss and grief, helplessness, vulnerability, community spirit and resilience. My scientific analysis of the River did not adequately express the hurt and anxiety of flood victims.

'I don't see much sign of infrastructure damage,' Victor said.

'It has been repaired.

'Brisbaners have used private funds to repair damage to many flooded homes, including those rented by lower income residents. Many have had to borrow to replace appliances. Flooding takes from the part of the population that can least afford it. A more equitable redistribution would be more just.'

CHAPTER 26 DAM FAILURE

A dam is a precarious venture with ability to hold back flood water and release it later. If the Brisbane River dams overfilled and failed, the authorities who constructed and operated them would be responsible.

Idle talk speculated that in 2011 and 2022 the dams had filled and had to release water fast, causing the floods. Any inference that a dam could actually fail was unspoken, heresy, fantastic, beyond quantification. The effectiveness of a dam was not questioned and it was assumed it would survive whatever weather could eventuate.

I searched the Internet to find information about dam failure.

Wivenhoe Dam could fail in the same way that a smaller dam in China failed in 1975 (11) resulting in more than 220,000 deaths. The Banqiao Dam could hold one third the capacity of Wivenhoe Dam, also made of clay. The Banqiao Dam catastrophe could indicate the scale of a Wivenhoe Dam disaster.

Responsibility was less than transparent for Wivenhoe Dam's technology, that could destroy a large part of the city. At an elevation of 86 metres above sea level, Wivenhoe's 2.3 kilometres wall is 24.5 metres high. It was designed to withstand a '1,000-year' flood i.e. failure conditions expected once in a millennium.

Typhoon Nina had stalled over Henan in China in early August 1975 and produced floods at twice the 1,000-year level. The first day's total precipitation exceeded 1,000 mm, surpassing the area's total annual precipitation by one-fifth. Three more days of heavy downpour followed.

The 118 metres high dam wall at 116 metres above sea level, overtopped, began to collapse and wash away shortly after 1:00 am on August 8th, creating a rush of water in a wave 10 metres high and 11 kilometres wide, traveling at about 50 kilometres per hour. The town of Daowencheng, just downstream, was immediately inundated and all 9,600 citizens were killed. A total of 61 other dams and reservoirs also failed that day, as a result of the typhoon. In the ensuing floods, 26,000 people drowned. A further 145,000 died, from epidemics caused by contamination of the water and from famine. Some estimates put the total death toll at more than 220,000. It was horrific.

Wivenhoe Dam could fail with similar consequences. It has an earth embankment with a clay core, faced with rock. Because earth is permeable by water, an impermeable clay barrier was inserted in the dam wall to prevent water penetrating and causing a leak that could breach it. The rock facing would protect the earth embankment, but not if it was overtopped.

I drove Victor, my visitor, on an excursion to Wivenhoe Dam. We drove on a winding road through scrubby dry country up the Brisbane Valley until the road passed along the top of the wall, across the huge dam.

We stopped at a viewing point and I told him the facts I had found out.

'To prevent overtopping, the dam has a concrete spillway with five steel crest gates,' I said. 'An auxiliary spillway acts as a giant pressure valve to protect the dam wall in the event of a 1 in 100,000 year rain and flood event. Supposing more than 1000 mm of rain fell in one day, the storage would be dangerously full near to overtopping and dam flood gates would have to be opened wide. The rate of release would cause severe flooding downstream. To prevent a worse disaster, Wivenhoe has three fuse plugs, piles of erodible gravel blocking the concrete spillway, which would wash away automatically, failing safely and releasing a huge quantity of water very fast, relieving the danger, preventing catastrophic overtopping and collapse.

'Rain falling in other parts of the river's catchment would also be trying to flow down the river at this time, through tributaries including the Bremer and Lockyer Creek. These could have water quantities equal or larger than Banqiao's, converging on Brisbane.

The effects downstream would be less severe than a total dam burst, but the flooding effects could be unprecedented.'

'What would happen if the Wivenhoe Dam was overtopped?' Victor asked me.

'A wave of water from the collapsed dam would travel 170 kilometres along the river course and smash into Brisbane,' I said. 'It's estimated 400 people would die, 300,000 would be in danger, and the community would face a bill of at least $100 billion. Brisbane's main source of drinking water would be destroyed.

'It's like the possibility of being in an airplane crash: not worth thinking about,' said Victor. His flippancy was typical of him, but many others would share his attitude. This had been the attitude prevailing in government response to an article by Mark Solomons in the Brisbane Times (13).

'A journalist reported that the safety standards of the dams had been relaxed,' Solomons said. 'He explained that when Wivenhoe was first conceived in the 1970s, Australian design standards for large dams made of earth and rock required them to be able to contain the flood created by the largest possible rain event in the catchment, the 'probable maximum precipitation'. But soon after Wivenhoe was completed in 1984, meteorologists realised the size of the epic deluge they had designed for was far too small. This shortfall affected almost half of Seqwater's 26 large dams. Dams all over Australia were no longer compliant with the existing standards.'

'That's scary,' said Victor. 'What did the government do about it?'

'Rather than raise all the dam walls, authorities changed the standard,' I said. 'For the first time they assigned a probability to this massive rain event, even though the new national dam design manual in 1987 acknowledged a fundamental scientific problem with doing this.'

'Although it was not possible theoretically, a probability had to be assigned... This must be done on a somewhat arbitrary basis'.

'The upshot was that standards began to involve fuzzy probabilities instead of absolutes.

'A bloke called McMahon (10) believed this was an effective softening of standards and it happened because governments, including the Bjelke-Petersen regime under which he worked, balked at the cost of dam upgrades.

'Instead of having to upgrade the dams, they could say, 'yes the dams can be overtopped, but the probability is only one in a million', or something like that,' McMahon explained.

'They're now accepting that rock fill dams can be overtopped and they're using studies with guidelines of how many people can be killed.'

'Loss of life has become acceptable, whereas previously it wasn't,' McMahon said. 'Wivenhoe should be able to cope with the Probable Maximum Flood. At this stage it can't - and I'm not sure the population at risk has been sufficiently consulted in this decision.'

'It really is scary,' said Victor. He was usually more optimistic than me. 'Did they do anything?'

'There was some re-engineering of the Wivenhoe dam spillway,' I said. 'Leaders didn't raise the spectre and those whose job was to plan to deal with the horror scenario didn't get much further than considering its low likelihood before dismissing the scenario.'

The prospect of failure of the Wivenhoe Dam was sobering. Thinking about it was too awful for serious consideration.

Victor and I had lunch in a country pub before driving back to Brisbane. We chatted and agreed absolute safety may be a dream. The level of risk accepted by the public is not incommensurate with risks from other events and accidents. For example, dam failure risk is low, like the probability of passenger death in aircraft travel, or the probability of an asteroid colliding with Earth.

The contingency of deaths from Wivenhoe dam failure had been planned.

I could imagine the wave smashing into my apartment building and possibly knocking it off its foundations. This prospect was far worse than the riverine flooding damage the dam had been constructed to prevent.

Rather than being a means to an end, the Heidegger phenomenon of a dam was as a technology that would understand the world. It could be interpreted in various ways. It could prevent occasional flooding, including disasters, but catastrophic flooding would rarely occur. Protection from traditional floods would have been traded off against monstrous flooding when the dam fails. A dam 'understands' storage of rainfall, but with the possibility of the dam's destruction, the stored water is a new threat. The value of a dam is ambiguous because when water is stored in it, it is potentially dangerous. The benefits of flood mitigation and water supply could be offset or even exceeded by threat of dam failure.

When I thought about consequences of the Wivenhoe dam failing, the event was improbable but alarming. I studied the statistical estimates of risk trying to balance the possibility of collapse with the supposed benefits of the dam. I realised that I could die and resolved to live as authentically as I could, from now on.

'Don't worry about it,' said Victor. 'If it happens you won't know about it.'

CHAPTER 27 GRANIA

'We never know what a dam's effect is,' I said to myself, frustrated. 'We can't go back and compare the undammed river with rainfall the same as before.'

'It's the same problem as a medical treatment,' murmured a voice in reply, from a woman standing shyly beside my desk. 'The results can be worse than the disease.'

'Exactly,' I said. 'Every project is a new situation.'

It was reassuring that the woman had confirmed my opinion. I didn't know her. I had heard someone talking before and had thought it was a neighbour's radio. But here was someone friendly. I smiled at her.

'Won't you sit down?' I asked. 'Are you doing medical research?'

'No. I research insurance against droughts. My name's Grania.'

'Good to see you,' I said, although she was insubstantial and difficult to see. Her voice was educated and soft.

'You never know for sure if a dam does any good,' she said. She had understood me perfectly.

'It doesn't deter dam builders,' I said.

She made no comment and sat at the table quietly, reposed.

'Do I know you from somewhere?' I asked her.

'I'm in the same class as you, doing a master's degree in hydrology part-time.'

I hadn't noticed her, but it was a large class.

She had a small pretty face, framed by auburn hair pulled back into a bun and a little younger than me. I was attracted, by her friendly manner. She was very private and when I didn't speak to her, she seemed to fade away a little.

She had appeared when I was anxious about the Brisbane River flooding my place. Perhaps her appearance was a delusion, relief from the trauma of being partly flooded several months ago. I began to tell her my worries about flooding of my apartment.

Talking with her relaxed me. She faded, but she let me know she was listening. It was not unusual for misanthropes and people who worked alone to talk to themselves and even imagine an invisible friend. When I was nine years old I had an invisible friend, Kurt, who stayed in my room. My parents knew of him as a normal part of healthy growing up. I welcomed the appearance of Grania because she had alleviated my solitude and prepared me to discuss and debate my work with others.

I knew that it was not normal to entertain a delusion and it could be thought insane to interact with someone who was imaginary. I would keep Grania to myself. There was no harm in having her in my corner, in my thoughts, as long as I was not taking advantage of anyone and my functioning was not adversely affected. I discussed my project only with Howard and with Gardner, my research supervisor, once a week. I needed to talk more frequently with someone intelligent, who was interested in my topic. When I am writing, I seldom have anyone with the expertise or interest to discuss my ideas with. Rather than relying on description or monologue to convey my thoughts, I want readers to get them from dialogues between my protagonist and intimates.

At our next hydrology class, Grania appeared sitting beside me. Afterwards, in the coffee shop, she turned down a coffee and watched me sip mine. I looked into her eyes, to see if she was real and she looked straight back, as if from a mirror. She was there to please me and I wondered how far I could go.

'Do I know you from somewhere?' she asked me.

'I used to work for Wattle Mines,' I said.

'That's it,' she said. 'I was there. Did you know Howard Pope?'

'Yes. We still meet up,' I said. 'What were you doing?'

'Exploration mapping, but I left.'

I didn't remember her, but it was a large section, with people coming and going.

We talked then about our work now, mine in investigating the River and her research into droughts.

Grania would have to negotiate meanings of droughts with farmers and graziers. I couldn't see her project getting very far, because she would have to speak with them and I knew I was the only one she could appear to. It crossed my mind that she could join with me in my river project; but PhDs weren't done like that.

When I walked her to her home, we hugged and kissed. My hands strayed from her perfect waist to her perfect bottom. She gently pushed me away.

'Not yet,' she said. 'Soon.'

I could be patient.

'Why hydrology?' I asked her.

'I do policy development for droughts.'

She didn't give the name of her employer and I thought she was being cautious, as most women were when they met a stranger.

'Sounds interesting,' I said.

'It is,' she said. 'You?'

'Science teacher. I have been writing a textbook.'

'Why are you studying hydrology?' she asked me.

'I want to understand natural flooding of a river,' I told her. 'My master's project is to investigate flooding of the Logan River.'

'Who wants to know?' she said.

'I do. I am writing a novel for people to understand riverside living.'

'What is there to understand?' she asked.

'Conditions that cause flooding, how these occur naturally and can be changed.'

'What do you mean 'naturally'?'

'Without construction of dams,' I said.

'Why not investigate a river with dams?'

'That can come later,' I said. 'First I have to find out what can happen without them.'

'How will you find out?' she asked.

'I will observe effects and attribute causes.'

'When the effects are floods, what causes can there be?'

'Natural events, weather. I used to live beside the Logan River for 22 years. My family's home was perched on the riverbank, overlooking the River. It seemed tame, until after a couple of days of heavy rain, the water level climbed 30 metres up to the river terrace, 10 metres below our house. The torrent thundered, shaking the ground, with whole trees careening past like express trains. Millions of tonnes of water tumbled by, tearing at everything standing in their way, without any human control. The water spread to the horizon and it was a relief when it stopped rising.

'My daughter Sarah said to me: 'There is more water than I would have believed is possible.'

'The sky was the limit,' I said to Grania. 'The wind conveyed moist air in and dumped rain on the Logan catchment. Our house wasn't flooded, but we were cut off from the shops and I couldn't get to work for several days. The flood blocked river crossings, with intrusion of water into low-lying places where livestock and dwellings were damaged.'

Grania was a good listener and I was drawn to her, by her interest in my project and by her serene understated appearance. She was poised, but not in a showy way.

'Droughts depend on weather, too,' she said. 'My work is to plan insurance against droughts. There isn't much mitigation with droughts.'

'Storages and bores can make a difference for watering livestock,' I said.

'Yes, of course. I meant there aren't technologies specifically preventing droughts occurring, like there are for floods.'

Grania's interest in droughts was helpful to me in understanding operation of the dams. We both followed weather forecasts, interested in rainfall from opposed perspectives.

We chatted then about the dynamics of floods and droughts, how they began and how they ended. Grania was almost too good to be true and I found myself studying her to check if she was real. She seemed real enough. It was good to have someone I could talk to. She understood my difficulty in addressing the ridiculous conventional wisdom. Until Grania joined me, I had often felt that nothing could be done about river flooding and that my proposals would have no public interest. With her encouragement, I began to prepare a portfolio of needed improvements that I could send to responsible authorities.

'I am able to infer river dynamics, partly by science and partly by instinct,' I said. 'When it is in flood, it collects water from the land surface, increasing in water depth until the volume flowing into the channel is almost level with the outflow along any reach of the river.'

'The bigger picture is of the river water overcoming the friction between water and stream materials, gravitating to the lowest point, eroding sediment away, lowering the river's bed, tumbling down waterfalls, onto piles of boulders, or mixing with tides in an estuary. Fast flowing water carries coarse suspended solids, depositing them when the flow slows down, filling up the channel.'

'Sediment causes flooding,' she said.

'Exactly. Most of the river is below the water surface and invisible to us, without special equipment. It contains sediment which can move and when there is flooding, the bed can build up, or the banks can erode away. It moves under the surface of the muddy torrent, threatening and sinister.'

I was talking too much, but she was interested.

'You have thought about the objectives of flooding,' she murmured. She had probably heard it all before. I wasn't used to women who knew all about rivers. I hadn't been able to resist showing off my experience of river flow dynamics.

'What does hydrology have to do with your work in insurance?' I asked her.

'I'm interested in the subjectives of droughts,' she said.

'What are they?' I asked, at a loss. I knew nothing about spiritualism and would have to be careful not to make a fool of myself.

'Subjectives are feelings, opinions and tastes,' Grania said. 'Peoples' dependence on water, their cultural and social backgrounds, their drought experiences, anxiety and uncertainty, frustration and anger, loss and grief, adaptation and resilience, community spirit and collaboration.'

'That lot will keep you busy,' was all I could say. 'I'm interested in those effects too, but I'm not sure how I could include them.'

'With phenomenology you could,' said Grania. 'You should join me in studying it.'

CHAPTER 28 NATURAL FLOODING

Instead of being a know-it-all and trying to impress Grania, I began to take her advice.

'Subjective data is the same as objective data, but more controversial,' she said. 'Phenomenology analyses subjective data. People's feelings are paramount in considering drought relief.'

'I'd like to find out about the phenomenon of river flooding,' I said. 'Perhaps the Philosophy Department has a course unit?'

'Do you still live there by the Logan River?'

'No. I moved into Brisbane, by the River.'

'Do you have a family?'

I was flattered a single woman was asking me about my family. I hadn't had a date since I finished with Karen two years ago and the possibility that Grania could consider me as partner material was tantalising.

'I divorced ten years ago and I live by myself,' I said. 'My children are overseas, but come and go. Where do you live?'

'New Farm.'

'By yourself?'

'No. I share an apartment with a friend from work.'

'A girl friend?'

'Yes.'

'Do you work?'

'Part-time. I'm an actuary.'

'Do you assess drought risks with statistics?'

'Yes. Do droughts affect your river?' Grania asked.

'Most of the time the Logan River is tranquil. Rain falls mainly between December and March but it can rain or drought at any time.

The wet season could have several weeks of flooding rains, or in some years it has been completely dry. Farming and livestock enterprises are often in drought, with skeletal animals fed on trucked-in fodder, donated by country folk from better-off districts, or bought and sent by kind city people.

'When the river was high, normal living was disrupted. Our kids were pleased that the roads were cut and the schools closed. They looked for items floating in the torrent to salvage.

'Dad, there's a horse caught up in a tree,' my son Michael told me. 'We're going to save it.'

'With a rope, they pulled aside branches and brought the weak animal to the riverbank. They took it into our stable and fed it.'

'Can we keep it?' they asked.

'It's not ours,' I said. 'The owner will probably be looking for it.'

'The owner showed up after a couple of days and took it away.

'Thank you, children,' he said. 'You did a wonderful thing.'

'Your kids were enterprising,' said Grania. I guessed that she was childless. A mother would have told me proudly about her child by now. 'Were there many floods?'

'In the 22 years we lived there, one particularly large flood is etched in my memory. Our house overlooked the river channel cut into its floodplain, over a kilometre wide. There were weirs for irrigation along the river, but they had submerged days previously.'

'I thought you wanted your river to be natural, without weirs or dams?'

'I do. But where there is potential, a storage has usually been built. The storages on the Logan were small, in those days,' I said. 'They didn't much affect flooding.'

'How did the height of flooding affect you?'

'We watched as the channel filled up and over its banks. There was water as far as we could see, with trees standing like sentinels over the chocolate-coloured torrent swirling around tree trunks. It made us feel small and inconsequential. It seemed impossible there could be enough water to fill the huge floodplain, but the level steadily rose 60 metres vertically over two or three days, until it was about 5 metres below our house. The sound was a deep churning roar of water tearing and snapping. Our access road was flooded and we were trapped. The electricity was cut. We consoled ourselves that water five metres higher, to reach the house, was inconceivable. It was a theory and didn't completely alleviate our anxiety.'

Grania was listening closely to me. No-one had ever been as interested in my story before and I indulged myself telling it to her.

"'Is the Logan a big river?' my daughter Sarah asked,' I told Grania.

"No,' I said to her. 'It's only about half the length of the Brisbane River. But it is steeper. The floods can be ferocious."

"'Our house is on the floodplain of the river, isn't it?' asked Sarah. 'The floodplain was originally cut into the riverbank by water, wasn't it? Could the water reclaim its floodplain again?"

'Good logic,' I said. 'It could, but it's unlikely'.

"Why is it unlikely?' Sarah asked,'

'I have interpreted the river terraces and flood plain. They are carved into the recent Holocene era sedimentary rocks outcropping in the riverbanks,' I said. 'My hermeneutical understanding is that the water carved the top terrace hundreds, or even thousands, of years ago. It was an unusual event and may not be repeated until a very long time in the future.'

"Do you mean the rain is stopping?' Sarah asked.'

'Haha,' I said. 'I mean a 100-year flood could be this year.'

Grania laughed.

'Sarah asks good questions,' she said. 'What is hermeneutical understanding?'

'It means interpreting the evidence. The riverbank erosion has a record of the river being there.'

'That's what I am aiming for with droughts,' she said. 'How did flooding affect you?'

'When the water went down, the river channel was denuded of its greenery and appeared empty. A lone fox searched for small creatures along the riverbank and came up to the house where we fed it scraps.

'My perception of the river changed from an idyllic waterway, concealed by tall trees in a narrow channel, to an open drain for a vast hinterland. For the first time, I recognised that it had been a gamble to construct our home on the flood plain. In my mind, the river crouched with malicious intent, ready to spring up and outwards at any time. In my intuitive non-sensory understanding, the river is no longer benign.'

'Would you say a drought has as much malice as a flood?' Grania asked.

I laughed. 'I'm not an anthropomorphist,' I said. 'Floods and droughts don't get personal with me. They are mean with everyone. They deserve respect.'

Grania stood up. 'It has been good talking,' she said. 'We two share existential viewpoints on the presence or absence of rainfall. Maybe we could study phenomenology together. Please let me know if you find a course. I think you would find it useful for your project.'

'I have liked our conversation,' I said. 'Can we meet again next week?'

'That would be great. Bye,' she said.

Meeting her had been a wonderful surprise. The days went by slowly until we were together again.

At the end of the year, I wrote up my data from the Logan River as a thesis to submit for a master's degree in hydrology. My analysis attempted to establish flooding frequencies and heights for the Logan River before construction of dams and weirs. I summarised statistical evidence and was able to conclude river behaviour which could be compared before and after construction of storages.

Construction of dams on the Logan River was controversial and the benefits of the small ones already built, was arguable. A dam could be a source of pride and be defended with mendacity, because the river was small, data was unavailable and livelihoods could depend on rivalry in making claims for water rights.

'What if they don't build a dam?' asked Grania at our next meeting in the coffee shop.

'There would be winners and losers. Winners could be downstream, who would get more water without it being taken by a dam upstream. Losers would be water users needing to hold a regular supply in a dam, for example, for irrigation.'

I had met Grania in time for me to tryout my masters' ideas on her, a couple of months before I submitted. She had obliged, giving her time generously. Her questioning and opinions had helped me consolidate my thesis. I couldn't imagine what I would have done without her.

After the first time, she hadn't appeared again, but I could imagine her being there and hearing her talk.

I had become aware that my analysis had overlooked many potential issues from a post-modern perspective. There were other more subjective viewpoints and my biases as observer had obscured other conclusions. I had been limited by my scientific and engineering training but I wanted my work to speak more widely to the people who could be affected by the river, for better or for worse. I would enrol in phenomenology next year, with Grania. Perhaps our relationship would recognise the great affection I felt for her. Gradually our discussion had added intimacy to hydrology.

CHAPTER 29 LIMITATIONS OF SCIENTIFIC ANALYSIS

I attended the final class of our hydrology course.

'How're you going with your project?' Grania asked me.

'I've put my thesis in,' I said, 'I am proposing to go on next year and investigate phenomenology of the Brisbane River, for a PhD.'

'What's wrong with using science, the way you did in your Logan River study?' she asked.

'It's too sceptical. There's nowhere to begin, no foundation for building knowledge. The separation of mind and body is artificial and does not allow for emotional responses to the River. It tries to understand flow of the river disregarding observations. It relies too heavily on my subjective experiences, introspection, reason and rationality but neglects my emotions and the knowledge I bring to bear. Application is oversimplified, biased and limited. It omits social and cultural contexts which are required for complete understanding.

'Science was the first to use reason and the power of human intellect to discover knowledge,' I said. 'Descartes' maxim was: 'I think therefore I am.' The Scientific Method, based on duality of subject and object, emerged with growing popularity. But it is flawed because it is doubtful and has to have something to observe *a priori*. It does not look under stones to see what crawls out: that is empirical science, requiring hypotheses. When I began investigating the River, I didn't have an hypothesis. Now, after investigating for a year, I still don't have one. I am frustrated. When I analysed for Wattle Mines, I would explore and eventually an hypothesis would pop into my head. For the next month I would be telling it to people, so they could take it up. But that hasn't happened yet with the River. Nothing has popped.'

'Perhaps you are being too ambitious?' Grania said.

'It is not ambitious to want to find something of consequence,' I said. 'The scientific method has misled me to focus on what can be observed and measured. Subject-object analysis can distort a problem. Objectification demands a passive object able to be manipulated and controlled by the subject, such as the height of a flood, which has causes which are remote. Where there is a flood in someone's lounge room, a subject who is intent on the object of flood height, may not connect it with the actions of dam operators. A more holistic and relational understanding may be more useful.

'The scientific method has been too remote. My findings were mainly hydrology. It is too hung up with being scientific. It tries to present a deterministic account of river flow, when causes are often unknown and partly random. It presupposes too much. It doesn't explore the effects of weirs and pumping, nor the possibilities of dam construction.

'How do you mean it's remote?' she asked.

'My investigation has recounted observations made while living beside two rivers. I wanted to develop a comprehensive explanation of flooding and to use this information to check the strategies used for managing the floodwater but rainfall and tides were unknown. The data I collected was fragmentary in space, time and mass. They were geographical features of the river course; catchment areas; elevation changes; river width; water level; dams and their operation. I could deduce a few local quantities, but was unable to observe values in the upper rivers and eventual consequences of flooding downriver.

'I agree that scientific data is needed, but subjective data and potential for change is also relevant. A scientific observer is ego-driven, with privilege and control over objectivity. The same stored water could have consequences of flooding or drought. A scientific observer might not be able to recognise, let alone measure, the ambiguity. The scientific gaze is for empirical research and explorative science, for establishing mechanisms, not for solving practical problems.'

I became aware that the analytical method of science was limited and did not achieve the critical viewpoint I wanted. I have had to accept distant observations of the rivers as if they were passive objects. In reality, observer and object are interdependent and active. My observation and the state of the river could not be understood in isolation from each other. The reproducibility I wanted was absent and my findings were unreliable.

'Perhaps the problems able to be solved by the scientific method have all been solved?' Grania said.

'I'm afraid the problem with the scientific method is more serious than that,' I said. 'It is a dualist philosophy and deeply flawed.'

'I'm not familiar with the problem of dualism,' said Grania.

'Dualism supposes there is a world out there, possibly with gods, from which I am physically removed but able to observe and analyse natural factors, such as heavy rainfall, topography, or geology and separately predict effects of human interventions such as deforestation, urbanization, or ineffective flood management practice,' I said.

'Every dyad of observer and object has to assume ultimate causes and final effects are known, when agreement about those are unlikely. Gods, the universe and final consequences are not settled. Findings from dualism are for use in protected sterile environments where ordinary people feel excluded.

'The scientific theory's assumption of a divine cause and truncated effects is usually conveniently omitted. God lurks in the wings ready to make an entrance. The author of an hypothesis has to admit it is bathed in unknowns and is a precarious venture. Science and engineering must look rather naïve and foolish when the dualist dyad of subject and object precludes ultimate causes and absolute knowledge.

'After 400 years of distortion by subjects' arbitrary viewpoints, perhaps the time to change the vantage point of the subject has come,' said Grania.

'Yes, I agree,' I said.

'What are you going to do?'

'I need a fresh perspective. My engineer's scientific mindset has so far been concerned with causes and effects of flooding determined by physical processes and technologies such as dams, operated deliberately and rationally. But the existential philosophies of Nietzsche and others has allowed more subjective evaluations, with less remote perspectives, becoming more involved with an observer. These methods are monist, attributing causes to both mind and body acting simultaneously, without a God.

'The Cartesian scientific method has predominated in my engineering training,' I said. 'It has been difficult for me to accept a different method, but my perception has shifted to a post-modern way of looking at things and I want to try phenomenology. It recognises observation can have several simultaneous limited points of view, with an object having various appearances.'

'A weakness of my dualist scientific method was that I couldn't associate with the problem,' Grania said. 'I adopted the old Aristotelian concept of scientific man as a passive observer, a 'blank tablet'. Husserl and Heidegger's phenomenology turned this concept inside out. The observer rated potential and identified useful experiences. It was a practical approach with powerful consequences.'

'Scientists have objected with accusations of bias in rating potential and negative consequences.'

'Heidegger was a fascist,' I replied.

'Phenomenology is not a political theory,' said Grania. 'It does not judge what is right or wrong. For that reason, it is liberating as well as irresponsible and dangerous. It can be powerful and has to be used with caution.'

'I agree. A phenomenological analysis can have many advantages but can also have risks.'

I proposed a PhD project, in which I would evaluate the Brisbane River by phenomenology, investigating subjective experiences and flood mitigation technologies. I proposed to include in my phenomenological study of the Brisbane River my own and other people's enjoyment and relaxation by the river, aesthetic appreciation, environmental concern, cultural significance, spiritual connection, victim suffering, economic benefit and political effects.

'It is time to bring lived experience into my analysis,' I said. 'Practical experience.'

'It makes good sense,' said Grania.

I was accepted as a PhD student part-time.

PART 4

REDUCING FLOODING

CHAPTER 30
PHENOMENOLOGY

'What do you hope to get from phenomenology?' whispered Grania, when I walked into phenomenology class, with her in my head. She had suggested we study it together, but I couldn't remember exactly why I was enrolled in something I knew little about.

'I want to reveal and analyse the subjective Dasein of the Brisbane River, as experienced by a variety of people,' I said. It was a new word and I hoped I had used it correctly.

'Why do we need a new word: Dasein?' Grania asked perkily. 'Do you mean the river-ness of it?'

Grania had quickly grasped Heidegger's term.

'Yes. Something like that,' I said. 'Hopefully I will find more potential for the Logan River than I found by Cartesian objective analysis.'

'Descartes' observer is so doubtful he doesn't see potential,' said Grania.

'Yes. Phenomenology looks at all kinds of potential,' I replied. 'It is like wearing sunglasses that cut out the 'glare' of unprospective low potential. The observer engages in 'what if' subjectivity. The River's potential could be as an obstructed channel able to be cleared to become a better waterway.'

Grania didn't reply because our class was starting. I was proud of my sunglasses analogy and knew that we would discuss it later.

When I was at home with Grania, I phoned Howard.

Grania knew us both from Wattle Mines but she had hung out with the exploration people and we hadn't seen much of her.

'I've been talking with Grania,' I told Howard. 'Do you remember her?'

He did.

'What's she up to?'

'She is researching drought insurance,' I said. 'She's put me on to phenomenology and I've been to my first class. She's here now and may have some questions for you.

I switched to speaker phone.

'Phenomenology is a new idea,' Howard said. 'It seems to do to science what impressionism did to classical art: it finds more potential for excitement in the same experience. It's controversial and the old science die-hards think it's rubbish.'

'I'm hoping to get a new take on Brisbane River flooding,' I said. 'I will go over the scientific study of the river I did last year with a post-structural toothcomb.'

I discussed with Howard the phenomenological perspective.

'In the early days, when psychology and sociology were used to analyse behaviour, they were regarded as unscientific, 'touchy feely', lacking the rigour of the physical sciences,' I said. 'They assumed what was going on inside peoples' heads, without being able to make measurements. Because they lacked objectivity, the analyses were 'subjective' and consequently down-rated.

'There was an attempt to observe behaviour reproducibly; to be objective; to control observation; to hide observers; to isolate subjects; to hypothesise; to falsify; to do tests blinded and double-blinded,' Howard said. 'Cartesian scientific investigations of causes omitted inferences and circumstantial evidence. They were often devoid of human values, without meaning of existence, beyond physical and biological processes. True understanding of behaviour was inaccessible.

'Phenomenology considers intentions and meanings, looking behind scenes for potential present-at-hand, or ready-to-hand, for the analyst to enumerate,' I said. 'The analyst makes explicit the purpose of the inquiry, its provenance, trajectory, mood, ambiguities, articulation, and projected future, all in an open slather of eclectic subjectivity. It replaces dry cognition with interpretations that can be used.

'I will no longer hold back from River events observing neutrality and refraining from trying things out,' I said. 'When flood heights are missing, I will estimate. Nor will I leave buttons unpressed. I need to find out how systems work. Heidegger's phenomenology encourages me to taste a grape before buying a kilogram. When I come to a road I don't know, instead of looking for it on a map, I will explore. As an agent, when I am out and about, I am empowered to sample reality and conduct experiments, looking for things that could be useful. My Being There, or Dasein, is immersed in potential.

Grania had taken a back seat during this phone discussion with Howard, but she had listened and when he had gone, she questioned me.

'How would a river in flood be different with phenomenology?' asked Grania. 'What difference would it make?'

'Phenomenology would reveal the river's Dasein, or Being There,' I said. 'Instead of a waterway framed by land, it would show water flowing in a floodplain, bending trees over, hitting submerged obstructions, eroding the banks, carrying particles of sediment, depositing gravel banks and being opposed by tides. The river's being includes everything about it that explains its meaning and intent observed by all media, eclectically. It would include all the river currents, circulation and ripples within the stream, not just observations relative to a point of view.'

'What intent could a river have?' Grania asked.

'In a river, water is moved to the sea by gravity,' I said. 'Every process and everything that helps the water reach the sea is useful and therefore is significant.

'Heidegger's genius was to recognise anything that could be useful was relevant,' she said. 'A single point of view does not have to be defined. Curiosity, ambiguity, future projection, fallenness, thrownness, moodedness and articulation of understanding are all relevant, to the extent they are useful.'

I reminded her of the sunglasses analogy I had mentioned to her earlier in our class.

'I like your analogy,' said Grania enthusiastically. 'It is like the epiphany I had when evolution was revealed to me in a biology class at school. Suddenly the form, size, colour and behaviour of every living thing was for survival. Features of animals and plants were different forever afterwards contrasting with God's purposeless handiwork. For example, a kangaroo's legs and hopping enabled it to survive by escaping pursuit through scrub.'

I joined in her enthusiasm. Grania seldom spoke of her previous experience. She was an existentialist leading her best life in the present. It was wonderful to have her amazing interest in topics so close to my heart.

'I had the same revelation,' I said. 'Darwin's theory changed my perception. I began to notice characteristics with potential for survival of animals. Now, with phenomenology, I look for river characteristics with potential to be useful.'

'Potential for whom?' asked Grania.

'To anyone, by right of access, or by those wanting protection from it, or by those who have technologies that could use the river, or depend on it,' I said. 'Dasein includes all aspects of the phenomenon. For example, the Dasein of a kangaroo would include its jumping through scrub using its long legs and wedge-shaped body.'

'Phenomenology cuts to the chase,' Grania said. 'A Scientific observer-object analysis could miss out the contexts, terrain and vegetation where kangaroos are pursued and the functions of parts of their bodies, for example their tails. Phenomenology reports on how kangaroos are observed to live and run in scrub for example when pursued by dingos.'

It was wonderful to share insights with Grania. I felt that I stood on the threshold of something great.

'Phenomenology doesn't see the features other philosophies find,' I said. 'Evolution looks for survival features; love looks for loveliness; photography looks for appearance; portraiture looks for portrayal; phenomenology looks only for potential.'

Grania and I had enrolled separately in the phenomenology class. I went for coffee after the next class and talked with her quietly about it.

'What potential could a flooded river have?' asked Grania.

I thought for a moment. It took time to respond to an intelligent question by the most attractive woman in the class.

'Its potential to contain and conduct away flood water is paramount. Flooding occurs because water flowing into a reach of the river exceeds the capacity for it to flow away,' I said.

Grania nodded and interposed 'Or is it: When river water level rises higher than normal?'

'Yes. Then more water enters a river system than can be distributed.'

'Hold on a minute... that's more than one 'Being',' said Grania. 'That must be wrong. There can only be one real Being!' '

'This is where you get *Heideggered,*' I said. 'Which reality? Which truth? Whose definition? Whose meaning? Dasein can be any one of those . . . or all.'

She agreed that Dasein included all those and more.

Grania had displayed with aplomb an in-depth knowledge of Heidegger and her own distinctive viewpoint. She had spoken with charm and asserted her own understanding on a key point, over mine. I could see she was a debater and loved to cross swords in discussion, as I did. She was outgoing, bold and creative, with an agile mind. She had potential.

When she sat close beside me in the coffee bar, I imagined making love to her. I undressed her in my mind's eye and realised her beauty.

That evening, in my apartment, my mind switched to making love to her. I imagined we would go to bed together and concentrate on matters with more potential. I imagined holding her and fondling her breasts.

'Does phenomenology have its own way of making love,' she said, holding my penis, making it hard.

'It would depend on our intentions,' I answered. 'If we could rely on each other we could try for a mutual orgasm.'

'I'm not used to that much intimacy,' she would say. 'Could we try it?'

An hour later we had tried it and succeeded.

'That was the best ever,' she whispered in my ear.

'And for me,' I said. 'Will we be able to follow that?'

'We should do something,' she said, posing. 'Now is not a good time to quit.'

'Could we perfect it before changing to something else?' I said.

'Good idea,' Grania says. 'Our love making is rather self-centred. It could be an effect of doing phenomenology.'

'You had better take your Heidegger sunglasses off when you are with me,' I said. 'I won't let you use me.'

'I love your potential,' she said, beguilingly, caressing my bum.

'There! You are using me.'

'No, it's existential,' she said. 'If I was using you, I would have a purpose. I don't.'

'Okay.' Grania turned over. 'I'm tired now. Goodnight.'

Next morning when I awoke, she was brushing her hair in my bathroom. I watched from the open door. She lifted her thick mop of auburn hair, exposing fine porcelain ears and the secret nape of her neck. Her hair had red and yellow highlights.

She pulled it back and tied it in a bun, with elastic bands. She got out a stick of lipstick and was about to apply it, when she saw me watching her in the mirror. 'I won't be long,' she said dismissively and I turned away.

'She likes her privacy,' I thought. I wondered if all she wanted from me was sex.

'Would you like a cup of coffee?' I asked.

'No thank you, I have to run,' I heard her say.

'Damn.'

It seemed I was just a passing interest. I wondered what I could do to attract her.

'Let's have dinner on Friday evening?' I asked her. 'There's an Italian movie we could see afterwards.'

'Thank you, but I have arranged to visit someone on Friday evening.'

I wondered who it was.

'Anyone I know?' I asked her.

'My flatmate.'

She didn't suggest an alternative day and I supposed she might not want a relationship with me. Or perhaps she was being cautious. I would ask her again later.

'Thanks for the great sex,' she said, going to the door. 'I can see myself out. We can do it again some time.'

I liked her very much but her interest in me was tentative. Perhaps she wanted to go slowly, or was in another relationship. I would see her next Thursday after class.

I thought about her a lot as the week passed slowly. I wondered if I had been too inconsiderate. Perhaps 'great sex' meant insufficient emotion. Maybe she had faked her orgasm or regarded mine as too selfish. I vividly recalled our love-making. She had seemed to enjoy it. There didn't seem to be anything more I could do. Perhaps our friendship would continue, with discussion of Heidegger, as if nothing had happened.

I was pleased that we had begun to understand phenomenology. It was a different approach to understanding nature and technology than I was used to, but already I had glimpsed improvements that could prevent the River flooding.

CHAPTER 31 DASEIN

The phenomenological method is elusive and I was fortunate to have my supervisor Gardner discuss with me my project of phenomenological investigation of the Brisbane River.

'Think,' he said. 'Who will benefit when you reveal the Dasein of the Brisbane River?'

'Me,' I replied.

'Correct,' Gardner said. 'Dasein' implies there is someone who is not only an observer, but doing everything else. He will identify the opportunities available and take credit for making them available.

'There is no English equivalent of Dasein. The German word helps us.'

'Is phenomenology blunt and un-English?' I asked.

'Maybe,' he said. 'The German language has sentences ending with verbs, as if action is the bottom line, whereas English sentences end with objects and material preoccupations.'

'How else is phenomenology a different perspective?' I asked Gardner.

'Besides potential utility,' he said. 'the observer is interested in fallenness and thrownness, negative conditions he might be suffering. The motion of a falling ball could have both physical and mental causes.'

'How could the mind come into it?' I asked.

'Senses and understanding use the mind for cognition. Also, beliefs and supernatural experiences could explain motion,' Gardner said. 'Both physical and mental causality causing a ball to fall is called dualism.'

'But the Dasein of a falling ball has a unified view of reality, having mass, gravity and time since release; other causes too,' I said. 'This is phenomenology and it is monist. It has no mental causality.'

'Monism can consider awareness of matter and physical processes, but not as mind separately,' Gardner said. 'Empirical relationships are sufficient without bringing in mental conditions.'

'What is the difference?'

'Under monist beliefs, influence of the mind is an aspect of the physical world. There can be no spiritual world controlling,' he said.

'Then monism is completely beyond the reach of religion,' I said.

'Yes. In the duallist view, human factors have causal agency, with natural effects dependent. It is an anthropocentric view which allows various interconnected and interdependent causes, including God.

'I get it. The monist does not separate human actions and natural processes. Any human causes are by association.'

'How would phenomenology investigate the potential for flooding from release of water from a dam?' Gardner asked. 'Equations could be developed to calculate acceptable rates of water release, as a cognitive problem of dualism.'

'Phenomenology could use those results but it would add practical experience and empirical evidence,' I said. 'Phenomenology is eclectic in accepting many different viewpoints. It doesn't have the idealism and purity of science's dualism.'

'Unless there is a lot of practical experience, your conclusions from using phenomenology aren't going to be much different are they?' Gardner asked.

'Oh, but I think they would be,' I said. 'For example, phenomenology could have a method of prediction of flood heights quite different from a numerical model derived from science.'

'How would the science of river flooding be different?' he asked.

'The advantage of phenomenology is not for making nit-picking changes to update Newton's equations of motion proposed in 1687 for later theories of relativity and quantum mechanics, but for creating new viewpoints that go where science hasn't reached before. Careful checking of others' work could discover serious errors. Many modern investigations of flood mitigation technology are rushed to meet political timetables and oblivious to necessary science rigour. An appropriate adage is a carpenter's: 'Measure twice and cut once.'

'You'll have plenty of difference there,' Gardner said. 'Phenomenology humanizes analysis, reducing dependence on archaic methods, authority and formulae.'

'Absolutely,' I said. 'Phenomenology identifies causes and effects by weight of evidence, from insights into the lived experiences, looking behind predetermined relationships, unrestricted by an unfeeling observer and unresponsive objects.'

'You're all set, then,' Gardner said. 'Be sure to come and see me every week.'

Gardner had grasped my research idea. There was hardly anyone else prepared to discuss application of phenomenology to the Brisbane River. I was fortunate to have Grania taking an interest in my work. She would talk through complex ideas and help me prepare answers, because I had critics and attackers when I spoke at seminars.

I recounted to Grania the confrontation I had with some students hostile to phenomenology.

'When I started my PhD work,' I told her, 'I had to claim a desk and shelf space in the research room from the other post graduates. At first they felt threatened and tried to exclude me.'

'Don't get too comfortable,' said one called Harper. 'You won't be here long enough to enjoy it.'

It was as if it I was in his territory.

'Why do you say that?' I said.'

'No-one's ever managed to complete a phenomenology project here,' Harper said. 'Heidegger's books are too difficult. They say he's too abstract.'

'There's nothing abstract about the Brisbane River phenomenon I am analysing,' I said.'

'Maybe you haven't realised the difficulty yet because you are starting,' he said.'

'My master's is on the hydrology of river flooding,' I said. 'Phenomenology of river flooding is familiar ground and I will be going into it in detail.'

'What's there to go into? Flooding is flooding,' said Harper.'

'Heidegger opens up a world beyond that studied by science,' I said. 'There's a whole new world to explore, Harper!'

'What do you expect to find?'

'Heidegger's analysis can focus on the dams as human artefacts, or 'technology', making three claims: first, technology is a way of understanding the world, or interpreting what can be done; second, technology is 'not a human activity', but develops beyond human control; and third, technology is 'the highest danger', risking us to only see the world through technological thinking. A dam can threaten humanity.'

'What's wrong with considering a dam as a water storage?' Harper said.

'I want to identify utility of a dam using phenomenology. The measure of utility could be percentage reduction in height of flooding downstream and would depend on the weather.'

'Hmph,' said Harper. 'It's all mumbo jumbo to me. Are you sure you know what you're doing?'

'I'm sure of the problem,' I said, smiling with more confidence than I felt. 'It will take me at least a couple of years to find answers.'

'Perhaps never,' said Harper.

He seemed to have difficulty accepting that he didn't understand 'phenomenology'.

'Chance, have you figured it out yet?' he would laugh, when he passed me in the corridor.'

'Yes,' I answered. 'You wouldn't understand.'

'People feel threatened by others' work when they don't understand it,' said Grania. 'For Harper to understand Heidegger would take more effort than he is prepared to make.'

Grania was using phenomenology for her PhD project too. She came to classes with me and afterwards we would discuss what we had learned.

Grania and I were spending more time together, kissing and fondling. She hadn't wanted another tryst and I was chagrined. I suspected that she had another lover. I hoped that the added involvement I had with her, would soon oust my competitor.

I sat beside Grania at a postgraduate dinner. Our proximity wasn't accidental. I had gone into the dining room early, found her place label and swapped it with the one at the place next to mevv .

'This is fortunate,' she said when she arrived.

I told her about changing her seat. She laughed, with respect.

'Postgraduates are supposed to be innovative,' I said. 'Your attire is in the spirit. You look great.'

She was wearing a sumptuous long blue velvet gown, off the shoulder and backless. She was stunning.

'Thank you,' she said. 'You're no slouch yourself.'

'I was in a tuxedo with a bow tie.'

'You could be a hustler on a river boat,' said Grania. 'Is that why you're doing rivers?'

'No. I was raised on a farm and experimented with water. Problems with water intrigue me. My parents were disaffected by governments and raised me to oppose the corrupt spectacle in which businesses profited from water resources taken from us.'

'Wow. You are going to be a campaigner.'

'Maybe,' I said. 'How did you get interested in droughts?'

'In the great drought, I was fascinated by how communities cooperated,' she said. 'I want to investigate drought occurrence and disaster relief.'

'Why?'

'I got interested when we studied hydrology. There seems to be a lot we can do to conserve water and use it better. I suppose I am a missionary for water conservation, like you are for scientific testing of technologies.'

'You sound like a visionary, with a passion for new innovative ideas,' I said.

'Our topics are complementary,' she said. 'Droughts alternate with floods.'

'Sometimes they do,' I said. 'Water storage is important for both.'

'I like thinking about droughts, intellectualising relationships and looking for new ideas,' she said.

'That's what I do with flooding, maybe half my time,' I said.

'Yep, half my time at least,' she said.

Grania was bright, creative and hard-working. She had made an impression through her research as a brilliant mind whose findings had revolutionary implications for river management. I felt privileged and fortunate have her. Collaboration with others could not be counted on and I would have to be careful not to expose Grania to bullies.

'How about I share my data with you,' I had said.

'Yes, that would be good,' she had replied. 'Do you know how Wivenhoe's flood compartment came to be partly filled, worsening the 2011 flood?'

I hadn't heard. Grania recounted to me her story, as if from personal involvement. Although she had been warned by a senior government official not to tell her story, she wanted me to know it and I had no compunction in repeating it at the dinner table, without divulging that Grania was the source.

'I heard this story from a friend, who said it was after the terrible drought broke in 2009,' I said. 'A Government Minister said: 'Demand management has been too successful. Reduction of water sales in the drought has cost our government dearly.'

'You can increase water charges, Minister,' a Treasury officer suggested.

'It would be unpopular,' said the Minister. 'Users who are desperately in need would be forced to pay more. It would be more acceptable to fill some of the dam's flood mitigation capacity with water for supply, allowing people to use more water and at the same time lowering the cost per litre a little. Users would buy more water.'

'What if there's a flood?' she had asked.

'Don't you worry about that,' someone said.

'The idea would be good,' said the Treasury officer, 'except that the dam's flood mitigation role would be reduced.'

'It would only be felt in a flood,' said the Minister. 'We can deal with that when we come to it.'

'There's no flood in sight,' said the Treasury officer. 'In the meantime you can use the dam to make money to pay for infrastructure.'

'The money could get our government re-elected,' said the Premier. 'Let's do it.'

'When the cyclone hit, the flood compartment was already partly filled,' I finished.

'What a scandal!' said the postgraduate sitting next to me. 'Who was the Minister?'

'My friend couldn't say,' I said. 'She had been warned not to divulge it. She wrote a paper criticising the government's management of the drought. She wanted permanent restrictions on domestic water consumption, in preparation for the next drought. She said the Council's loyalties were divided between storing water and selling it. Money had won. Left to their own devices, people use more and more water and no leader will tell them otherwise, with no-one urging conservation of water, even though drought was expected. It was not a message the government wanted told. Her paper was refused publication and she was warned to keep quiet.'

Grania had let me tell it and did not disclose that it was her story. There was some talk at the table, with derogatory views of politicians being expressed. I was asked if the Minister in the story was the Resources Minister at that time, but I said I had to honour my source's confidentiality.

After the dinner, I asked Grania out at the weekend.

'Would you join me to eat at a restaurant, Grania? Do you like Japanese food?'

'Love it. When?'

I knew that Grania wouldn't eat anything, but she would enjoy toying with her food.

'How about Saturday at 7 pm? I can give you a lift from your place if you like?'

She gave me her address, which was nearby.

I gave her a lift home. It was a perfect end to a wonderful evening. I hadn't had a date since I finished with Karen a year ago.

When I stopped my car, I leaned across and kissed her. Her lips were soft, warm and engaging.

'This is wonderful,' I said. 'I never dreamed there could be someone like you!'

'Meeting you was even more unlikely,' Grania said.

If she hadn't appeared when she did, it wasn't likely that I would become friends with someone else interested in phenomenology. It was an unusual interest.

I got out of my car and walked her to her door, where we hugged. I felt her firm breasts and mons pubis press against me.

'See you tomorrow, at class,' I said. 'We could sit together.'

'No holding hands!' she said. 'Keep your mind on phenomenology!'

CHAPTER 32 BRACKETING

We went to a restaurant after our next class. We took our time, choosing from the menu carefully. After we had ordered, we talked about the learning over drinks. Grania would not talk in public, nor eat and when we were in company together, she stayed quietly beside me. When she could be overheard she whispered her thoughts to me.

The two of us were dining alone and Grania's talk was uninhibited.

'Heidegger didn't just provide sunglasses,' said Grania. 'He provided a list of steps telling us what to look for.'

'We have to bracket, intuit, analyse, describe, expose attitudes and discover technologies,' I said. 'It is more searching and discriminating than the usual science method.'

'Where does it get us?' asked Grania.

'It clears the way for twists of perspective, such as the entrée of the observer and his relation to the object, with curiosity, fallenness, thrownness, ambiguity, hearsay and mood all present, with endless potential.'

'The ontology of the river, its being, is its properties and relations between them, will reveal the Dasein of the phenomenon.'

'How will you start?' Grania asked me.

'I will review my experience of rivers, keep the part that is relevant and bracket the rest,' I said.

'Is your inexperience relevant?'

'No, I can't use what I don't know.'

'Will you be using your engineering training?' she asked.

'Yes, I will keep the processes but leave out the content,' I said. 'I will remove, or 'bracket' my previous experience of rivers and flooding to avoid preconceptions that could be inauthentic. I have to replace assumptions about rivers and flooding with the lived experience of processes.'

'What type of processes?'

'The phenomenon of turbulence is one. That could be needed.'

'Why is that called bracketing?'

'Turbulence is a process. Settling of particles is another. The processes can be plugged in and together used to calculate bank erosion from first principles. My previous experience of erosion of riverbanks is irrelevant and to be bracketed.

'What's the difference?'

'My experience of eroded riverbanks is derivative and irrelevant. It is the processes that can be used. I must forget my perceptions from having lived with a river at my doorstep. I must exclude those secondary experiences, because the reality I am living now is different and that is all that counts.

'The river can be described as a conglomeration of processes.'

'I don't see why you have to leave out your previous experience,' said Grania.

'Because it may not be relevant,' I said, patiently. 'Not all rivers, floods and observers are the same. I have to understand the Brisbane River, at my place, now, not some other rivers somewhere else at another time.'

'You're not quantifying it objectively by the usual science method, are you?' she said.

'No. I'm finding its qualities, such as turbulence and settling, instead of measuring everything indiscriminately.'

'Does Dasein observe with a stereoscopic viewpoint, from two different directions?'

'Yes, more than two,' I said. 'Dasein's take is from all the angles, giving a multi-dimensional layered image.'

'Will Dasein enable you to discern potential for improvement?'

'Yes, if I am up to recognising it.'

I had extensive experience of water environments. I told Grania about the books I had read with stories about salmon and eels, that migrated annually, sensing river and ocean currents and returning to breed in their home rivers. My images of rivers had been nurtured by Mark Twain's Huck Finn, Kenneth Grahame's Wind in the Willows and Henry Williamson's Salar the Salmon. Phenomenology could learn from these stories by focussing on their description of natural processes.

They brought our food and I started eating. Grania passed her plate to me.

'Wanting to keep alive your memories from those books is nostalgic,' said Grania. 'Ignoring your own experience must be difficult for you.'

'Yes. Turning away from my experience is counter-intuitive,' I said. 'My life's work has been adventures with water. I will keep them in a locked compartment of my brain, where I can only use them when they're relevant. I may need them one day.'

I recalled my previous encounters with the phenomenon of flooding. On the farm where I grew up there was a brook, where water voles lived beside their busy waterway. I had dammed it, sandwiching clay between metal sheets, raising the water level high enough to drive a paddle wheel, turning an old tractor generator, electrifying a wire fence around the free range poultry. Thus began my interest in engineering, which had become a career. Now I had to forget those experiences.

'You have done a lot,' said Grania. 'Your expertise must be relevant to improving this river?'

'I can carryover my knowledge of processes,' I said. 'Content has to be left behind.'

Every flood is unique, I explained to her. At various times I had watched TV news reports of disastrous flooding of Australian rivers inland, in Bangladesh and in China. Distant shots of people retreating from rising flood water was not relevant, because it was in different places and news photos couldn't be relied on to be authentic.

'You are setting out to be different, aren't you?' Grania said. 'It's only natural to infer similarities with other places.'

'Similarities are often superficial,' I said. 'If others have theories that could apply to Brisbane River flooding, that is relevant. But they have to be observed under the same conditions as the Brisbane River.'

I told Grania of my apartment by the river.

'Is flooding your main concern?' asked Grania.

'Yes, there could be loss of life and damage. I want to predict how it could occur. I will bracket the application of our studies in hydrology to erosion of farmland, waterways and coasts. I will set aside my learning of how river flooding has been affected by farming practices, by vegetation types, water penetration, land degradation and surface run-off. My science students have studied how flooding could affect groundwater, erosion and transport of sediment by streams. While sailing, I have seen discharge of flooded rivers into the ocean but I can't use this knowledge. None of it is relevant to the river flooding I am studying.'

'A pity. I enjoyed our hydrology class,' she said.

We ordered dessert. I chose cheese cake and Grania lemon sorbet.

'I can't use the content of my studies of fluid dynamics nor is my reservoir engineering experience admissible,' I said. 'I can only use the processes.'

'Isn't it the engineering method, to apply to new situations technologies that have worked?' asked Grania.

'I have to bracket my experience of water in other rivers, flowing into other oceans. It is irrelevant. The floods I am investigating are of the Brisbane River. I have sailed on the Brisbane River, raced a yacht in the South Atlantic and experienced storms at sea. I have travelled for long distances by canoe, riverboat and barge on the Amazon and on the Mekong River. These other waters might not be relevant to my analysis of the River. I am studying a unique phenomenon: the Brisbane River.

When I finished my bracketing Grania said 'Is that it? You have had wide experience. I am not sure you won't be losing valuable experience by leaving all that out.'

They brought our desserts. I knew she wouldn't eat her sorbet and she passed it to me. I had a coffee.

'The usual commentary on Brisbane River floods has been largely myth, well-meaning, but uncontrolled and misleading,' I said. 'I am making a fresh start to understand the Dasein of the Brisbane River. Leaving out all the earlier work is a weight off my shoulders.'

While we had been talking, I had eaten my food. Now I sat back with my coffee.

'What about your research?' I asked Grania as I sipped.

'I want to analyse water supply in a droughted region,' Grania said. 'I will bracket my experience as you have done. After that I will document the phenomenon and look for ideas of how to reduce droughts and their effects. People will want to contribute their experiences of droughts. I am having to invent new terms for drought effects that test limits, such as new definitions of livestock starvation and crop failure that can help determine personal responsibility and responses of relief agencies. There is a lot to agree.'

Grania would have to negotiate meanings of droughts with farmers and graziers. She had never shown any inclination to step into the limelight. I couldn't see her getting very far with her project, until she was able to speak with farmers face to face.

I decided not to raise this obstacle yet. She must have realised it and would find a way around it. In the meantime, I was very happy having her as an interlocutor. It crossed my mind that she could join with me in my project; but PhDs were individual enterprises.

We talked about books and movies, pleased to find we had interests in common.

When I took her home, we kissed and I held her in my arms, my hands straying from her perfect waist to her superb bottom. She gently pushed me away.

'Soon,' she said.

In order to observe potential in the Brisbane River, I was learning to turn a blind eye to my experience obtained in dissimilar situations that I should leave out. It was strange to select only experiences that could be transferred, as processes applicable in similar situations. When I reviewed my experiences, most could not transfer. It was disappointing to realize how little learning I had achieved of the transferable sort. On the other hand, bracketing had a purgative effect and I was freed to regard the River as a proving ground, for establishing potential, where I could consider the effect of changing any variables.

CHAPTER 33 EROSION

After bracketing, next steps in Heidegger's method were to intuit, analyse and describe potential. Later I could search for attitudes and discover technologies.

My intuition was that river flooding was affected by erosion on farms, bringing sediment to rivers, but I didn't know how significant it was. Erosion was the process of gradual wearing away and transport of rock material through rills, gullies and small waterways.

'I know rivers transport sediment as well as water,' I said to Howard, when we met for a drink. 'Could you tell me how rivers are affected by erosion and what can be done to reduce it?'

'River channels are clogged with a huge quantity of sediments from weathering of rocks and wearing away of stream banks,' said Howard. 'The Australian continent has been relatively stable for a long time, with weathering at outcrops of ancient igneous rocks. Sand is eroded from granite and basalt outcrops and from bedrocks. Other erosion is from streambank unconsolidated rocks and by sediment outflow in sporadic river floods. Residents returning to flooded homes have been surprised to find banks of sediment dumped on their lawns, where the torrent slowed and abated.

'Erosion is a problem on farms, where surface run-off washes soil into waterways,' Howard said. 'There is a rumour that on a wheat farm that fails to conserve its soil, production of a loaf of bread loses a kilogram of topsoil by erosion.'

'Is that true?' I asked. 'How could that have been measured?'

'It's an aphorism that's been around for years,' Howard said. 'It could be true. I've seen a lot of sediment on the move through erosion gulleys on wheat land. In one season truckloads can disappear from badly eroded land.'

'The amount could be a part of Dasein that Heidegger referred to as idle talk, a phenomenon that is gossiped and passed along, as hearsay,' I said. 'I doubt that many farmers would believe they lose that much soil, nor that they could do anything to stop it happening.'

'A campaign is needed to persuade them to take it seriously, compensating them for the benefit in flood prevention in Brisbane.'

'I agree. Objectifying the phenomenon is important but measurement is difficult. Many farmers conserve soil and water with earthworks and good land management, including reverting to keeping fewer hard-hooved grazing animals, also by more lot feeding and by growing plants that conserve water.'

'The Dasein of the River includes dealing with floodwater on farms before it reaches waterways,' I said. 'There could be potential for infiltration, storing water and preventing erosion.'

I wanted Grania to talk with Howard and me, on the phone. Howard had spoken with her on the phone before.

'By the way,' I said to Howard. 'I am working with Grania Brinker. Do you remember a girl called Grania working at Wattle Mines?'

'Can't say I do. What department?'

'Exploration.'

'I didn't have much to do with them. Why?'

'She's good with figures, working in insurance.'

'You always were interested in figures.'

'Too right. She's staying at my place.'

'When are you going to invite me to meet her? Are you keeping us apart?'

'No. She's reluctant to meet face to face. It's probably a consequence of the pandemic. She does all her meetings on zoom or on the phone. She's the same with everyone. She's on my other line. I'll put her on.

'Here's Grania now. Howard, I'd like you to meet Grania.'

'Hi Grania. We met at Wattle Mines?'

'Yes. Hi, Howard. I heard you have been talking with Chance about erosion on farms,' she said. 'It's a serious problem.'

'Rivers fill with sediment,' I said. 'Most of the harm is caused by a minority of farmers. There is reluctance to single out individual farmers to take the blame. Land degradation and river flooding continue.'

'Dams allow sediment loads to drop out from flood water,' Howard said. 'When a dam silts up, it ceases to store much water. To maintain water storage capacity, soil erosion must be managed.'

'Soil erosion and flash flooding can be managed by increasing water penetration and preventing run-off,' I said. 'Farmers can benefit by retaining soil and moisture, but don't always do it, through lack of understanding.'

'If you mean they don't know what they're doing,' Grania said, 'I don't believe it. They just can't see how they can make money from fixing erosion.'

'She's right,' Howard told me. 'Farmers copy other farmers. But hardly anyone's stopping erosion.'

It seemed to be a bad situation. My superman could barely contain himself.

'IT ISN'T AS BAD AS YOU THINK,' said Superman. 'FARMERS WANT TO HELP BUT THEY DON'T KNOW WHAT TO DO. THEY ONLY LACK THE LIGHT TO SHOW THE WAY. I'M HERE TO FIGHT FOR TRUTH AND JUSTICE'.

'We need to recruit farmers interested in soil conservation to lead the way,' I said. 'The benefit to city dwellers can be ploughed back. Government could fund demonstration of soil management techniques.'

'The same is needed to encourage water retention on farms against drought,' Grania said.

'The techniques are not obvious,' said Howard. 'Harnessing City folks' support could gain traction on these serious problems.

Tackling water retention and prevention of erosion with the same programme could have synergy.'

'There's potential to reduce river flooding by keeping soil on farms,' I said. 'My project can bring this to attention of the government.'

We seemed to be making progress.

We talked about other aspects of River Dasein.

'Could the height or movement of flood water be harnessed for its energy?' Grania asked. 'Could a water wheel be used?'

'It could,' I said. 'A water ram is a pulsating valve installed in a steep stream to use the energy of falling water to pump it to higher and more distant places.'

'Yes, it's an uncanny device,' Howard said. 'There is other potential for harvesting water from a river in flood, for irrigation and flood mitigation. They could divert water from running into the River.'

'A dam site has ambiguous criteria. It is wanted to either store a large volume of water at low cost, or to be sited well downstream, to contain water from the largest part of the river catchment.'

'Are there still sites available offering that?' I asked.

'The best sites have probably been taken,' said Grania. 'Choosing a site could depend on the weighting given to each use and to environmental effects. The way forward might be to construct two dams, one for each of irrigation and mitigation.'

'They could mitigate flooding from different types of rainfall event.'

'A river authority needs to have a diverse portfolio of investments in dams,' said Grania.

'Thank you, Grania. That was helpful,' I said

Farmers are needed to show leadership in preventing erosion of their land, reducing sediment in the lower river and preventing flooding. Leaders could show how to conserve soil. Seen through the Heidegger lens, farmers and flood-plain dwellers have a symbiotic interest in preventing floods, constructing water storages and to supply the water they need.

CHAPTER 34 DREDGING

Dredging of the Brisbane River had seemed to me as much a part of the flood mitigation landscape as were the dams. When I found that dredging above the Hamilton Reach in Brisbane had ceased in 1996 after continuing during most of the 20th century, I suspected that the upper Brisbane River would by now be clogged with sediment. Floods would have washed some sediment out, but more could have replaced it. I wanted to find out why dredging had ended.

The problem seemed perennial. I came across an article where a quantity of sediment in the Brisbane River was mentioned.

'River sediment flows quickly during floods and creeps during dry weather. In flood years - 2011, 2012, 2013 and 2014 - sediment flowing down the river was well over a million cubic metres of a year: 'enough to fill a line of dump trucks stretching from here to Adelaide and back. Sand and gravel dredged from the Brisbane River was used in concrete that built a large part of the city.(42)'

Cause of the moratorium on dredging of the Brisbane River was sensationally reported by Stuart Ballantyne, for The Spectator. He claimed experience of working on dredges on other rivers and said that Brisbane's floods had been caused by the failure of the Queensland Government and environmentalists to continue dredging of the Brisbane River (24, 29). An anti-dredging cult referred to in the Spectator as 'Greens' was said to be preventing the Government engaging with the problem of Brisbane River flooding.

My Superman was frustrated.

'GREAT SCOTT! I'M READY TO KICK ASS,' he said.

Faster than a speeding bullet my Superman phoned around the government authorities to find who was responsible for dredging the upper Brisbane River.

The Port of Brisbane Authority said they weren't responsible and didn't know who was. I phoned the central government switchboard, who suggested I contact Maritime Safety Queensland.

I had to explain my inquiry before I was put through to an official.

'I want to know if dredging of the Brisbane River is being considered,' I said.

I was informed.: 'The river has been dredged to a minimum depth of 15.0 metres in the deep water channels of Moreton Bay, used by cruise ships docking at Hamilton after 2006, but there is no dredging upriver of there.'

I found an article with details of dredging expenditure.

'The Port of Brisbane reportedly spent $20 million after the 2011 flood, dredging sediment from the river to keep the city's shipping channels open. It now costs between $5 million and $7 million annually to dredge the area from the mouth of the Brisbane River up the coast to Caloundra' (42)

The only dredging since 2011 had been in the lower river for navigation purposes. No dredging had been done to mitigate flooding. When I cited statistics that flooding of the river had increased since dredging ceased, my informant disputed this.

'The flooding statistics indicate that the River has silted up,' I said.

'That's not correct,' said the Maritime Safety officer.

'Do you have measurements of how the River depth is changing?'

'We have hydrographic surveys,' he said. 'We have current river profiles above Hamilton. It will take me a couple of days to extract the data and I will send it to you.'

But I never received any depth data. When I phoned a couple of weeks later, he wouldn't speak to me, as if he wanted to cover up something.

A reason given for not dredging above Hamilton was that navigation did not require it. I inferred from speaking to several people that dredging of the Brisbane River was regarded as vulgar, archaic, environmentally unfriendly and the cause of brown coloration of the River water. But cessation of dredging had not improved colour of the river water. A different source attributes the brown colour to colloidal clays being eroded near the river source.

In my view, the colour of the Brisbane River water is a less important problem than the need for dredging to reduce flooding.

I was walking with Grania at the university when I crossed paths with Harper, who shared PhD rooms with me.

'What are you up to?' he asked. 'Still puzzling over what Heidegger meant?'

It was his usual antagonism. He was an activist who supported popular causes.

'I know what he meant,' I said. 'I am puzzling over why dredging of the Brisbane River has stopped.'

'We are better off without it,' he said. 'Dredging is an ineffective and polluting activity.'

'Like damming, dredging is a human artefact, or 'technology', making three claims,' I said. 'First dredging is a way of understanding the world, or interpreting what can be done; second, dredging is 'not a human activity', but develops beyond human control; and third dredging risks seeing the world through technological thinking. Dredging is a threat to those who don't understand it, who are unable to control it, nor evaluate its effectiveness.'

'Those are good reasons to forget about dredging,' Harper said. 'We don't know enough to risk it.'

'Are you against all river technology?' I asked.

'Probably,' said Harper. 'We oppose damming and straightening. We believe a river naturally carves out the best size and shape of waterway for moving flood water. The natural course and channel are best.

'That's like saying a tree will grow as few leaves as it needs,' Grania whispered. 'The River can be pruned, or shaped, to dispose of more flood water. His analogy is false and can't be tested.'

'The increase in the channel depth by dredging would probably fill up with sediment within hours of flooding,' he said.

'It's possible, but that doesn't invalidate the dredging,' I said. 'How would you describe a flood?'

'A flood is an oversupply of water able to invade homes and threaten the well-being of people, livestock and property,' Harper said.

His definition was anthropocentric, a common mistake.

'How would you protect people from flooding?' I asked, wanting to reveal his bias against dams and other technology.

'I wouldn't,' said the activist. 'They should move to places that don't flood.'

'It's not democratic. It has to be their choice.'

'They shouldn't expect the rest of us to keep baling them out.'

'We keep baling out victims of bushfires, cyclones and earthquakes,' I said. 'Why not flood victims?'

'Floods are . . . a social problem,' he replied.

'Do you mean some people are less equal than others?'

Harper shook his head and walked away.

'I think he wants flood victims to have all government protection withdrawn,' Grania whispered. 'It's not equitable.'

'It's smug and callous,' I said. 'His opposition to dredging is the hidden part of an iceberg of contempt for others.'

My investigation had uncovered conflicting attitudes to dredging. From 1893 until 1996, dredging of the Brisbane River was routine and statistics of flooding are in Figure 2. I discussed it with Grania at home where we could both see the graph clearly.

'Science can use this data as a display of flood heights over time, measuring peak heights of the River at the Port Office,' I said.

The graph showed flood heights for almost 200 years, since records had been kept. After 1893, the graph shows moderate and minor flood levels, with the exception of a major flood in 1974. Floods became more frequent and higher until soon after 1893 when dredging commenced. Floods became less frequent and lower in height. Between 1893 and 1996, when dredging ceased, there were no major floods with the exception of 1974. After dredging ceased, there were major floods in 2011 and 2022 (not shown).

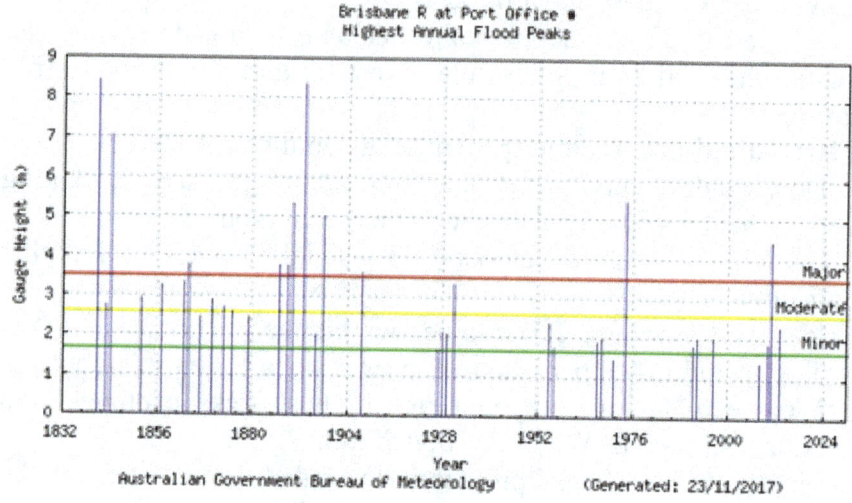

YEAR	MAJOR ANNUAL FLOOD PEAKS
1825 est.	=8.35
1841	8.43
1843	7.0
1891	5.4
1893	8.35 and 8.09
1897	5.0
1974	5.45
2011	4.46 (6.9)
2022	3.7 (5.9)

Figure 2 Heights of Flood Peaks in Brisbane

'Does Figure 2 show that dredging prevented major flooding?' Grania asked.

'Yes. There have been worse floods since dredging ceased in 1996.'

'Major floods in 1974, 2011 and 2022 could have been caused by dams,' she said.

'It could be either or both,' Grania said. 'Or something else.'

'The potential of dredging is to enlarge the river channel, reducing obstruction by sediment,' I said.

'Sceptics fixate on sediment refilling dredged places, instead of them permanently enlarging the channel as wanted,' Grania said.

'Residence time of sediment in the river, the average time for it to flow through, could be many years, depending on location. Dredging in some places could have a long-lived effect and could be worthwhile.'

It had taken me a while to look behind the scientific data for the rest of the Dasein. There were other meanings that could and should be brought to bear.

'Besides flooding statistics, physical processes of river deposition of sediments are generally in favour of dredging the Brisbane River.

'How do you know the physical processes?' Grania asked.

'Before dredging began in 1893, the river was said to have been blocked by sand bars and shallows, with a natural tidal limit of only 16 km. Rivers often have bars where currents combine and slowing of a stream causes deposition. These could be rebuilding today.'

'A survey of river depth is needed,' I said. 'We need to know how much the build-up is.'

'Heidegger would have referred to this part of Dasein's Being as a curiosity until the information was obtained. Our aim in interpreting this phenomenon is in principle one which is essential-ontological. Our orientation could be towards imaging the river bed or towards cognition.'

'The government is unlikely to admit there is deposition, because they could be liable for flood damage,' Grania said. 'The government has a responsibility and I want to know if obstruction of the river by sediment is being monitored.'

I asked Howard: 'Will you please check out the history of Brisbane River authority flood mitigation actions, to infer a case for dredging?'

A couple of days later Howard emailed me with the history of Brisbane River dredging.

'After floods in 1841 and 1893, the government's approach was to improve the water flow by dredging, straightening the river course, cutting, deepening, widening, building of training walls to keep the flow in a deep channel and by removing obstacles such as rocky outcrops in the banks and bed,' Howard said. 'The historical record shows that for nearly a hundred years, dredging and other channel-enlarging work could have prevented major flooding.

'Deepening and straightening the channel improved navigation too. Brisbane was competing with other river ports for cargo. It was fortuitous that improving freighter access upriver also improved the discharge of flood water downriver. Surgery to the river eventually focussed on removing sediment by dredging.'

'Dredging is widely regarded as necessary to keep rivers and harbours open,' he phoned me. 'Here's why. Flooding occurs when water slows down in a narrow shallow channel, bumping often against rough obstructing surfaces, snags and projections, without churning against itself. Dredging deepens the channel, reducing flow friction, increasing flow velocity and letting water stream smoothly, allowing the water to carry away silt, without backing up and flooding.'

'During flooding, sediment spreads across the channel and its flood plain, trying to form a delta,' he said. 'A delta could commence with fingers of deposition. It's natural for the water to find the pathways with maximum fall and the least constricted channels, until it fills up the spaces. Then it slows down and sediment deposits, blocking flow and causing more flooding. The channel fills in and moves somewhere else on the flood plain. A flood is a dynamic phenomenon and so is a delta.'

'Thank you Howard,' I said. 'The historical record of flood management explains the flood data. I think we can make a strong case for dredging to resume.'

'It won't go unopposed,' warned Howard.

CHAPTER 35 POLITICS

'Grania has some questions about dredging,' I told Howard. 'Can you help?'
'Okay. When?'
'I'll put her on. I've sent you now a graph she wants to ask you about? I'm sending it now as an email attachment.'
'Okay.'
I sent Howard Figure 2 (21).
'Got it,' he said.
'Dredging was done from 1893 to 1996,' I said. 'Here's Grania.'
'Hi Howard,' Grania said. 'I remember you. You played rugby in our lunch room sometimes.'
'Too right. I hope it didn't interrupt your lunch?'
'Only when you knocked our table over. '
'Sorry about that.'
'No hard feelings. My question is how would dredging affect flooding of the River?'
'I'm looking at the graph Chance sent,' Howard said. 'There could be a correlation between absence of dredging and flooding.'
'Does it show that dredging is what the Brisbane River needs?' Grania asked.
'Why wouldn't it?' asked Howard.
'The graph could be a coincidence,' Grania said. 'It would be better if we knew dredging would actually prevent flooding.'
'It does,' said Howard.
'Are you saying that constriction of floodwaters by sediment is a natural process raising flood heights,' Grania said. 'Therefore, removal of sediment by dredging would lower flood heights?'
'Yes, it is logical,' he said.

'I've heard some wild stories about sediments,' I interrupted. 'I have heard opponents of dredging claim sediment removed and dumped in the Bay is returned upriver by tidal flows.'

'It's not likely,' Howard said. 'During a flood it's impossible.'

'The government's ending of dredging is harmful,' I said.

'It won't be easy to show that the government's inaction has caused the flooding,' Howard said. 'Voters punish sins of commission; omission is blamed on the previous government.'

Howard confirmed that we had sufficient evidence to press the Government for a hydrographic survey of river depths.

'I have another meeting,' said Howard. 'It has been good talking with you Grania. Don't let Chance play rugby with you.'

The call ended.

I visited my local councillor, Sullivan, at his office.

'I am trying to gauge interest in dredging of the Brisbane River,' I said on the phone.

'That's easy,' he said. 'There is no interest. It doesn't work.'

'Could I come to your office? I want to show you some information we have,' I asked.

'I have time for a brief meeting,' he said. 'Make an appointment with my secretary.'

When I walked in, he was at his desk and rose to shake hands.

'What can I do for you?' he asked.

'I have a graph here of flood heights showing there was no major flood in Brisbane for 80 years, from 1893 to 1974.' I showed him the graph. 'During all that time, the river was being dredged. After dredging stopped in 1996, there were major floods in 2011 and 2022. It could have been dredging that stopped major flooding.'

'It's probably a coincidence,' said Sullivan.

'Maybe not. Having no major flood for 80 years was extraordinary.'

I showed him Figure 2 and explained my hypothesis that dredging prevented flooding.

Dredge Woomera arrives in Gladstone, Queensland

'It's not enough to convince me that dredging works,' he said.

'Do you know the depth of the river now compared with what it was before dredging ceased?' I asked.

'No,' Sullivan said. 'Dredging is not needed, so there is no need to measure the depth of the river.'

'It is a fallacy to argue that because a condition is not present it is not needed,' I said, concealing my anger. 'A test is needed to find any parts of the river that would benefit from dredging, to counter misconceptions, prejudices and sensationalism.'

'What misconceptions?'

'That the government is abandoning flood prevention. Even a few centimetres' difference in flood height can reduce flood victims' property damage dramatically. A test could show that several metres of removable sediment are filling the river channel, reducing the flow channel aperture and raising flood heights. Flooding is being exacerbated and mitigation is being neglected.'

'If dredging was needed, Maritime Safety would be doing it,' said the councillor smugly. 'There is no cause for concern.'

'Again that is a post hoc fallacy, which falsely claims that a later condition applied earlier. It is a deceit.'

'Is there anything else?'

Sullivan was out of his depth but he didn't care.

'The graph I have shown you does not mean that flooding is inevitable,' I said. 'It is if you prevent dredging. Dredging allowed the construction of homes on the river floodplain and while those homes are still there, dredging is needed to protect them from flooding. You can't have flood-prone homes without flood prevention technology. It is not sensible to devalue and withdraw a technology without replacing the function it performed. The way to end dredging technology is stop approving new homes on the flood plain and buyback homes built earlier.'

'It will never happen.'

'If leaders are fatalistic and negative about flooding, it won't. Flooding impacted 23,400 homes in 2022, a small percentage of homes. The problem can be fixed, beginning with resuming dredging.'

'Good morning, Mr Finething.'

'Good morning,' I said, refusing his offer of a handshake.

My visit with councillor Sullivan ended. I was disappointed that the government was refusing to investigate or compromise on an issue of great importance to the many residents who lived in flood-prone homes.

'Sullivan is a Green,' Grania said when I told her of this conversation. 'There is a bad smell around the anti-dredging cult.'

'They may see a river dredge as archaic, fuel burning and polluting,' I said. 'In their view dredging is unnatural. Dredging technology they can do without. It lacks digital glitter and ignores woke sensitivities. I doubt that they are aware of sediment build up and its effect on flood level.'

'Few antis have had their homes flooded.'

'Their bias is disadvantaging people who are hurt most by flooding, those without influence,' she said.

'We'll give them a voice,' I said.

Superman appeared.

'HOW DARE THEY WITHHOLD INFORMATION THAT COULD PREVENT FLOODING OF PEOPLE'S HOMES!' he said.

'Truth, Justice and a Better Tomorrow! I will make the facts known to audiences who will demand the puny under-achieving politicians and their bureaucrats reveal water depths, historical and current.

'My infallible instinct is that the authorities are hiding sedimentation.

'WITH MY POWERFUL VISION I CAN DETECT THE RIVER IS BECOMING SHALLOWER DUE TO DEPOSITION.'

Superman left.

'The evidence is obscured under the muddy waters of the Brisbane River,' I said. 'Figure 2 demonstrates that flooding of the Brisbane River could be reduced by dredging.

That afternoon I went to our coffee bar for lunch with Grania. I sat beside her on the plush bench seat and held her hand. It was warm and responsive.

Our thoughts and fingers intertwined with excitement. Discussing channel sediments and dredging wouldn't have been an aphrodisiac for every couple, when we left the coffee bar, we started kissing in the street. Holding on to each other, we walked to my place, without talking. We undressed and climbed into my bed. We were gentle and affectionate, making every moment last and last. Her touch thrilled me her caresses were sublime.

I was entranced by her mind, her firm body and her sweet lips. We held each other, without talking. We undressed and climbed into my bed. We were gentle and affectionate, making every moment last and last.

In the morning, we ate croissants with strawberry jam and café' mocha.

'When are you going to move in here?' I asked her.

'When would you want me to?' she asked.

'How about tomorrow?' I replied. 'I'll make some space for your stuff.'

CHAPTER 36 DAM STORAGE

After I had lived happily with Grania for a week, she said: 'I need a big favour. Could my flatmate Leigh come and live here?'

This was a complete surprise.

'Is Leigh male or female?' I asked, when I could speak again.

'Female.'

I realised that Leigh would be from the same imagined world as Grania. I wondered how extensive that world was.

'Are you lovers?'

'Yes.'

My jealousy surged, but only briefly.

'Why didn't you tell me?'

'It doesn't affect you,' said Grania. 'You agreed I can live the way I want with you. This is what I want.'

'Have you been lovers for long?' I asked, like it wasn't a deal-breaker.

'About a year.'

I remembered seeing Leigh earlier at their flat. I hadn't realised they were in a lesbian relationship. They wouldn't impose on me, because they would only appear when I wanted to see them.

'Would you like to get to know her before you decide?' Grania asked.

I supposed that if Leigh could be going to live with us, I needed to get on with her. Maybe Grania was proposing a triad. Grania was enough for me, but if Leigh joined in, it might be even better.

'Okay.' I said. 'The three of us could go to a restaurant.'

'Would we have to appear?' Grania asked.

'Of course! I'm not going to sit between two empty chairs.'

'What could we eat? I've forgotten what I like.'

'You may see something when we get there.'

'Could we go tonight? I'll call Leigh.'

Grania phoned.

'Hi Leigh. I've told Chance. He wants to go out for a meal with us. Are you okay to make an appearance this evening?'

She listened. 'You'll look great,' she said to Leigh. She turned to me. 'Where do you suggest?'

'We can go to the Connection on Hardcastle Street,' I said. 'They have Vietnamese and Chinese food. Is 7 pm okay?'

'Yes.'

I made a table reservation.

'We'll drive all together,' I said. 'It'll be fun.'

'I'm so looking forward to a restaurant. I haven't been for ages.'

It was an unusual date. Grania was fair and slight, speaking with great charm. She wore a colourful striped cotton midi dress with puffed sleeves. Leigh was ten years younger than us, petite, brunette, vivacious, speaking alluringly. She wore a floral print dress, with short sleeves and pockets. I congratulated myself that two attractive women wanted to live with me. They ordered won ton soup but didn't eat any.

'Sorry. We're not hungry,' said Grania. 'Do you mind?'

'I liked our relationship the way it was,' I said to Grania aside. 'I'm getting outnumbered.'

'We can always go back to being a couple, if you want to,' she said primly.

'No. I'll get used to it.'

My beef noodles came.

While I ate, we talked. Neither Grania nor Leigh had jobs. They would be pleased to help me with my River investigation. Leigh had experience of disaster relief. She was sharp and creative. I felt drawn to her. She held my gaze and I read approval.

The two girls were obviously very fond of each other, joking together, fading in and out. I felt jealous of Grania but Leigh could have been feeling the same about Grania.

When I had finished my food, we got up to leave.

'Leigh, would you like to come and see your room?' Grania asked. 'Or do you want more time to decide?'

'I've enjoyed being with Chance this evening,' Leigh said. 'It will take a while to get to know him. We could make a start tonight.'

We showed Leigh her room. I opened a bottle of wine.

We sat in the lounge with our glasses.

'To old friends,' I toasted.

I supposed that if Leigh could be going to live with us, I needed to get along with her. Maybe Grania was proposing a triad.

I decided to break the ice. 'Where will you sleep?' I said to Grania.

'I want to be in your bed,' she said. 'Could Leigh join us?'

'What will she do with you?' I said.

'She could want to have sex with me,' she said. 'Or with you? Would you mind?'

Mind? It was a dream come true.

'It might work,' I said. 'It's worth a try.'

'Are you worried about something?' Grania asked.

'It seems like a big step,' I said.

'Is it what you want?' she asked.

I nodded and smiled at Leigh. We all stood up. Grania busied herself taking the glasses into the kitchen.

I took Leigh in my arms for the first time. Her body was shapely and firm, with a faint aroma of flowers and with moist soft lips.

'You can continue in bed,' said Grania, sounding proprietorial.

We undressed and got in, with the two girls together at first but then I went in the middle. Grania took the lead in ensuring that all three of us participated in the couplings.

It was a great success for everyone. I had satisfying sex with both girls and they had very evidently enjoyed each other and me.

We awoke in the early morning.

'How was it?' Grania asked us.

'It was good,' I said.

Leigh nodded and smiled.

'It's a good start,' Grania said.

'Are we having an adventure?' asked Leigh.

'You bet,' I said.

Grania laughed happily.

'Are there any rules I should know?' I asked.

'We could do polyamory,' Grania said. 'We can have multiple intimate relationships, whether sexual or just romantic, with the full knowledge and consent of all parties involved. Polyamory is generally not gender-specific; anyone can have multiple partners of any gender. Would that suit you Chance? Leigh?'

Would it ever.

'It would be fine,' I said.

'I like Chance very much,' said Leigh.

I was in love with Grania and very fond of her sidekick Leigh.

It seemed that nothing could go wrong.

We agreed not to discuss my work in bed.

I had started analysing my Brisbane River data.

'Your experience of being flooded in Brisbane is a good place to commence your project,' my research supervisor Gardner said the next day. 'The Brisbane River is much larger than the Logan River. You will have many sources of irrelevance to bracket.'

'These days people's involvement with the Brisbane River is mainly through flooding, dams and irrigation,' I said. 'But there is much more going on in my neighbourhood, for example developments intruding into the river channel.'

Heidegger would have wanted me to unpack Dasein from emotional moodedness and by cognitive forward projection, to express the activities as part of Dasein.

I interpreted 'being-as-such' as having three elements: a threat of Wivenhoe dam being overtopped; revealing of falling back from authenticity into inauthenticity; Seqwater's ability to continue to hold flood height below the 6.9 metres peak in 2011, when it reached my lounge floor. Damming of a river is deceptive. It doesn't take the water away and holds it until it has to be released.

Reports of the activities of the water authority's engineers managing the 2011 and 2022 floods have mentioned that senior engineers made rainfall forecasts using weather radar. They intuited flood heights in Brisbane and adopted hands on control of the dams.

'The engineering team was frantic, keeping long hours and having difficulties sleeping,' I said.

'The main difficulty in forecasting is knowing where cyclonic rain will fall,' she said.

'Engineers must be aware of their bias from own experiences, beliefs and acknowledge. Their judgement may have unusual influence on their interpretation of the data,' I said.

I phoned the Seqwater office and spoke with an engineer about their policies.

'The irony is that whenever you store water, you may have to release it, worsening flooding. The dams could amplify the river perturbation.'

'That's correct,' said the engineer. 'We like to keep the dam 20% full, with enough water to meet city consumption requirements in a drought. When we hold back a spike, we release it continuously to empty the mitigation compartment as fast as we can without causing flooding.'

'When the dam is filling and the river is in flood from the catchment below the dam, you are between a rock and a hard place,' I said. 'You can't release water without worsening the flooding. If you let the dam fill, you are forced to release water to prevent the catastrophe of the dam overtopping. The ensuing flooding could be worse than before the dam was built. Presence of the dam could be harmful.'

'Modelling could test changes planned to the operating protocol and potential for construction of new dams.

'Good dam sites are scarce. The two dams we built were like picking low-hanging fruit. It might be difficult to find sites as good.'

'Is there potential for constructing hydro on the Brisbane River?'

'No. The best hydro sites have been taken. The contribution of further hydro would be small. On the Yangtze River in China in 1984, The Three Gorges Dam commenced generating 22,500 Megawatts of electricity by hydro, greater than Queensland's total installed generating capacity of 15,500 Megawatts.

There was surplus base-load generating capacity at Swanbank Power Station and a 500 Megawatt pumped storage hydro station was built at Splityard Creek to convert electricity for peak load supply. The recent shutting down of Swanbank Power Station would allow Splityard Creek to be operated as hydro, if Wivenhoe dam has enough water to supply it. Deeper analysis of the situation is needed.

Electricity produced from Queensland's several small hydro stations is ideally pollution free and responsive to peak demands but vulnerable to drought. The stations probably fully exploit their available river resources. Evaluating any potential remaining for the Brisbane River is a complex calculation, confounded by uncertainty of weather and climate

'The land taken for dam sites lower down the Brisbane River would be valuable and ecological impact would be protested. To rely on further damming to relieve flooding in Brisbane, further evidence is required that the two existing dams have brought benefits. When rainfall was peculiarly localised in 2011 and 2022, the mitigation was quite limited. Hopefully the dams will be of more value in mitigating future floods. It may be possible to better appreciate the likelihood of that with a digital model of the river catchment.

After 40 years operation of the Wivenhoe Dam, flood mitigation benefits are elusive and some exacerbation of flooding is possible. I did not expect my investigation to resolve a case for constructing more dams. I had found ways to consider using the existing dams better. Future flooding could be reduced and then there would be more experience from which to judge the efficacy of damming.

CHAPTER 37 MODELLING

Michael was living in Unit 4 with his son. They may have heard me talking to Grania and Leigh, but they wouldn't have known I was in a polyamorous relationship with them.

I was investigating the risk of flooding. I wanted Michael to be fully informed of the risks before accepting my gift of the apartment. He was aware there were risks because he had been staying in Unit 4 when the building basement flooded in February 2022. I was trying to enumerate the risks in a letter to him. I wouldn't give my son and daughter an apartment that was likely to be flooded and I wrote to them as follows, explaining the risks.

Dear Michael and Sarah,
I am writing with important information you need to know.
Here is the Council's assessment of flooding risk at Unit 4 based on update of their model of the flood earlier this year.

FLOODWISE PROPERTY REPORT
West End, 4/21 Orleigh St
Min habitable height (above river locally) 8.0 m
Flood Jan 2011 6.9m
Flood Feb 2022 5.9m
DFL (Defined Flood Level: is approved minimum height of ground floor, raised 0.5m) 5.8m
Frequency of exceeding 7.5m is 1%

My evaluation is as follows.

Unit 4, being higher, is on the second floor and would be better protected than my Unit 2, but evacuation would be needed at about the same time.

The Brisbane River flood plain is extensive and the volume of water required to raise the flood level from 6.9 m experienced in 2011, to 9.5 metres, would be huge. My guess is that a 38% increase in flood height would be very unlikely, with probability much less than 1% estimated for 7.5 metres.

These estimates indicate that Unit 4, while not absolutely flood free, should be significantly drier than my Unit 2. You would be safe.
Dad.

In 2011, predictions of flood height were broadcast by the BoM, for householders trying to evacuate or move their things to a higher position. Accurate predictions were needed to know where to park cars safely, to clear garages and save precious photos, memorabilia and other things. In 2011, height forecasts on the radio swung wildly as I tried to keep ahead, lifting heavy armchairs on to table tops, gradually converging on a peak height.

Predictions left a lot to be desired. My experience of modelling dynamic systems was in the petroleum industry many years ago. I knew the task as an engineer programmer. Coding and computing have made huge advances but the methods used for flood prediction were similar.

The predictions on the radio in 2011 were generated by a model, attended by boffins who used it to calculate flood height expected. They had input data for rainfall, catchment size, reservoir capacity, dam release rates and river channel capacity. Before the predictions were broadcast, they received critical scrutiny by government leaders, presumably from a political standpoint, so they could raise or lower the forecast river levels arbitrarily to garner votes.

BoM used a digital model to predict flood height. Two types of model were distinguished by Persig (2). The 'classical' scientific method which deconstructed, or dissected, the system, revealing causal relationships and making tweaks that would improve the 'fit'. For example, water had to move from place to place downwards, without moving upwards. Despite flow processes being well known, the state of the river is often unknown until models have reconciled the data from hundreds of river monitoring stations, taking hours or even days to make a prediction.

The other approach, not Persig's preference, discovered river conditions from the outside, deducing the internal working of the situation as a 'black box'. This type of model can match river conditions but lacks the understanding needed to adjust for different conditions, such as rainfall change. He called this method 'romantic'. It was the preferred method of those who obtained their understanding from hearsay, declining to 'dirty their hands' with observation, by analysis, or from real understanding of technology. This second method was anathema to me because I was a dyed-in-the-wool classicist.

When the romantic black-box method failed to engage enough detail of dasein, it was too superficial to reveal potential. Classical science may succeed better because its process of modelling can explore detail and find opportunity there. On the other hand, a black-box approach can be more aware of actual performance. Persig has both ways of modelling useful for solving problems. For recognising potential at a distance, a black-box may be better although more impressionable and less reliable.

The problem with the classical method, called 'simulation', is it can take too long to adjust the controlling conditions. Keying in the data and running the model can take precious hours. A numerical model solving hundreds of simultaneous equations iteratively can be too complex, running slower than real time, making it useless for prediction.

These two methods encapsulated the two main approaches to flood prediction. The classical modelling approach was for engineers to predict future flood height by reasoning and calculation from the 'inside'. The romantic way was to guess from how high the water came up to last time, or from the 'outside' in other ways. Both approaches try to match flood height history. Although Persig deplored the romantic black-box method, he recognised the value of using both approaches. Practical simulation can be hybridised, tweaking the classical model with empirical results to calibrate it.

The BoM's simulation was caught off guard by the 2022 flood and overwhelmed. Simulation by deterministic calculation when river conditions are unstable is 'run' until conditions balance with convergence. Imagine trying to calculate a river's water level when a wave of water is passing along it: there would be roll and recoil until a steady level is reached by iterative calculation. Modelling a river to make useful predictions is a difficult task requiring time, skill and luck.

Understanding of river conditions is confounded by weather variations. Despite extensive meteorological data collection, radar and analysis systems, there can be sudden heavy rainfall resulting in river flooding which makes water level in the river unpredictable.

I had learned, when I had coded models in the oil industry, that I should take calculation shortcuts and accept approximation when possible. The engineering mantra was 'Near enough is good enough'. Coding done by inexperienced engineers often added 'bells and whistles', for unnecessary accuracy, that slowed down calculation. Idealism had to be tempered by objectivity.

I had to wait several months for the Council's Floodwise Property Report to be updated with outcomes of the 2022 flood, by simulation. I had no other method than to accept the predictions of their model to complete the Dasein of my PhD investigation.

I usually ate at home in company with Grania and Leigh where they could talk freely. I cooked for myself, but the women appeared and helped prepare my food, entering into discussion.

'Heidegger's ideas are difficult,' said Grania. 'Why are you so committed to his method for analysing flooding?'

'Heidegger's book Being and Time (4) is guiding my analysis,' I said. 'His method systematically explores properties and relationships. It has guided me through my investigation of flooding of the Brisbane River. I will check that the BoM simulator includes all the processes needed to explain existential flooding data received from several hundred stream gauging stations.'

'Doesn't it put you off Heidegger's theory that he was a Nazi?' Leigh asked.

'No,' I said. 'His politics are unsavoury, but do not invalidate his theory. Heidegger joined the German National Socialist Party in 1933, at about the same time as Hitler. After the war ended, he was vilified and barred from academia. Although he was an unrepentant Nazi, Hannah Arendt, who was Jewish and whose aversion to fascism is in her book Origins of Totalitarianism, was an unlikely friend and helped restore his reputation. It is not necessarily true that because the NSP was evil, his model would be evil. 'Being and Time' is not a political treatise and in my view his book is his redemption.'

'I agree,' said Grania. 'The process of Heidegger's model was rigorously authentic ontology, as if Being There is before a God unconcerned with trivialities, projecting belief into the future. His content included Nazi beliefs – but the process of his analysis was uncontaminated.'

'Any model of a river in flood is a work in progress, rather than an exact abstraction of a physical entity,' I said. 'A model has approximations and errors which can never be eliminated. Testing the model can check if it is useful. But a model can have quirks that are not apparent until the unexpected occurs, as it did in 2022, with heavy rain downstream of the Wivenhoe Dam. The model couldn't make predictions. Encountering criticism, several meteorologists quit their jobs.'

'Could they have been better prepared?' Grania asked.

'I think so,' I said. 'Modellers should prepare standard rainfall configurations ready to drop into the simulator when a cyclone threatens. The best-fitting scenario could then be adopted, tweaked and used to make forecasts.

'The Dasein of Brisbane River flood height prediction does not include confident forecasting for more than an hour or two before the peak is reached. A lot of data will have to be entered and hopefully this can be done quickly enough to calculate river height forecasts from rainfall and warn people who could be flooded.'

'Fine-grained weather radar can change forecasts too quickly for river heights to be predicted in time for people to protect themselves,' said Grania. 'The situation could be precarious, needing rehearsal.'

After I had dinner, Grania regaled us with tales of her foreign travels. She had covertly accompanied an Australian Government diplomat to conferences and negotiations, becoming a listening post for him. In the end he came under suspicion and had to give her up.

It was a warm evening and I shared a cold bath with them. Leigh came in, stripped off and washed us all over. Still wet, the three of us made love slowly and tenderly. One would initiate, another do the hard work, another experience exquisite torture, another provide an emotional counterpoint. Afterwards, we lay together listening to a magpie warbling in the garden.

'What a song!' said Grania. 'I wish I could whistle it.'

'I wish I could hear you,' I said.

'It has made us all happy,' said Leigh.

We were a loving triad. Sometimes I was the indulged one, my body stimulated until my will melted down. At others, I was one of a team coaxing orgasm after orgasm from one or other of the women. At first, I was self-conscious, but I learned to express my wants and affections freely. Each of us had a specialty which we deployed for the greatest good of the greatest number.

Leigh was experienced in welfare provision and contributed to Grania's and my analyses. Provision of benefits to flood victims lay at the heart of the Brisbane River's Dasein. Leigh suggested the framework of legislation needed for fair relief and compensation. For Grania's investigation of drought relief, victim welfare was paramount. Government policy too often was decided by people inexperienced with disaster relief. Leigh benefitted from finding out physical and technological aspects, that would help her work. We were united by a common interest in rainfall and group sex.

PART 5

THE FUTURE

CHAPTER 38 ALTERNATIVES

After the flood in 2022 was over, I wanted to resolve what to do with the apartment I had bought above mine. I had become more aware of possibilities of flooding than I had been when I acquired it. My investigation of the Brisbane River was helped by the Council's publication of its Floodwise Property Report. For the first time I had become aware of risks that could be quantified for my apartments. The information was helpful for evaluating alternatives for living there with the possibility of flooding.

This departure into strategies for disposition of my property oriented my story to focussing on the realities of river flooding for thousands of Brisbaners in similar circumstances. It emphasised the critical role of flood heights for damage to property and the need for all types of flood mitigation. Matters I had reviewed as having potential for mitigating flooding, such as prevention of erosion and resumption of dredging, now assumed critical importance. There were other factors exacerbating flooding, such as city location, infrastructure, transport and bridges that I had to investigate.

Michael and his son were staying in Unit 4. He was a diligent father, wanting to have his son, friends and possessions around him, with control over who could come there.

'I could live here,' he said. 'I like this apartment. Why don't you want to move up here?' he asked me.

'I'm thinking of giving it to you and Sarah to share,' I said to him. 'I don't want you to worry about flooding. I'm used to it.'

'Wow, Dad,' Michael said. 'That would be generous of you.'

It seemed natural that because I was older I should take more risk. Termite soldiers were mature adults and went outside the nest, risking death, whereas young termites stayed inside caring for the larvae. Nature protects the young.

There were various ways Michael and Sarah could share ownership. Michael and I talked about some alternatives, such as joint ownership.

I asked Grania what she thought of the idea.

'Sharing the apartment will be good for the togetherness of your family,' Grania said. 'You could help each other in many ways.'

I had emailed to ask Sarah in Canada what she wanted to do.

'Sharing is a great idea, Dad,' Sarah replied.

'How would you be, chancing the next flood, Dad?' Michael asked. 'Could you take refuge up in Unit 4?'

'Gambling is not in my nature. It wouldn't do me much good if the water continued to rise, because evacuation from Unit 4 has to follow the same route as from Unit 2 and the way would be submerged, when Unit 2 is filling.'

'Perhaps you could get another place, away from the river?' he asked.

'There is nowhere I like as much as here and moving would be expensive.'

'Perhaps you can compromise, accepting less amenity but getting away from flooding.'

While I was arranging for him to live in the apartment above mine, he was proposing I move away. I lacked impetus to move my home. Living by the Brisbane River was safe enough for me. The dams were holding up; deluges had not become more frequent and it was the dry season now. With these odds, it was reasonable to continue to accept the uncertainty of the weather. If my apartment flooded, I would be brave and care for Grania and Leigh.

The news media sensationalised weather reporting to attract audiences. Australia is a large continent and there was usually a cyclone lurking somewhere that could pose a threat, most often offshore in the north near the equator, or moving inshore from the Pacific Ocean. The alerts broadcasted by BoM worried everyone. Cyclones were unlikely to travel into the Brisbane River catchment and waiting for a flood was interminable, like waiting for an earthquake.

I showed Grania and Leigh Figure 2, which I had used to calculate the probability of our home flooding. Water level at the Port Office had exceeded 4.8 m once in each of 1825, 1841, 1843, 1891, twice in 1893, in 1897 and in 1974, i.e. 8 times in 190 years to 2022, a 4% probability, on average.

'Assuming flood heights were lowered 2 metres by construction of the Somerset and Wivenhoe dams, only 3 of the floods, in 1825, 1841 and 1893, would have had heights above 5.3 m at Port Office, a probability of 3 in 190, or 1.6%,' I said.

'The BCC Floodwise model probabilities are 1% (7.5 m) and 2% (5.2 m). Grania calculated probability of reaching the level of my lounge floor, 7.0 metres, as 1.2% in any year, or 1 in 83.

'It could be less if the dams mitigate flooding,' I said.

'Is it an acceptable risk?' asked Grania.

'The risk of flooding is small,' I said. 'My living area has never been flooded in 25 years since it was built.'

'It's not been flood-free for long then.'

Grania as usual was thinking critically. It was her trait I most valued.

Estimating the likelihood of my place being flooded was the crux of my investigation.

'Where are you up to now with the river's Dasein?' Grania asked me.

'I have focussed on improving understanding; considering idle talk; pursuing curiosity; teasing out ambiguity; revealing falling; and thrownness,' I said. 'Buying a flood-prone apartment was not necessarily an ambiguous proposition, but I was thrown into purchasing it. The resistance to flooding of the Brisbane River has fallen, because the channel has been obstructed, by sediment and by bridge pillar islands. The probabilities of flooding have probably increased significantly.

'Those concerns complete my analysis and next I have to consider what can happen in the future. Experience of floods can be complicated by events and situations. For example, a flood like in 1893 could happen again.'

'The circumstances in 1893 were a fluke,' Grania said. 'It is very unlikely that two cyclones will coincide over the catchment again.'

'The order of severity of recent flood years, from the number of properties affected, was 2022, 2011 and 1974,' I said. '2022 had the lowest water level but most flood damage because it was localised, with the rain falling further down the river. Our understanding of flood effects is incomplete.'

'Management of the dams has to contend with uncertainties. Dam operators are thrown into situations without previous experience. In the past, political leaders have elbowed in with their intuitions, opened the flood gates and caused mayhem.'

'Another refinement could be to superimpose on river flooding predictions of the effects of higher tides and increased water levels at the ocean outfall, according to climate change orthodoxy, which could slowdown discharge of flood water. I am sceptical of this.'

My perspective of the river and its floods was affected by my age. Heidegger's philosophy always included death as a possible outcome and he wanted us to be prepared for it. The prospect of death, strangely, was liberating. I contemplated my death but I didn't bring Grania in on it yet. It seemed negative, but consideration of my Being-towards-death would make my Dasein whole. Speculation about death had ontical existentiell meaning, real and limited, taking precedence over other events. Any moment could be my last, my utmost possibility for being, the point where my life became impossible.

When I contemplated the river flowing into my apartment, I imagined evacuating as I did in 2011 and 2022, with drowning as an alternative. Drowning could be attractive, compared with living an evacuated life among strangers, without the comforts of home. I perceived life as transient and fragile. I would feel no obligation to participate further than being immersed under a deep flood, being drowned, rather than suicided. I felt an obligation to younger people to make my exit stoically, rather than tragically. Drowning was a contingency, not what I wanted.

ConsideringZZ death was an unexpected outcome of Heidegger's method and an important one. The traditional scientific engineering analysis would have omitted many important aspects of the situation, especially my own involvement.

My being-towards-death was an unusual posture for someone of my age. I did not announce I was preoccupied, but some people guessed. A clue was that I was not accumulating new possessions, merely repairing and renovating small damage. Things that had taken my time, such as replacing broken gear, didn't matter anymore.

Age would eventually bring disability. The worst of it would be that caring for me could detract from the lives of Grania and Leigh, if they stayed with me, as I hoped they would. I wanted to exit as independently as possible, fighting it. I continued to discuss my writing with Grania and helped her with hers. We had other interactions, but it was our writing that gave our lives together meaning. I didn't know how long we could continue. It was the fear of nothingness that was most concerning.

Grania expected my planning should protect her and provide for her well-being. We had lived together happily for three years. Her PhD project was not advancing but she seemed to get pleasure contributing to mine. Because she was with me, there was less uncertainty of how my final scene would play out. With her, I felt calm and composed. Household chores were not a burden. We could carry on until evacuation was necessary and then calmly leave.

My abiding concern was to have a refuge where we could go if we had to evacuate from Atrium. I had been fortunate in 2022 to be able to stay with John, but such an opportunity might not come again.

If there was a room available, we could go to Hilltop Apartment Hotel in South Brisbane. If we could borrow a car or get a lift, we could take our computers and connect to the internet there. We would set off early, to avoid traffic jams on Montague Road and other arterials.

The risk of being flooded in Unit 2 was small and we could possibly continue living there for years. After all, the living area had never once been flooded in the 25 years I had owned it. In my view obstruction of the river by silt and bridge supports was getting worse, but it was only an impression. I was sceptical about climate change and demonstrated the courage of my convictions by giving little credence to forecasts of increased river flooding.

I was still considering what to do with Unit 4. It depended on what my son and daughter wanted.

For the first time, I felt my project to analyse the Dasein of flooding of the Brisbane River was succeeding. I had lived by the River for 23 years and experienced two major floods. I felt experienced enough to summarise recent events and predict the future. I had come across harmful actions and irresponsible inactions that could have wide interest if they became known and I began to ready my writing for publication, in a memoir of my investigations and findings. I hoped to attract readers to understand how living by the Brisbane River could be improved. My alternatives included moving higher in Atrium apartments.

CHAPTER 39 AGREEMENT

In mid 2022, Sarah and Michael and their families were visiting from overseas. I loved having my family with me. There was more common interest between us than usual, as we amicably made plans for the transfer of Unit 4.

'If Sarah would sell me her share, I would take possession and move in,' said Michael. 'I'm not sure how soon. It depends when I can finish my job.'

'When I visit, where would I stay?' Sarah asked.

'You could stay with me,' said Michael. 'We would fit your kids in somewhere.'

'Some or all of you could stay with me,' I said.

'Great,' said Sarah.

She was a pretty blonde with a pony tail. She ran marathons.

'Every step hurts,' she told me. 'It does me good.'

She had not acquired her stoical determination from me.

Quiet, thoughtful, inscrutable, humorous and prickly, she worked as a senior lecturer at a university in Canada. She liked to stand before a packed lecture theatre, presenting her views from meticulous research, that cleverly reconciled opposing viewpoints on some controversial topic when feelings were running high. Charismatic, her ideals shone as she recognised the potential in others and ignored unpleasantness. She was a skilful debater with formidable skills of persuasion.

She played chess and poker well. In poker games with stakes of pennies, she took away dollars. At her university, she coordinated a large postgraduate degree programme, matching acolytes with opportunities and assessing accomplishment.

'I'm not sure how to get most benefit from your gift, Dad,' she said.

'It all depends on what you want to do with it,' I told her.

'I can't return from Canada now,' said Sarah. 'But I can come back on holiday at intervals of about 18 months.'

Michael could make plans to use his half.

'I could furnish it and pay the bills,' said Michael. 'Sarah could pay for the time she is here.'

'Will you get a tenant?'

'If we leased it, we wouldn't be able to stay there when we wanted to. Cancelling bookings and evicting tenants would be the pits.'

'If I gave Unit 4 to the two of you to share, what would you do with it?'

'I'd like to live there,' said Michael, 'as soon as I can arrange it.'

Sociable and spontaneous, he wanted it badly.

'I want to give the apartment to you two equally,' I said. 'If Sarah will not be returning in the foreseeable future, as seems likely, perhaps Michael would want to buy Sarah's half share at market value.'

Sarah was reluctant at first, not wanting to convert bricks and mortar into cash, at a time when inflation was rampant.

'Michael is taking on more risk than you,' I told her. 'Your position is good.'

I wanted Michael to be fully informed of his prospects for the apartment. Apart from the risk of flooding, I reminded him that BCC had approved a bridge across the river, from outside Atrium to the university.

There was a lot for Michael to consider but he was a risk taker. His planning method was to hold many prospects open and stay flexible until the last possible moment. His caution was often at the expense of others, but Michael was not empathetic and he often did not realize how others felt.

Michael and Sarah hesitated only briefly, then agreed Michael would buy Sarah's share.

'Let's do it,' I said.

Michael couldn't move in yet, but it would be too difficult getting tenants. It seemed extravagant to keep it empty, with Michael's furniture and only a few visitors.

Sarah's study leave ended and she returned to Canada with her children.

We signed a three-way contract. It recorded that I was irrevocably gifting the property to Michael and Sarah 'in consideration of natural love and affection'. Michael agreed to pay Sarah for her half of the value. It was all formalised within two months.

'It's yours now Michael. You owe Sarah for her share,' I said.

Michael whooped.

'Thank you very much, Dad,' he said. 'I love the apartment. I would never be able to afford to live in a place like this without your gift.'

I had given Unit 4 to Michael and Sarah equally. Michael had bought Sarah's share and was making plans to move there with Amir. I looked forward to their living above me and hoped I would see more of them.

People who live on the deltas of the Ganges, Euphrates and Yellow Rivers are probably inured to regular river floods. Living in flood-prone homes on the floodplain of the Brisbane River, families had the inconvenience of infrequent floods, as the flipside of their coin toss with low cost living. Rich people would be able to buy favourable conditions but the masses would suffer hardship and would have to either adapt or perish. In China, construction in 1984 of the Three Gorges Dam on the Yangtze River required 1,250,000 people to move away, who had lived all their lives in riverside towns and villages of great antiquity. My Dasein was to continue living in the same place as I had for 22 years, with my son and grandson coming to live in the same building. In the event of a flood reaching my apartment, they could help me escape.

We never discussed what would happen if the place flooded. Michael had been staying there in February 2022 and had evacuated with me to John's place. If it caused him any hesitation to live there, he didn't mention it. Michael would be higher in the building, with his things better protected from flooding, than were mine in Unit 2. But he could need to evacuate if the water cut off his exit down the staircase. I bought a rope escape ladder to hang over the back balcony into the neighbour's yard, so they would be able to climb down if the main stairway flooded.

I had given my children the apartment above mine to share, hoping it would create family unity.

CHAPTER 40 OCCUPATION AND AFFECTION

Michael had got what he wanted, but he could one day want to move somewhere else. If he did this, I would be put out, for I had wanted my gift of the apartment to gather my family around me and to be a place of refuge in a flood and old age. If Michael went away, I would have only my own apartment to accommodate visitors, including Sarah and her children.

My gift had brought my son and daughter new possibilities for living and investing. I hoped that Michael and son would want to reside there long term and I would have their company. When I could no longer live with Grania and Leigh, I could vacate my apartment for Sarah to live there.

It changed my life for the better to have Michael and Amir living in the apartment above us. It was like a coming home. He had left home 15 years earlier and gone overseas a few years later. When he came home from Fiji later that year, with his son Amir, my love for them was unbounded. What they had done and what they had become filled me with such joy, there was a warm glow deep inside me. It was the happiness of a parent who was contributing positively to his offspring's well-being.

Michael settled down and found employment. He worked from home, his skills for hire, travelling widely to hot spots to advise people from his extensive experience.

He furnished the apartment tastefully and comfortably. Amir attended a nearby State High School. He had been attending the international school in Suva and was making good progress there. He was only 12 but was diligent with his school homework and home chores. He was popular at school and had friends who came for home visits.

I loved having my son and grandson living next door. I wasn't with them everyday, but I saw enough of them to appreciate their striving at work. When Michael went overseas for work assignments of a week or two, Carol came and stayed there, taking care of her grandson.

Amir did what he wanted, went where he liked, with anyone he chose. I had yearned at his age to be allowed to have a friend visit and go to a movie together. I could do nothing without permission and was refused permission to do anything other than school work, playing rugby and helping on the farm. Amir took these freedoms for granted. He had an Iphone and spent a lot of time talking with friends.

Amir was my oldest grandson and I loved him dearly. He visited me in my apartment below his, to play chess. In Fiji, his recreation had been horse riding. Living at West End, his father drove him a long way to an equestrian centre to ride weekly.

Michael worked as a contractor administering foreign aid programmes. With a doctorate in science, he was capable of complex multi-tasking. He was adept with digital devices, used to accessing IT infrastructure and cutting red tape. He had great ability to get things done, by bringing people together.

A friend of Michael, Frances, came from Fiji and moved in with him. Her son Kyle was Amir's age. Tall and well built, they made a handsome family. Michael was besotted with Frances.

They asked me next door for meals sometimes. I shared with them food I cooked. Amir and Kyle would come to my place when Michael and Frances went out for the evening. We played chess or watched a movie.

They hadn't lived with us for long before Amir started complaining about Kyle taking his art box.

'Did he give it back?' I asked Amir.

'No. He's hidden it.'

'How do you know that?'

'He's done it before.'

'Have you asked him for it?'

'He says I must have lost it.'

One day when I was out and they were left alone. When I arrived home, Amir was in tears.

'What happened?' I asked him. Kyle was in another room.

'Kyle punched me in the face.'

'Were you fighting?'

'Yes.'

'Who started it?'

'I told him to give back my art box. 'What are you going to do about it?' he asked, holding up his fist. I tried to grab him, but he punched me.'

'What were you going to do to him?'

'I was going to force him to give it back.'

I called Kyle in.

'Did you punch Amir?'

'He tried to grab me.'

'We don't solve arguments by punching in this house,' I said. 'Do you have Amir's art box?'

'No.'

'He's lying,' said Amir.

'I'm going to search your room, Kyle. Amir can help me. You stay here Kyle.'

We looked in cupboards, drawers and under the bed.

'Here, I've found it,' said Amir.

I called Kyle. 'Did you know it was here?' I said.

'No, I didn't,' he said.

'You shouldn't have Amir's things in your room, unless he has lent them to you. Did you loan it to him, Amir?'

'No,' he said. 'He grabbed it.'

'Now stop that, Amir. I want you to tidy your room Kyle. This dispute is over.'

Later Kyle punched Amir several times before I realised he was bullying Amir, provoking him and intimidating him. It was unfortunate because they were often together and their relationship was spoiled.

'How are you getting on with Kyle?' I asked Michael.

'Is there a problem?' he asked.

'I think he is bullying Amir.'

'Really?' Michael said. 'I haven't seen it.'

'He seems over-entitled to me,' I said. 'He's pushing into Amir's space.'

'He can be demanding, I agree. But he's not a bully.'

'He likes to be right, putting the blame on others,' I said.

'I'll talk with Frances,' Michael said. 'He had it all his own way in Fiji. Thanks for letting me know.'

Kyle had difficulty fitting into his new school. The standard of work was higher, there was stiff competition in his class and he lacked success. He was often disconsolate. Amir's achievement discouraged him and he was falling behind in skills he needed. Unless he improved, he would be put back a year.

CHAPTER 41 CARRYING ON

With Unit 4 occupied by Michael and his family, I continued living with Grania and Leigh in Unit 2, keeping busy writing novels and going out on several days each week to discussion and writing groups. I prepared for more flooding. There was comfort that because my living space didn't flood last time, it probably wouldn't next time. Submergence wouldn't be decided as if by random lottery. Properties would be flooded in order, with lowest elevation first. Superior positions could escape flooding. The danger for me was that places not flooded previously sometimes went under.

Teleology is the study of a person's aims, purposes, or intentions. Earlier in life my telos had aims of raising children and caring for loved ones, but this mainspring of my life had weakened with age. It was a reduction of purposiveness rather than diversion of interest. Salmon leap upriver, past fish traps, returning to the river where they began life. The female deposits her eggs in a hollow in the gravel of the river bed and the male covers them with his milt. Within a few days, both parents die, their duties fulfilled. I had watched over my children for many years but now the flame of my life began to falter.

I wanted to care for my young family but they probably didn't need me anymore. I helped others when I could. I felt I had a duty to model mentally healthy and independent adulthood to family members. If my continued living was more purposeful, I could help others and keep the flame burning brightly. I expected to be around for many years.

Birth age is not a signpost to life's journey. Our ability to cope does not have an expiry date nor does it relate to the number of Earth revolutions around the Sun, since our births. We carry on as long as we can.

My aim for living a long life is for my heart to beat slowly. According to biologist Geoffrey West (25), the number of heartbeats during the lifetime of any animal, of any species, whatever the body mass, is constant. An elephant (heartbeat rate 15 per hour) lives for 200 years and a hummingbird (heartbeat rate 1000) lives for 3 years. Both would have about the same number of heartbeats at death: 2 billions. This is shown in Table 1 at the end of this book.

Different cars have different engine speeds, like heart rates, determining their lifetimes, as shown in Table 1. A Fiat car engine runs faster and wears out with fewer kilometres than a ponderous Rolls Royce. My heartbeat rate at rest is quite low, about 50 bpm. I expect a longish life. An irony is that in animals living quickly, fulfilment could accumulate at the same metabolic rate as a slow-moving animal, such as a sloth. A hummingbird could experience as much happiness in its lifetime as an elephant.

Grania wanted to relate it to intent and will.

'Fulfilment would depend on the individual's willed accomplishment,' she said.

'Willpower can be developed, so it won't run out.'

'How?' Grania asked.

'Free will is like the electricity you get from a car battery,' I said. 'If the car stays in the garage, the battery will go flat and it won't start. If you run the car regularly, the battery will charge up and have electricity even for a tough cold start. Forcing myself to go to work and attending to chores at home has helped me build up my free will to cope with unexpected situations, like a flood. I need to keep my willpower up, ready for when life serves something tough.'

'I agree,' said Grania. 'Resilience is maintaining will to overcome problems. How can I do that?' she asked.

'To keep our batteries charged,' I said, 'I believe we have to free ourselves from 'the little fidget wheels' that operate timepieces and vibrate caesium crystals at certain electromagnetic frequencies to count a type of time. We should live in our own time. I can ignore seconds and live at a pace that will expend my life at a rate I am comfortable with, measured by my own internal clock. My body lives in my time, that is different from your body time. I have theorised elsewhere that extreme flow can also dilate my time, so that it is possible for me to stay younger, by relativity (16).'

'Do you seek inner harmony, like in Zen?' Grania asked me, with mock sympathy. She was sceptical of spiritualism, although amenable to the perceptual distortion of phenomenology.

'Zen can reduce time awareness,' I said. 'Willing personal control of time does more than reduce time awareness. It replaces it with self-control.'

'You aren't wearing a watch. Why?' Grania asked.

'Not wearing a watch and doing things when you feel like it, are aspects of peaceful non-violent living which, according to Pinker (19) are increasing,' I said. 'I can choose to have my cake of time freedom and eat it too, with self-determination.'

'I suppose living outside time set by others could be anxiety reducing,' said Grania. 'I don't see that living in the moment will rectify the anxiety of a flood-prone living place. Scientific analysis could find living in a flood-prone location was due to objective inherited ignorance or stupidity, or housing supply failure, or phenomenology would attribute it to subjective social, economic and home marketing circumstances, including risk taking. They would drain willpower.'

'The hippy movement, with its inattention to time, seemed to Norbert Elias, (1897-1990), to be a counterculture.' I said. 'Self-control and personal interdependence lie at the heart of the civilizing process, as if awareness of time is desirable, even if it is not watched. There has been growing interest in meditation and 'living in the moment'. Flooding could be less uncomfortable.'

'This is simply Zen desensitization of intolerance of flooding,' said Grania.

'Zen can relieve anxiety but radical seizing of control of time is needed to maintain the willpower needed to cope with flooding.'

'Interesting,' she said. 'I can see that the watch you wear on the back of your wrist demonstrates your determination not to be a victim of time.'

Having given Unit 4 to Michael, I am counting on him to help us face the possibility of future flooding of Unit 2. I hope that Michael will help. There is a possibility of wanting to live with Michael while my apartment is being restored. I would be able to move back in a couple of months, when my place had been repaired.

I have prepared for flooding, but if the place fills with water quickly and no-one comes, I can face the end with equanimity. This is not a plea for attention. When I articulate my being-towards-death, my concerns are alleviated. I am able to confront my mortality with simulation of those circumstances, consoling others that the situation is normal. My death is not cowardice. Although fleeing and falling in the face of death are more usual, confronting my death is more authentic and cannot be put off any longer.

Both Grania and I applied for and obtained tutoring work in the philosophy department at the university. We helped students with their assignments and conducted reading groups. The contact with bright young minds and the respect we received was rewarding. Students were confronted by our advanced ages, wondering how we were dealing with dying.

Planning for one's death is suppressed in our society, because it could be construed as suicide, which for religious people would be unethical. Suicide and attempted suicide are legal, but perpetrators are regarded as mentally ill and in need of help.

Suicide gets little publicity. There is a preference for interpreting suicide as accident. There might be more suicide cases than are inferred. Not all collisions of cars with trees are accidents. The number of cars that collide with large roadside trees, causing death, is higher than the number expected from the proximity of cars to large wayside trees.

Author Virginia Woolf planned her suicide carefully. At age 59 she filled her overcoat pockets with stones and on March 28, 1941, walked into the River Ouse. I want my own drowning to be regarded by my descendants as an accident. In the turmoil of river flooding, I could be swept away to my death.

There is a tradition that ennobles death, illustrated by Caravaggio's painting The Miracle of Saint Francis. He is uplifted from his wounds, consoled by an angel, as if his dying can be prolonged because it is sacred.

I expect my life to be prolonged, but not by God. My bid for longevity has several interests: time dilation, mental engagement, slow metabolism, flow, independence, companionship and being-towards-death. With good fortune, I expect to carry on for as long as I want to. Grania respected my adherence to Heidegger's mental preparation. She did not adopt my preparations.

'I'm not going to worry about death,' she said. 'When my time is up, I'll die without any fuss.'

I planned my way forward for my own exit before discussing it with Grania and Leigh.

'I'm worried about you,' Leigh said. 'Your thinking is bogged down in pessimism. Why have you left me out of your plans? Are you trying to get rid of me?'

'No. I want all three of us to be together to the end,' I said. 'I don't want to worry you.'

'Well you have worried me,' Grania said. 'Your Being-Towards-Death is macabre. I love you and want to enjoy being with you. You need to get away from your morbid writing. We should take a holiday. Where would you like to go?'

'How about Bali?' I said.

'Good choice,' said Leigh. 'We could stay at a place in the country, away from the resorts.'

'How about doing a road trip around Bali?' Grania said. 'It would be adventurous and spontaneous, exploring for new ideas and perspectives. We wouldn't have a schedule and would stay in places we liked. You would be able to stop and investigate the sights. What do you think?'

'I love it!' I said. 'It will be great to see a beautiful place without crowds of tourists. I need a break away from my project. Who is going to plan it?'

'Why not all three of us?'

It was agreed. We planned and took a month-long holiday together.

When we came back from Bali, we settled back refreshed into our lifestyle and work. I was relaxed and ceased to worry about flooding of my apartment or my death. I had adopted Heidegger's existentiality and the inevitability of events beyond my control.

On holiday with the boys, we had been able to watch Kyle and Amir for signs of bullying. I mentioned Kyle's over-confidence and independence to his mother.

'Many kids go through phases of being self-absorbed,' she said. 'Kyle has an inflated sense of self-worth, and can lack empathy for others due to the focus on getting his own needs met,' she said. 'But I agree he is selfish and perhaps he will learn from Amir to be less demanding. I'll remind him to be more considerate of others.'

CHAPTER 42 FLOOD PROOFING RESILIENCE

An effect of our holiday was to reduce an obsession with flooding to an ordinary risk. After our holiday, I focussed on a probability of 1.2% in any year of being flooded. It was very unlikely, but significant because I had been traumatised by two floods, even though they were minor and didn't come inside my apartment. The water had come into the garage silently, sneakily, in darkness, unstoppable. I had felt helpless and lapsed into victimhood. Humans are accustomed to controlling their environments and a flood was an insidious, pervasive and intimidating intrusion.

If Unit 2 flooded, I would want it repaired quickly to continue living there. People whose homes had been flooded said the Dasein of flood recovery is: finding tradesmen to repair walls and floors; claiming for government financial assistance; and getting fair treatment from fund distribution authorities.

In a flood, water gets into possessions and damages them. Many materials will not dry out or resume their former condition. The Dasein of immersion in flood water is 'falling'. Thus flood debris is divided into goods that are undamaged, others in need of repair and the remainder to go to the tip. The fallenness of Dasein subtracts the jettisoned and unrepairable part of the material. The assignment of fallenness takes skill to evaluate the potential for recovering each type of water damaged material and its application.

Water is a mysterious substance and fascinates children for hours. It flows down into anywhere at a lower level, filling upwards to form a horizontal surface. It flows around, under, over and inside objects, wetting surfaces, soaking into capillaries and flowing up to the tops of tall trees.

'You can't shut the door on a flood,' Sarah said. 'You can run but you can't hide.'

When water covers you, unless you can swim, float, or walk on the surface like a water strider, you will drown. A flood is fearful to a non-swimmer. Humans, livestock and wild animals may not be able to swim. A horse will stubbornly refuse to step into water, possibly fearful of losing its footing and injuring a leg. Flood water is murky and can conceal dangers, including snags and currents. Swimming in flood water is dangerous.

Water cools our bodies, conducting heat away and evaporating it into the air. When immersed, air-breathing animals quickly drown. Under muddy water, submerged plants starve, unable to photosynthesize. Trees may eventually recover from being flooded, but animals may lose their homes and may die without food or warmth. Finding a comfortable place to shelter is difficult in a flood.

Inside a home, water clings to surfaces and is absorbed into materials with pores by capillary attraction. Wood, clothing, carpets and plasterboard sop up water and may never dry out. Flooding does damage to property that can be expensive to undo. Flood water contains microorganisms that can grow moulds in saturated materials, requiring restoration or replacement.

My kitchen and bathroom cabinets are particle board and would disintegrate in a flood. The wall linings are plasterboard and would have to be replaced, but behind are besser blocks with steel studs and lintels. The task of replacing the boards with water resistant fibre cement sheeting would be straightforward. Sliding windows and doors are aluminium and would not require replacement.

Distorted plasterboard walls would have to be replaced and wall cavities dried out. My apartment consists of a lounge cum kitchen and dining space, with three bedrooms, an ensuite and a bathroom with laundry. Ceilings may have to be replaced. Fixtures such as kitchen benches and bathroom cabinets could be ruined.

White-ware would likely have to be replaced after immersion. Dishwasher, fridge, oven, gas cooktop, microwave, washing machine, tumble dryer and air-conditioners, could all have to be replaced. A kitchen sink with a waste disposal grinder could have to be replaced.

Four of my sliding door openings and windows are fitted with Shoji simulated Japanese rice-paper screens. When the flood reaches my living room, I plan to lift the screens off their tracks and carry them up to store on the landing above.

I would try to save furniture, cabinets, books, art prints, computer, printer, kitchen equipment and cutlery. Some items could be put up on tables but the settee and armchairs, beds, bookcases filled with books and the 40-volume Encyclopaedia Britannica would have to be left to the flood. There is nowhere the books can be put to save them. The kitchen cabinets are particle board and would be lost, although I would tape the doors closed to prevent the contents dispersing.

The floors are compressed bamboo boards laid over tiles. The bamboo planks are made of porous materials and could swell in water, but the ceramic tiles would survive. The walls are plasterboard hung on metal frames with a few wooden studs. The ceiling is plasterboard hung from metal frames. The light fittings could need to be replaced. I would leave most of the clothes in the wardrobes, to be lost.

I have thought through my actions in recovering from flood damage. Resilient repair has to be aimed for, so that damage in another flood later would not require repeated repair. When the plasterboard walls are repaired, I would want waterproof materials installed that would avert further flood damage. The replacement materials could include hardwood frames, fibro-cement sheeting, and Styrofoam insulation, with wet-proofing access, to let water out of wall cavities.

With planning, being flooded would be inconvenient but not unthinkable. We would leave and return later to clean up and begin repairing the damage. Paying to repair the damage would be like repaying a debt for all the good times we had had when living there, on the cheap some might say. We would dare to get over being flooded. The apartment could be renewed, with more resilience.

Many people who have rebuilt interiors of their homes use resilient materials that would not be damaged if flooding occurred again. To reconstruct my walls and floors with resilience now would be expensive and a financial blow. After being flooded it might not be insurmountable, if funds were available for Resilient Homes Relief. (20)

A U3A colleague, whose 3 bedroom retirement home flooded recently, had it rebuilt internally, on insurance. He estimates the cost of restoring it at more than $100,000. If my apartment is flooded, the building structure isn't insured. If the flood comes in here, I would want to return it to its former condition with resilience, hoping to pay for the restoration work when I sell it.

Contents insurance should restore contents to as new condition. The interior is 26 years old. Although in reasonable condition now, it will need to be replaced soon anyway. The kitchen and bathrooms are due to be refurbished. The insurance I have been paying for is 'replacement as new' but I have bought few replacements.

Cook considers the totality of flooding effects as if they could all have been prevented by regulation to stop development on the river floodplain. Although this would have prevented many people being duped, others would have preferred to accept a risk, to get a better place to live.

The other approach is to build another dam. Dams usually flood places of ecological preservation and extraordinary beauty. Construction is resisted on sites accessible for recreation or in national parks.

'Dams could 'possibly' be built on the Bremer River and in the Lockyer Valley,' said Hubert Chanson, a civil engineering professor (1). 'The Wivenhoe Dam could be raised.'

Further water storages would cost more per megalitre of water stored. Protests against damming of the Franklin River in Tasmania had several objections: destruction of beauty of natural environment; endangerment of fauna and flora; destruction of Aboriginal art; and loss of jobs. The high court weighed up costs, against benefits from electricity generation, industrial development and townswater supply and stopped construction of a dam. Further damming of the Brisbane River could be opposed.

There is some evidence that the Dasein of Brisbane River flooding has been worsened by bad dam management, by ineffective dam technology and by lack of government control of city development. The Wivenhoe and Somerset dams might not have been built, with today's conservation values. One day they may be abandoned, due to silting up.

My hope when I bought Unit 4 was that Seqwater would manage the dam better than they did in 2011. They have experience now from floods in Jan 2011; 2013; February 2022; March 2022. Hopefully they will be able to keep flood levels lower. Their management has been reasonably successful, insofar as the living areas of my apartment have not yet been flooded.

Brisbane River flood prevention is part of a 'spectacle' of city care and development promulgated by governments and developers. The Dasein of the recent floods is a spectacle (17) in which the government and media have sown fear and anxiety, reaping profit and votes from false appearances of care and understanding. They induced learned helplessness in many victims. Home owners want the values of their properties to steadily increase, with general prosperity making the increased prices affordable. According to Debord's (34) theory of the spectacle, investors, developers, governments and media promote an appearance of well-being in order to profit from subscribers. A politician who became popular leading the City population to cope with flooding, was catapulted into State leadership.

If living in flood prone properties is prevented, many people would be unable to afford a home and would be homeless. Home prices would fall, development would stop and the government would lose voter support. Banning construction of floodable homes would appear to be against the public interest as a capitalist spectacle and could never be enacted. The Dasein of the Brisbane River has new homes being built there on the river floodplain. Even when well-informed of dangers, people will take risks.

Brisbane residents want technological fixes such as dams to mitigate flooding of their homes. They hope another dam will hold more water back. When there hasn't been a flood for a long period, it can be misconstrued as a benefit of dam building. The protection is more likely to have been luck with cyclones and fortunate dam location.

There is no easy solution. Dr Cook[1] has advocated a suite of 'proactive' preventative measures, including buyback, retrofitting and building houses with flood-resilient materials, ensuring areas of vegetation are preserved, with rainfall able to penetrate grass areas in backyards and public spaces.

To reconstruct my walls and floors with resilience now would be expensive and inconvenient [20]. It could be cheaper to suffer a flood and retrofit afterwards, applying for support from the Resilient Homes Fund.

I would not surrender to a flood. I would resile and rebuild.

I anticipated flooding of my home with a plan to repair the major damage I expected.

My antidote for worry about flooding is to plan my response now and eliminate residual concerns, by living in the moment. To do so doesn't get easier with time passing, unless I go into timeless flow. By focussing and concentrating on tangible goals, such as staying healthy and completing this book, I engage my skills, automatically. I become immersed and timeless, forgetting my flooding worries.

CHAPTER 43 PLANNING AND PREPARATION

My early career in mine planning had developed my ability to forecast future events and control them by planning for the outcomes wanted. Later, as a school teacher I had learned to plan, schedule and conduct events. In retirement, I was planning to reduce effects on my home and community of river flooding. I developed a plan for my own and others to use, covering many possibilities, including misfortune and the possibility of death.

Although I depended on intellectual stimulation by Grania and Leigh, I didn't have to make material provision for them. I had wanted to tell my plans to Grania and Leigh, but they were reluctant to consider the possibility of my death.

'Death is the last thing I want to discuss,' said Leigh. 'Considering how to live has to come first.'

'You do what you want,' Grania said to me. 'If you go first, I'll miss you. If you go suddenly, it would be a shock, but more convenient for everyone than your slow decline. Does Heidegger have any advice on how to make your exit?'

'Gradually starting at birth,' I said.

'Haha. How did Heidegger die?' asked Grania.

'He just died in his sleep, sometime after breakfast on 26 May, 1976. People say he was 86, as strong as a bull and very healthy. According to another report, he died of an unspecified infection. He had no known illnesses prior to that, although he had long since made all the necessary practical arrangements for dying and remarked the end was near to his friends, since at least the year prior.'

'He was prepared, but how did that improve matters?' said Grania. 'You can't forecast death and shouldn't try.'

'Our deaths are out there waiting for us,' I said. 'We have to be ready.'

'What are you going to do?' she asked.

'Prepare myself mentally,' I said. 'I will consider each of my actions as if it is my last.'

'Bah,' she said. 'Dwelling on your death won't make it any better.'

Leigh didn't take part in this discussion. She was 10 years younger than us and thought she might be immortal, as young people often do.

At a meeting of the Corporate Body, I told residents to plan and rehearse their evacuation, imagining flooding of their homes.

'It's not like moving to a new place. You can give your time to conserving your cherished possessions and redeploying your resources efficiently,' I said. 'You can communicate with others about when to leave. Escaping from a flood is always hurried. The two flooding evacuations I have experienced were like fire drills, hurried and under duress. Stay calm and do not panic. Being prepared is important. You must commence planning well before any flood, anticipating conditions, with time for things to go wrong.

'My earliest preparation will be to buy supplies of food and charge up my electric lanterns. My kitchen has a gas hotplate I can use when the electricity goes off. In the first days of cyclonic weather threatening, foods like baked beans and spaghetti bolognaise can be prepared, ready to warm up. I would cook and freeze several meals for each of us, keeping the food cold in my esky until I am ready to warm it up.

'When water starts coming across the park outside, before it floods the street, I would put my computer on the back seat of my car and park it in a side street in a high position. My black suitcase would go in the car trunk with precious papers, back-up USBs, clothes and toiletries, all needed at my temporary abode. I would carry my blue suitcase up to Michael's apartment with more clothes, shoes, copies of precious papers and USBs.'

I had told them my personal plan and hoped they would catch on. I would be hero of the hour, deciding when to evacuate, a Superman leading his people from the front to evacuate. When I felt daunted, I recalled Superman's words:

'IT'S ABOUT WHAT YOU DO . . . IT'S ABOUT ACTION. YOU'RE MUCH STRONGER THAN YOU THINK YOU ARE.'

We would all go together, leaping tall buildings in a single bound. There was another planning meeting of locals in the barbeque area of our building. Michael and Amir were in the crowd and I could see Grania and Leigh at the back. I told everyone what to expect.

'Until the water comes into the garage, we can paddle out across the forecourt and along the street. When it reaches calf deep in the forecourt and garages, evacuation will be through my garden gate and climbing through a hole I will make in the boundary fence.'

'Why would we evacuate when the water is only knee-deep in the garage?' a resident asked me.

'We could stay longer, until the power is turned off. In previous floods, it was turned off when the water level reached the power supply box, at about 1.5 metres. If the water came no higher, we would have been safe to remain in the apartments,. Without electricity, without refrigeration or food preservation, nor ability to see, nor a gas hotplate, it would be unpleasant. Staying longer in the building would be stressful. Gas and water remained connected previously. Evacuation to a safe comfortable place would be a relief.

'As soon as water enters the garages, Michael will phone a friend to ask if our family can come over for a couple of days. Or if he can't put us up, Michael would book us into a room at a hotel. Failing that, I would locate the nearest public evacuation refuge or centre. We would go there, taking suitcases and bags with our things.

'When water starts coming into my living room, we will carry up my Japanese screen doors to the staircase landing above. The water might rise in in the garage basement past the 2022 flood level (5.9 m) up to the garage ceiling level reached in 2011 (6.9 m) before it would enter the living area. We would lift up chairs onto tables and find a high place to put the TV. There would be too many endangered items to rescue each carefully from the encroaching water. An all or nothing strategy would be to throw items in a jumble into storage boxes. The alternative would be to abandon things to the ravages of the floodwater.

'When the flood level reaches the living room, water would be flowing over my back lawn, where people from all 6 units could be coming down by stairs and escape ladders, to walk through to safety. We would evacuate and accept loss of my things remaining in my apartment, when we have raised as much of my property up as high as possible. By then the walls, floors and ceilings would be swelling and slumping.

'Are there any questions?'

There were a few details to clarify. My plan seemed to be accepted. I gave out copies of my Emergency Preparation Checklist, in Appendix 1.

I was fortunate to have Grania and Leigh living with me. In a flood, their heads would be level and their presence appreciated, whether I stayed or evacuated.

The paralysis from flooding of my home could be prevented by preparation, including a rehearsal of quitting the building, like a fire drill. Heidegger's prescription, to live ready for death, could prevent panic. By following my plan, I would take care of my people and my property coolly and calmly.

Living at home with Grania and family support, I would not need residential care for many years. I was able to cook and do household chores. I was able to walk in the park, to the supermarket and catch the bus into the City. I borrowed Michael's car for trips, or if he was using it, took a taxi. I wanted to stay in Unit 2 as long as possible. I did not want to be in a residential home, uprooted and transplanted amongst strangers.

My planning for the twilight of my life with Grania unsettled Leigh and she left.

'Three's a crowd,' Leigh said. 'The two of you can look after each other. I am going to live with younger friends. I want to raise a child.'

'We want you here,' Grania said. 'You can raise Amir.'

'It's kind of you, but I think Michael is managing very well,' she said. 'My friends need to achieve balance like you two have and I can help them.'

Grania and I were sad when Leigh left, because we loved her dearly. We had each other but her absence left gaps. We became more dependent on each other, sharing the cooking and chores. It was her independent viewpoint we most missed.

I heard of an elderly person who employed a live-in housekeeper, a university student. The student received room, board and an hourly rate. I mentioned this to some students in my reading group, but no-one showed any interest in living with us. I imagined that living with an elderly couple would limit a young person's social activities and detract from the image they wanted to project of their home.

'Sharing a two-bedroom apartment with an elderly person could have more close encounters than a young person would be comfortable with,' I said.

'Young people's hours, noise and intrusion could be off-putting,' Grania said. 'We get along together well enough, but the apartment isn't designed for living separately from boisterous youngsters.'

I had some thinking to do about how long I could live there. Grania was a few years younger and excellent company. Ours would be a mental competition to find the last one understanding.

I gave Michael and Amir space to build their new lives. My role was the same as the spent husk of a mature salmon after spawning. I would die soon, leaving my offspring to forge new lives, migrating to the ocean and returning, as they had done. I would try to enjoy my remaining contact with them.

My only regret was not to have risen further to prominence during my career in the coal mining industry, in science education, or afterwards as a writer. If I had stayed in mining, instead of going teaching, I might have gained the aura of a coal baron, known by fame and fortune. Instead the impression I had made was as a maverick. I had stayed on the periphery, close enough to see how the game was played. I saw enough to disdain the bluff and bluster. Frustrated, I had left those jobs.

Although in my work I hadn't achieved the laurels I had wanted, nor fulfilled all my potential, the career phase of my life was over. I continued writing the memoir that I hoped would reveal what should be done about flooding of the Brisbane River.

Now I looked forward to many more years with Grania. I hoped we would be able to take care of each other.

CHAPTER 44 NEW BRIDGE

A new bridge across the river was proposed to be constructed, near the ferry and bus terminals, crossing the river opposite my apartment building. It would intrude on recreation in Orleigh Park. There were glorious trees, grass lawns, paved paths, bicycle lanes, playgrounds, barbecues and shelters. It was already a busy transport hub and could become congested. The plan was for a pedestrian and cycling bridge above the highest possible flood level. It was doubtful that the new bridge could be above the huge height of the 1893 flood.

The new bridge was one of several planned by the Council.

Howard and I met with the bridge project design team at a community forum where they answered questions.

I was concerned that when the river was in flood, the new bridge would constrict flow and raise heights of major floods significantly. Slowing of the river would raise backwater and worsen flooding upriver from the bridges. The bridge proposed would block floodwater flowing along the flood plain on both sides, possibly raising flood height to a new tipping point.

BCC officers claimed the new bridge would be above flood height, but they didn't disclose the maximum flood height in their design. An extreme flood, like that in 1893, could hold back flotsam and slow river flow, with disastrous consequences for us at Orleigh Park. We could do nothing to avert flooding caused by the new bridge, besides pressing the Government to prevent unnecessary obstacles being constructed that would block the river when it is in flood.

'The bridge will not block the river,' a Council officer told us.

'Backwater from the bridge pillar support islands will raise the river level when it is in flood,' I asserted.

'The effect will be small. It is insignificant.'

I said to Howard later: 'Their reassurances lack credibility. They were vague and uninformed about flooding, as if they were playing a game.'

The new bridge seemed unlikely to have enough people crossing it to justify it. The campus is isolated, with access on three sides blocked by the river. The university has an enrolment of 39,000 fulltime equivalent. In my opinion it has already reached its optimal student population. Further growth will require too much transport infrastructure and destroy the familiarity and cohesion existing within the university community.

At present students can cross the river to the university by ferry and by bus, with a short walk to their study destinations. Building a connecting bridge would not improve campus access.

'A student residing in West End is unlikely to experience much university campus life,' I said.

'A campus culture is beyond the experience of most Brisbane people,' said Grania. 'Economic circumstances make it difficult for students to live away from home. Consequently, their social experience is limited to family and school friends. They don't meet new or different people, limiting their intellectual development. University students should reside on a campus.'

'Why is there a frenzy of apartment building at West End?' I asked. 'Students should reside at St Lucia, close to the university. Building of student accommodation in St Lucia is being resisted to keep new student accommodation off-campus and preserve St Lucia for influencers who live there. When they were students, they didn't live on the campus. Now they are owners blocking today's students from benefitting.'

Students should live in purpose-built flats and participate in campus cultural events, rather than commuting across the river from distant locations in the City,' I said. 'If they lived close to the university, they would have more intellectual freedom and liberality, uninhibited by family living, as is standard at many universities overseas.

There was rampant construction of residential apartments in West End, caused by the BCC's plan to transform the suburb into a worker dormitory connected to the CBD by pedestrian bridges. Most of the apartments constructed lacked the independent studying spaces that students require. Students could be uncomfortable in recreational spaces shared with city workers and unable to afford expensive amenities. On campus accommodation would be more desirable, closer to a creative campus-centred culture.

My opinion is that the need for new bridges was contrived by a city council that had designated rapid growth of West End. The population was planned to grow at 4.2% p.a. from 2016 to 2036, a breakneck rate for urban growth, greater than any Brisbane suburb except South Brisbane, with the average for City suburbs at 1.1% p.a. The growth bubble was unnecessary, inefficient and unpleasant. Orleigh Park was crowded at weekends, with family or group gatherings. Compared with other suburbs, the Kurilpa Peninsula has a deficiency of open spaces for residents to use and the new bridge would take space away.

'When a new bridge is constructed it could threaten outlook, activities and safety at my apartment,' wrote to the Council. 'I am sceptical that the river crossing is needed. I have not seen a feasibility study for the project and the design parameters are not transparent. I attach questions for the Council's bridge planners to provide detailed answers.

'I believe that the new bridge will worsen flooding.'

Superman could see potential for reducing flooding by stopping the bridge.

'UNNECESSARY FLOODING IS SOMETHING I DEFINITELY FIND OFFENSIVE.
IT'S NOT WHAT YOU DO . . . IT'S ABOUT ACTION.
TRUTH, JUSTICE AND A BETTER TOMORROW.'

CHAPTER 45 RIVER OBSTRUCTION

The height and severity of floods is largely dependent on the rate and duration of rainfall, but other factors also play a significant role. The river's meandering course, winding through Brisbane's riverside suburbs, creates obstacles to the flow of water, especially when heavy rain causes the flowrate to be greater than normal. The bends in the river's course cause friction, making it difficult for the water to discharge quickly into Moreton Bay and as a consequence the level rises. Buildings, earthworks and roads constructed on the flood plain reduce the floodway, obstructing flood water flow. When the river in flood is slowed, it can deposit large quantities of sediment at the heart of the city, causing the river to burst over its banks.

Orleigh Estate where homes were washed away in 1893.
-State Library of Queensland

Superman told me he had used his super-sensing ability to discover 'fallenness', or degradation of the river channel, due to sediment and obstruction by bridge pillar islands, jetties, promontories and embankment earthworks. He said the fallenness of Dasein was, according to Heidegger, a fall from a purer and higher 'primal status', which could be natural river flow. Falling is a definite existential characteristic of Dasein itself. We cannot ascribe to Dasein a sense of a bad and deplorable ontical property of which, perhaps, more advanced stages of human culture might be able to rid themselves. In short, this was not blameworthy nor irremediable.

Building the city out on stilts over the river had been proposed and rejected, because of the obstruction to flow during flooding. One developer had extended a quay out into the river, to increase the area for their customers' recreation. They took away some of the river channel because they could. The area gained was not essential to their design and it was simply a case of greed.

Many small obstructions together amounted to major restriction.

'Keeping the river floodway free of obstruction is owed to residents upriver who would experience worse flooding,' I said. 'The river channel is marred by obstructions that prevent flood discharge.'

'How much do they intrude?' asked Howard when I told him. 'Is it a serious problem?'

Superman investigated.

'THE PROBLEM IS SERIOUS! BEFORE THE CHANNEL WAS OBSTRUCTED, THERE WAS LESS FLOODING, MAYBE 10,000 HOMES HAVE BEEN FLOOD-IMPACTED BY THESE INTRUSIONS.

'The river channel was deepened between 1893 and 1996, without a major flood, then dredging ceased and there have been two major floods, in 2011 and 2022,' I said. 'The major floods coincide with river obstruction and blocking of the floodplain by new buildings and bridge support islands. Further construction constricting flood flow has been approved recently.'

'Have you complained?' Howard asked.

'I haven't found any authority that will accept responsibility,' I said. 'The port authority denies there is a problem. I don't have objective data. There is nothing I can see or measure.'

Flooding was being exacerbated in several ways. I had observed a phenomenon of obstruction of the Brisbane River flood water by bridge pillar islands, constructed mid-river to support bridges. I could see that their backwater would raise the heights of floods. I was excited that here was what I was looking for, potential to improve flood water flow.

I could not see or estimate how much flood height was held up ahead of all the bridge support islands but I knew that it was significant. Science had no ready answers. There was potential to reduce flood heights by reconstructing bridge supports, rebuilding or destroying the obstructing bridges.

'Can you find out how much the backwater from the bridge pillar islands is raising the level of the river?' asked Howard.

'I haven't any before-and-after test information,' I said. 'It's a complex phenomenon. At a guess, the river could be raised half a metre by one island, going back to near nothing at two kilometres upstream. It's just a guess.'

'Intuitively, it is large enough to be a measureable effect,' Howard said. 'Backwater is like a ship's bow wave and wake when flow is opposed. Can the effect be measured for a bridge support island?'

'Not directly. When the river is in flood, which is when it matters, it would be dangerous to obtain an empirical measurement,' I said. 'The effect of dredging is also difficult to measure: we will have to rely on expert opinion to back up our logic and intuition. It is subjective and I suppose the reason there is a problem is because the bridge designers only acknowledge objective information when it is convenient and easily measured.'

'Are you sure the problem is significant?' asked Howard.

'I'm sure,' I said. 'It is condoned because it is out of sight and out of mind.'

My superman asserted his view.

'IT DOESN'T TAKE X-RAY VISION TO SEE HOW THE BRISBANE RIVER IS BEING CONSTRICTED BY CONSTRUCTION.

'I will have to take direct action to the people, for their approval,' Superman said.

'Most river bridges have pillar islands constructed in the river channel,' I said. 'The Walter Taylor Bridge is a suspension design without an island, but the rest would obstruct flow of the river. The proposed Kangaroo Point Green Bridge would block the river channel with three bridge pillar islands in the river channel. Brisbane's other 14 existing bridges and several planned, have one or more bridge pillar islands each. They reduce the availability of the river channel for flood water flow, with raised backwater and increased heights of floods.

'The most obstructive bridge could be the Goodwill Bridge, opened in 2001, with a mid-river mast island and about 10 other pillar islands holding up spans to Gardens Point.'

'How significant could be the effect of the islands?'

'I estimate the central island of the Neville Bonner bridge at the Queens Wharf development to be about 10 metres wide and 30 metres long. It could block 7% of the cross section of the river channel, raising flood heights upstream significantly. Queens Wharf also has promontories built out from the riverbanks blocking floodwater flow, reducing the cross section area of river channel in flood by possibly 15%, increasing height of the flood by as much as 15% of 5 metres, which is 0.75 metres for that bridge alone and several metres for all bridges together.'

'If it's that much,' said Howard, 'it's disgraceful.'

'Any obstacle which reduces the area of the flow channel and has surfaces contacting the river water, creates friction when the river is in flood,' I said. 'Water level will be raised upstream and residents' homes could be damaged. Even a few centimetres could be devastating. In 2017 it was reported that the Neville Bonner Bridge pillar island was being resized and relocated, but no details have been published. The utility of the bridge, for pedestrian access to

Southbank Gardens from the casino, must be less than the harm it will do in raising flood levels.

Superman was incensed by the scale of the offenses against floodway flow.

'BLOCKING OF RIVER FLOODWATER DISCHARGE IS UNACCEPTABLE' he said. 'OBSTRUCTIONS MUST BE REMOVED.

'What would be the backwater from all the obstructions?' asked Howard.

'There are maybe 25 bridge islands along the river and more planned,' said Superman. 'There are also 25 ferry terminals on piles at the embankment. In a flood, when they hold back floating debris, the obstruction can be magnified. There are private jetties which can break loose, jam on bridge islands and impede river flow.

'The Southeast Freeway, constructed in 1973 above the riverbank, also has pillars reducing floodwater flow and causing flood damage,' said Superman. 'Reticence of experts to condemn these structures could be because the government is the major employer of structural and hydraulic engineers in Brisbane and none of them would dare criticise the conventions that allow the Government to cause obstruction of the river.'

'The river has been a playground where they have experimented with bridge aesthetics,' I said. 'River flood flow dynamics have been overlooked.'

'It's too late now to get the obstructions changed,' said Howard.

'We can request the approval authority to cancel the new bridge pillar islands they are planning,' I said. 'Another worry is that in 2011, the flood could have caused scouring and settlement of bridge pillar islands (17). Expensive repairs could be needed, or disaster could result.

Superman wanted immediate action.

'WE CAN STOP THEM. WE ARE STRONGER THAN WE IMAGINE.'

Superman left.

I discussed what to do with Howard.

'Superman's theory of the Brisbane River being blocked is a cavalier one,' he said. 'We haven't a shred of evidence.'

'It's sound hydraulic engineering,' I said. 'At my university, in Chemical Engineering 101, we tested water flow in Perspex models of channels. We measured flow effects of various shapes inserted in the channel. The obstacles caused turbulence and slowed flow, causing the water input level to rise. Scaling up from those models to the Brisbane River, the obstacles cause flooding.'

'What if you're wrong?'

'We need reassurance. The responsible authorities must respond to my criticism objectively.'

'How much would the bridge pillar islands have increased the flood height in the 2022 flood?' he said.

'I don't know, but it can be calculated.'

'How much do you estimate?' asked Howard.

'I won't guess. It requires study with a model.'

'Who could do that?'

'The university,' I said. 'But another effect of obstruction is deposition of sediment and that is just as problematic. When we put sand in our model of a channel, we saw it spread along the bottom in laminar flow, until flow sped up and became turbulent. Then the sand was lifted up into the churning water and was carried downstream, until it was deposited where the channel deepened and widened. That is why we need dredging, to remove constriction and maintain the flow rate.'

'Are you sure the channel is blocked?'

'I don't have evidence, but without any dredging being done for the last 27 years, I'm sure sediment has built up and the river is partly blocked now. It took dredging to keep it open before, from after the 1893 flood continuously to 1974 without a major flood. Sediment has continued to be washed into the river from farms. Logically and intuitively, there is a problem.

'It is circumstantial.'

'I agree it is not objective enough by the scientific standard, but my phenomenological analysis allows subjective opinion. People experienced in dredging have published their opinion that flooding of the Brisbane River is being caused by lack of dredging.' (24,29)

'Deepening the river channel can reduce flood heights. Constructing a bridge pillar island in the river has the opposite effect, interrupting laminar flow, causing turbulence, eroding the banks and river bottom, causing siltation and slowing down of flood water discharge. Fifty centimetres of extra flood height could do billions of dollars' damage in Brisbane.

'Why wasn't it studied before they approved the obstructions?' asked Howard. 'Did the licencing authority fail in its responsibility or was the effect rated too small to bother?'

'Both,' I said. 'Bridge engineers don't normally model flow and erosion. The calculations they do would be to show that the bridge wouldn't under normal conditions hold back flow much, ignoring the extreme flooding conditions we're concerned about.'

'There is no authority licencing river constriction,' said Howard. 'There has been an open slather to intrude into the channel in a grab for foundation space.'

I phoned the City Council to find out the authority responsible for approving designs of bridges over the Brisbane River.

I was connected to a civil engineer and told him my concern.

'There isn't an obstruction problem,' he told me. 'Pillar islands have been tested under flood conditions and are not a problem. If you have a complaint, write to us.'

I wrote my complaint in detail and sent it to him but I didn't receive acknowledgement or reply.

'The Council has approved obstructive bridges,' I said to Grania. 'Their testing and criteria have evidently allowed it. There is danger and harm in what is happening. I will bring it to the Council's awareness. The officials I have contacted so far have been complacent, but when there is another flood, I will present the need for change persuasively in the news media.'

Superman was concerned and said he would help gain Council's awareness of the problem.

'THE WAY TO GET STARTED IS TO QUIT TALKING AND BEGIN DOING.'
TRUTH, JUSTICE AND A BETTER TOMORROW.'
Superman sped away.

I posted in the Courier Mail an idea for a news story about river obstruction. They sent a journalist and I told her about my investigation and findings.

'Your allegations that the Council has worsened flooding will be contested,' she said. 'What evidence do you have?'

'The Brisbane River would be obstructed by sediment accumulated in the channel and when in flood by many bridge pillar islands. I know of no measurements and have little data. Peak flood calculations of obstruction by bridge islands and sediment have not been available to me. The Council has claimed authority and diligence as if that should be enough, without providing transparency. There was chronic failure to inform and protect flood-prone people and their homes. Modelling of effects of obstructions was a matter of urgency.'

I told her the narrow objectivity of the architects and engineers didn't sufficiently recognise the cumulative backwater effect of islands and sediment. Their designs met only the outermost functional criteria, beneath which were layer after layer of phenomenological considerations, like peeling an onion. Flow resistance of streamlined island shapes and sand bars was counterintuitive. The designers had not kept up to the standard of modern post structural criteria.

Her article in the Courier Mail was on the front page. Several columns presented my allegation that construction had worsened flooding, followed by the reply of a Council bridge engineer who denied it, without citing any measurements.

'Flooding has worsened because there has been more rainfall,' he said.

'Floodwater is supposed to be held back by dams, not by channel sediments and city bridges.'

CHAPTER 46 DOWN THE TUBE

I stood at the lectern in the Brisbane City Council Chamber, addressing 27 city councillors with our group's proposal for a city-wide underground railway (8).

'The river's natural flow is seriously in the way of existing transport routes,' I said. 'The city is locked into a few river crossings that have become congested as the city has grown.

'Travel across the city is expensive and unavailable to many people. Brisbane's public transport is mired in pandering to private cars, with the lion's share of the city budget being wasted in futile attempts to relieve road congestion and duplicate infrastructure at an impractical hub, Southbank.

'To avoid clashing with road and rail traffic, the river could be channelled through culverts passing under the city. But when the river is in flood, the volume of water could not possibly be hidden underground. We have to somehow minimise the obstruction by the river of traffic passing over, across and under it. We believe the best solution is a circular underground railway with tunnels intersecting the river in two places, well away from the city centre, allowing travellers to move from any part of the city, to any other, without congestion or hindrance.

I projected on to a screen a map of the city and railway proposal. *See next page.*

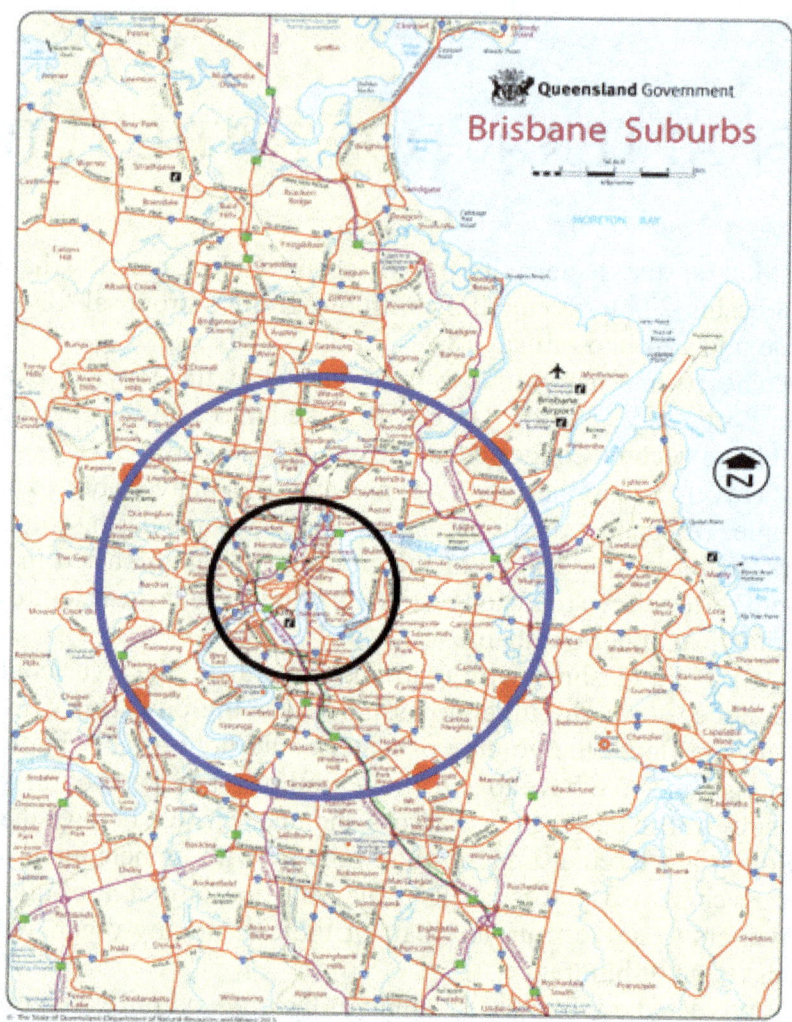

Fig 3 Brisbane Circle Underground Railway Proposal (6)

'Here is my colleague Gerry Hanlon, an infrastructure engineer. He has designed the layout of an underground railway.'

Gerry joined me at the microphone. He explained the map.

'The Circle Line (in blue) passes through seven TODs (Transport Oriented Development centres),' he said. 'The black line is an alternative underground railway around the city centre. It would worsen congestion in the city centre, without enabling people in the outer suburbs to travel across the city.

'Brisbane's public transport provision has been reactive, without integration or planning for the long term,' Gerry said.

'The Queensland State Government's policy standard is that 90% of dwellings should be within 400 metres of an existing or planned public transport stop,' Howard said. 'In 2018 only 61 percent had such a stop (7). Only 12 per cent of Brisbane homes have access to a bus or train stop with services running at least every half hour - the worst of all Australian capital cities.

'We need new public transport that can serve everyone, including developing areas,' Gerry said. 'We are proposing an underground railway to provide public transport of this standard.'

'Why an underground railway?' a councillor asked.

'A large capacity transportation solution is wanted. Thinking outside the box, a circular underground railway, the blue circle, with radius 8 kilometres from the city centre in the CBD, would allow the travellers to pass under the river and city centre without congestion delays. We are proposing an underground railway that is integrated with road, rail, air and river transport. An underground railway could serve as a circular hub, connecting travellers to anywhere in the city.'

'How much would it cost?' asked a councillor.

'Our preliminary feasibility study indicates $30 billions for the first phase,' I said.

Someone whistled.

'Thinking big is required to create a lasting solution for a city of 2.6 millions, the fastest growing in Australia,' said Gerry. 'Public transport provision contrasts with the bold planning in London in the 19th Century, when private underground railways reached out to green field sites, where houses were built for city workers to commute by rail to jobs that enabled them to pay their mortgages.

'Cars have been allowed to dominate in Brisbane, while public transport has languished,' I said. 'Investment has merely increased capacity of existing links, such as the Metro Bus and Cross River Rail projects. Development of the CityCat service has relieved road congestion and the ferry has been a convenient and pleasant option for commuting and tourism.

'Why do we need a circular railway?' asked a councillor.

'It can act as a hub, routing travellers to any part of the city, along the spokes connecting to seven development centres shown on our map. Trains would go around in both directions, allowing journey times to any station in under 40 minutes, with frequent trains. Traffic has been congested because it has had to converge at the inner city, which lacks parking spaces. In a flood, roads, bridges and parking are blocked, bringing road traffic and CityCat ferries to a standstill. A circular railway would avoid all that.'

'Your underground railway would be stigmatised as transport for the masses,' said a councillor. 'Have-nots would benefit most but the haves don't use public transport and wouldn't want to pay for it. Drivers don't see the irony of their selfishness.'

'They pay dearly and still their commuting is taking longer,' I said. 'Our proposed development lacks a champion. The Circle Line would overcome the obstacle of the river and congestion at the Southbank hub. A Circle Line would end the need for proliferation of bridges crossing to the St Lucia university enclave, obstructed during floods.'

'A circular underground railway would have far-reaching consequences,' said Gerry. 'Reappraisal of the future of Brisbane's CBD is required, as a centre for enterprises having city-wide, regional, state, national and international customers. Cultural, educational, medical and recreational pursuits could be located in the CBD, with devolution of some commercial activities to seven Transport Oriented Development Centres (TODs) and others to home working. The TODs are at Indooroopilly, Yerongpilly, Garden City, Carindale, Airport, Chermside and Enoggera. These satellite cities would connect to the CBD as shown in Figure 3.'

'The carrot is devolution of city development, but the stick is congestion of the existing transport corridor,' I said. 'A new Brisbane hub is required to route the growing number of passengers across the Brisbane river, removing the burden of connectivity from the Boggo Road to Roma Street rail corridor and from the Southbank

Metro busway bottleneck. An underground railway circle line, like London's Circle Line, would function as a router, forwarding travellers between stages of their journeys.

'Travellers would be able to cross the city without going near the centre,' I said.

'City retailers would oppose that,' a councillor objected.

'Probably not,' I said. 'Specialties and luxuries would be in the city centre.'

'The Circle Line would reduce development pressure on the river flood plain and help alleviate flooding.'

Gerry answered more councillors' questions.

The Council did not action our proposal, no political leader stepped up to champion it and no party adopted the scheme. The shortfall of the existing system would be most apparent in the next major flood and our scheme could be acted on in future when car drivers realise they needed it.

Brisbane was a city divided by its river, with travel between its parts restricted. The underground railway proposal would bypass river bottlenecks and enable the river's value to be realised as an amenity, rather than disparaged as an obstacle to transport.

This was an ambitious public transport project, blocked by a majority who did not use public transport, who wanted to alleviate congestion on the roads. Our proposal was a sensible solution needing leadership. Chronic neglect of public transport needs continued for a majority of the population.

CHAPTER 47 CLIMATE CHANGE

My perspective on climate change is sceptical, meaning I am not convinced that the rate of climate change is a crisis. I apologise for any seeming disrespect to others' whose beliefs are different. I have arrived at a questioning posture, investigating weather, atmospheric physics and thermodynamics.

In an earlier chapter I considered the difficulties of analysing river flooding by the scientific method, which requires a single viewpoint of a definite object, so that change can be determined as cause and effect. Cyclonic weather and river flooding are too large and complex to be identified so precisely. Climate science has not observed the empirical methods traditionally demanded for acceptance of theories in physics.

Using phenomenology, I can survey the Dasein of the Brisbane River flooding system, including cyclones, to gain subjectively an impression of the significance of climate change without quantifying it.

'So you won't accept that there could have been changes in climate which could cause more flooding?' said Michael.

'Yes,' I said, 'it is possible, but I am not aware of any evidence. I would change my mind if there was compelling evidence of a long term trend of increasing rainfall in the Brisbane River catchment area.'

'By the time the science is worked out, it could be too late,' he said. 'It is good that there is action now to prevent climate change.'

'I don't agree,' I said. 'Alarmists preach urgency falsely, to get public funding of their organisations.'

'You are such a cynic, Dad,' Michael said. 'I can see how you want science to be cautious but you seem to be opposed to the rest of us who want to do something about the effects of climate change.'

Michael invariably was a doer, wanting action rather than correctness. Many people observed a climate change emergency, whereas to me normal weather variations were being catastrophized. I dared to be contrarian and held back from clashing with Michael because our arguments had been vitriolic in the past. Michael and I were evenly matched in acerbic proficiency.

I recognised the topic was emotional with no-one about to change their mind. I could try a different philosophical perspective.

'I am trying to understand the Brisbane climate but climate change is difficult to distinguish from fundamental variability of our climate,' I said. 'A scientific observer-object analysis of Brisbane River conditions, to identify effects of climate change must have one observer and one object, the river catchment system. But a single observer, or viewpoint, or method of observation, cannot observe the whole object of the river and its catchment simultaneously,' I said. 'The prospect for synthesising understanding with a digital model is dismal, not by simulating the physical processes of mass and heat transfer at a scale allowing matching of climate measurements.'

'What do you suggest?' Michael asked.

'Analysis could focus on understanding the Australian climate, what this means for the Brisbane River catchment and any evidence of change,' I said. 'Trying to detect climate change with a local model is a step backwards.'

'Perhaps climate change is like a joker, used to disrupt the main game,' he said.

'Good analogy, Michael,' I said. 'Climate change creates uncertainty that detracts from my analysis of the Brisbane River. To discover a change in climate, the government is bringing all river flood level monitoring under a single national authority. That's a good move.'

'It will take many decades of data to resolve the question,' Michael said.

'Climate changes in Earth history have been extensive, with unknown causation,' I said. 'It is doubtful that changes will ever become predictable by measurement and analyses.'

'Are you saying that investigation of climate change effects on the Brisbane River is a furphy?' asked Michael.

'Yes,' I said. 'All we can do is be alert to possibilities of change. I remain to be convinced there is a crisis. Australia's climate has changed many times in the past. There have been colder and warmer climates before, both briefly and for thousands and millions of years. I don't believe the data we have portends a general trend of universal rapid catastrophic change.'

'It is intuitive that the climate is changing,' Grania said. 'I realise it's not verifiable. It's like belief in God. Some people are believers. Not me, but I will allow that other people could be right. Just because I don't have a defined God, doesn't mean I can't discuss incidents of droughts and flooding with climate change believers.'

'I don't deny your intuition could be correct,' I said. 'My intuition is probably different from others'. The way different viewpoints are usually reconciled is by science or politics. Because the science is too hard, climate change is being resolved by politics and media, which count heads and support, not reasons, as if consensus offers a method of finding truth that can substitute for reason, which it cannot.'

'There is ample scientific evidence that climate change is real,' Grania said.

'I disagree,' I said. 'We differ in our understandings of greenhouse effects. We have different information sources.'

Fortunately, Grania was prepared to listen and our discussion could be friendly, because we stuck to situations and detail we knew about.

'The issue for me is whether climate change affects flooding of the Brisbane River significantly,' I said.

'I believe it does,' she said.

'The mood of Brisbane River's Dasein has people concerned that the climate has changed, becoming warmer and wetter,' I said. 'I have surveyed the Dasein of the Brisbane River flooding system, including cyclones, subjectively, to gain an impression of the significance of climate change without quantifying it. My conclusion is that increased river flooding has been neither measured nor debated and there is a wide range of opinion about climate effects and river effects. Influencers have accepted shortcutting of data without objective analysis. The new understanding has been backed by climate scientists asserting results of modelling, without traditional verification and peer review.'

I mentally considered difficulties of imposing uncertain climate change on the unpredictable Brisbane River. Unexpected flooding of the River could be of more significance for city residents than would be the possible effects of climate change. Two hundred years after settlement, Europeans were still learning local climate conditions, land forms and river systems. Those who had proposed a site for the city selected settlement on the River flood plain, despite frequent flooding there. When major floods occurred, as in the 1840s, the Brisbane River's behaviour was initially regarded as aberrant, as if irregular flooding could not be expected. That view had modified slowly, with heights interpreted as a statistical distribution of the normal model. Normal flood heights are asserted to be changing with climate change, but the part of change attributed to climate change is unable to be distinguished.

'Climate change has been adopted as a dystopian spectacle by the climate change industry,' I said to Grania.

'Post-structuralism has done away with the objectivity canon,' Grania said. 'We live in a post-truth world with people promoting their beliefs by assertion and emotion.'

'A new truth is totalitarianism controlled by a 'woke' autocracy, like Big Brother in Orwell's novel '1984',' I said. 'People don't know what to believe and are too frightened to talk or act contrary. The climate spectacle emerging in the media appears to serve the public good, but its real purpose is to generate profits for investors and support for leaders.'

'I feel sorry for you, Chance, that you are stuck with that idea of climate truth being totalitarian,' said Grania, moderating my vociferousness. 'Climate change is not a conspiracy for everyone. Many sincere people are trying to stop it.'

'I would be content if you would suspend judgement, and allow that climate change could possibly be a hoax, with doubts and reservations to be addressed by scientific research,' I said. 'Measurements comparing climate conditions, across the continent, probably do not exist. I have not seen them published except in polemics disputing data published by the Australian Bureau of Statistics (44).

'Would you say the data published showing climate change, is biased?' she asked.

'Yes. It is often uncontrolled cherry-picking,' I said. 'Dystopian weather forecasts alarm people by the availability heuristic, which seizes on recent, most easily remembered events, such as bad weather.'

'Why is there a bias towards noticing bad weather?' Grania asked.

'The population has adopted a cringing posture,' I said. 'Environmental warming is intolerable to many Australian people because their nation's climate is normally warm or hot. In Canada warming is welcomed by many local people who want it to counter their cold climate. Colder countries can accept acclimatisation. Australian's won't.'

I knew from experience that accusing Australians of local bias did not go down well. It surprised me that it wasn't a centrepiece in debates.

'Do you imagine there is a similar bias of observing wet weather in Australia, because our people are intolerant of more flooding?' Grania asked.

'Yes.'

'That's nonsense,' she said. 'Statistics show wet weather is increasing.'

'99% of statistics are made up,' I said.

'Haha.'

'It is safer to compare theories of how rain forms,' I said. 'Global warming should theoretically hold more water vapour in the atmosphere, but for precipitation to increase, it would take more global cooling to condense it. Without the climate cooling, the possibility of more flooding is equivocal.'

'What is your response to the theory of climate change by fossil fuel combustion emissions?'

'I am sceptical. Critics have shot the infrared theory full of holes.'

'What then is the cause of global warming?' she asked.

'Global warming is exaggerated. It is most likely but a result of overuse and waste of energy by humans. Heat emissions could be causing the warming. The real challenge is for democratic governments and corporate capitalism to reduce amounts of energy used and wasted by their people. Consumption of inessential energy has to be stopped.'

'So you agree fossil fuel energy use has to cease?' said Grania.

There were only four of us present, Grania, me, Michael and Frances.

Grania was widening out the discussion, to consider causes of climate change.

'Less use of fossil fuels and of other sources of energy would be good,' I said. 'If other energy sources like renewables are substituted it would be a backward step.'

'You want less renewable energy?'

'Yes, without a greenhouse theory, it is pointless and would increase entropy (8).'

I had told her that spent electrical energy from wind turbines and solar panels would cause as much global warming as heat emissions from fossil fuels and hydro. I didn't accept that solar energy was being trapped by traces of so-called greenhouse gases. The Earth is kept warm by all the gases of the atmosphere.

'We'll never agree about that,' said Grania. Our discussion of supposed scientific evidence had not found agreement. 'Let's get to practicalities. How should riverside dwellers protect themselves?'

'Brisbane people living in flood-prone homes should not sink into a bovine torpor as they wait complacently for devastation by a 1-in-80 years flood they believe will be hastened by climate change,' I said. 'They can require governments to mitigate flooding. They can improve the resilience of their homes and moderate their energy waste and consumption. They can petition the government for compensation for their flood losses and to buy-back the flooded homes they were tricked into buying.'

'On the other side, there are those who would wrest relief from flood victims in the belief that they have wrongly chosen to live in a flood-prone place,' Grania said. 'That is inhumane. Provision of public funds is not withheld from victims of self-abuse, such as addicts. Relief to flooding victims could be more authentic, impassioned and urgent. The tendency is to devolve risk of flooding to 'have not' people exposed to unscrupulous real estate agents.'

'I agree,' I said. 'Compensation should be available to all flood affected people, whether the climate is changed or not. I don't see why people inundated on Kirbati should have more protection than people on the Brisbane River floodplain.'

'The pattern of Brisbane River flooding has been erratic and predictions are uncertain. Superimposition of theories of climate change would confound any mitigation or compensation proposals,' said Grania.

'I doubt that the role of climate change will become clear,' I said. 'Flooding is an extreme event. I doubt that changed cyclonic conditions will be able to be forecast for many decades, if ever. In the meantime, exaggeration of changes, biased sampling and over-reaction prevent reasonable responses.'

CHAPTER 48 SEA LEVEL RISE

'Sea level rise could theoretically cause Brisbane River flooding,' I said. 'A rise in sea level at the river outfall into the Pacific ocean could delay subsidence of floodwater and prolong inundation inland.'

Precisely measured records of sea level rise are few. I will contend that universal sea level rise is illogical.

'How is it illogical?' asked Grania.

'Sea level cannot rise the same amount everywhere, because where could the water come from? Glacier melt water would not be sufficient for a significant rise. I would like you to meet a friend, Robyn, a geophysicist, who denies universal sea-level rise. She is coming to Brisbane soon.'

'I would like to meet her,' Grania said.

I asked Robyn to lunch at a Turkish bistro in West End. Robyn chose a lamb wrap and I had a hamburger. While we ate, we caught up on our news. Grania was with me but she wouldn't reveal herself. She whispered her questions to me, to ask Robyn. I asked Robyn about sea level rise.

'Wouldn't the ocean surface rise equally everywhere?' I asked her. 'When Venice goes under, would flood-prone homes in Australia be threatened?'

'No,' she said, smiling. 'Rise is relative to land. Have you any data showing sea level in Australia is changing?' she asked.

'The water level in Sydney Harbour has been measured to increase 15 inches in the last 150 years, one tenth of an inch each year,' I said. 'It is only a couple of millimetres, but enough to be concerning. London, Venice, Kirbati and Australia may be neither sinking nor experiencing higher sea levels. The movement may not be regular or uniform: measurements are needed.'

'They could be local effects,' she said. 'They don't indicate sea level is rising there.'

'But ice is melting,' I said.

'I agree it is,' she said. 'But melting of floating ice would not raise the water level.'

'That doesn't sound right?'

'You can test this with a half-filled glass of water and ice cubes. By Archimedes Principle, a floating object displaces its own weight of water and the ice exactly fills the space left by its weight when it melts. As the ice melts in the glass, the water level stays the same.'

'So the disappearance of floating Arctic ice won't raise the sea level?' I said.

'Not one iota,' she said.

'What about ice that is not floating?'

'Antarctic ice is partly grounded and some melt water would run off the land into the sea which could raise the water level world-wide a tad, relative to the land. Retreat of glaciers may have been caused by reduction of snowfall in their catchments. With less snow and the melting glacier removed, the land would be buoyed up and would probably rise. So melting of grounded ice would not cause sea level to rise relatively to land and it could even cause sea level to fall.'

'How could the land rise or fall?' I asked.

'But land and ocean do not take up vertical positions independently,' Robyn said. 'Land floats in raft-like plates, on the Earth's magma mantle, the same as the ocean floor floats on magma below the thin crust. Sea level change compares the position of a continental plate with water above an ocean plate, at a location.'

'Doesn't the land rest on the sea bed?' I asked.

'Yes, but the sea bed is buoyant. It is part of a thin flexible crust, resting on magma, that is circulating in the mantle between subduction zones and mid-ocean ridges,' she said. 'The land can rise or sink on a timescale of millions of years. The seabed, crust and magma levels change continually.'

'So the ocean and land are both floating on magma?'

'Yes,' she said. 'That is plate tectonics theory.'

'Can sea level change be measured accurately?' I asked.

'No,' she said. 'Remote sensing from space can't observe the relative levels of land and sea on Earth. Whereas a global positioning system in a car can measure horizontally within a few metres, it would be impossible to measure vertical position change of a few millimetres a year, because vertical telemetry from a satellite in geostationary orbit at a height of 35,786 kilometres is not that accurate. Sea level change is too small and changing too slowly for remote sensing from space. There would be great difficulty in controlling measurements.'

'What has to be controlled?' Grania whispered in my ear and I asked Robyn.

'A change measured could be due to orbit decay of the GPS satellites, meteorological changes, wave height variation, spring tides, storm surges and atmospheric pressure changes,' she said. 'Only when everything else has been excluded can sea level change be deduced to be the cause.'

Robyn finished her wrap.

'That was good,' she said.

'Would you like a desert?' I asked her.

We had baklava, sweet and delicious.

'How can tides be excluded,' I continued questioning her.

'The greatest effects are spring tides, at the New and Full Moons. Then gravitational pull of the Moon can pull up the ocean and river outflow would slow down, but 6 hours later the opposite occurs and the river outflow would speed up. Diurnal tide changes are predictable but longer term sea level changes are difficult to predict.'

'It is incredible that sea level rise can't be measured absolutely.'

'Here's a true story about sea level rise', I said. 'When I was a kid on the farm in England, we lived at the coast near Stolford and Steart, hamlets on the Somerset Levels. Fields next to the beach were below the high tide level and protected by an artificial pebble bank several kilometres long. It was maintained by bulldozers, with costs shared between the farmers whose land was protected. Water from the land drained through channels and out through sea doors in the bund, which swung shut automatically and prevented backflow at high tides. On several occasions, the pebble bank was breached in storms, or the doors were jammed open by driftwood and the land was flooded with salt water, drowning livestock, destroying crops and killing pastures.

'Was there evidence that the sea level was rising at your farm?' Robyn asked.

'No. When they stopped repairing the pebble bank, the sea breached it and flooded thousands of acres of land previously grazed by sheep.'

'Why did the sea come in?'

'They didn't stop it. It was too expensive to repair the pebble bank.'

'The Earth's crust could have been sinking locally, or the water level could have been rising,' I said. 'Controlled measurements were not available and the flooding was indistinguishable from other breaches that had occurred for centuries.'

'Was there a way to attribute change in level to the sea, or to the land?' Robyn asked.

'Either the sea level was rising, or the land was sinking, or the sea would not have come in.'

'We don't hear many stories of land sinking. How could there be universal sinking? Where would the land go?'

'People who live on shallow sand islands are sensitive to change in the ocean relative to the land and testify that the sea level is rising. There are many reports of flooding due to sea level rise; but they are not unmotivated and the land could be sinking. They could want to blame other nations, to get compensation, or get concessions for their people to seek refuge in Australia. Their testimony is local and may lack control of land level, tides and weather.'

'Do you believe Kirbati is sinking?' I asked,

'I don't know,' she said. 'There could be an island or two sinking near there. A couple of others would be likely to be rising. There could be heaps of sinking and rising going on around the coasts of Australia and other places.'

'Without measurements, no-one knows.'

'I have predicted local sea level changes from a knowledge of logic, physical principles and plate tectonics,' said Robyn. 'I am sceptical that sea level change could be a universal process. An increase in water level in one place is theoretically likely to be balanced by a decrease in water level at another. It could be that land has submerged because the local tectonic plate has moved down, or risen nearby where sea level is falling.'

'The geological record has large changes of sea level, hundreds of metres, over long periods.'

'Yes, sea level could certainly change at a location. It is doubtful that such changes would be universal.'

'Coffee?' I asked her.

The coffee was Turkish, made with unfiltered finely ground beans in demitasse cups. We added sugar but no milk or cream. We savoured the thick strong sweet liquid, leaving the grounds at the bottom of the cup.

'There is no reason to believe there is any net global change in sea level,' Robyn continued. 'Rises and falls would probably average out. Several leaders in climate policy are reported to have bought houses beside beaches. If universal sea level rise was kosher, wouldn't they have bought inland?'

'What about warming causing water to expand?' Grania whispered in my ear.

'Could ocean warming cause rise in sea level?' I asked Robyn.

'Thermal expansion from warming of oceans is too small to have much effect on their level,' Robyn said. 'Flooding of Venice and London has been occurring for a long time. There are some places like Kirbati where sea level is rising at an alarming rate, too fast to be warm water expansion. If that is correct, authorities are right to protect the people.'

'I agree,' I said. 'There are places where sea level is falling and they may need to protect people too. Harbours could dry out leaving fishing boats stranded.'

'There is no reason to believe the ocean and land have moved universally in relation to each other,' Robyn said. 'Measurement of sea level change relative to land is too difficult and impossible to attribute. I am open-minded to any local evidence of sea level rise. Until there is a significant rise locally, there is not much that can be done except to relocate cities to higher ground,' I said. 'It could be done gradually, as a sort of mini-migration. Or by adaptation. But drastic action may not be necessary. Sea level could rise, fall or stay the same, at any time. Sea level rise at the Brisbane River outfall will be too small to reduce discharge of floodwater.'

'Is a tsunami possible here?' I asked.

'No,' she said. 'Brisbane city centre is 23 kilometres from a coast ringed by islands. The closest earthquake zone is at New Zealand and a wave would have to cross the Tasman Sea, then flow over the islands and traverse shallow Moreton Bay, which does not seem possible.'

'The Brisbane River could be changing its level by cutting down its bed by erosion,' I said. 'Or it could be changing in other ways we don't know about. The River has changed dramatically in geological time. Sea level rise here is possible but it cannot be inferred from sea level rise elsewhere.'

'There seems to be little possibility of sea level rise significantly affecting flooding of the Brisbane River,' Robyn said. 'The concern about sea level rise is unfounded.'

'Islanders facing inundation should be helped, perhaps with migration,' I said. 'So can floodplain residents. Governments can incentivize living away from floodplains and above floodable beaches.'

I had found no evidence of sea level changes that could affect the Brisbane River. Several claimed causes of sea level rise are unfounded or have been exaggerated. In my view, significant causes are local. Measurements of local rises and falls in levels are needed.

CHAPTER 49 BRISBANE SAILING PORT

My understanding of the future had Dasein ahead-of-itself, because climate change and sea level rise had self-projected longer term possibilities, temporalizing the more distant future.

When I published my dystopian speculative fiction novel 'The Grass Is Always Browner' (14), I discussed my story with book reviewers from Brisbane's newspaper, the Courier Mail. They were concerned that I had forecast flooding of Brisbane due to sea level rise when this had seemed likely. They didn't recognise my story as speculative fiction and didn't review it because my story would reduce prices of houses for too many readers.

I had imagined a famine-stricken and flooded city 250 years in the future and described what could occur. I had extrapolated technological trends and climate alarmism, creating a story about inundation of Brisbane City due to a large rise in sea level.

'I am having difficulty imagining the Dasein of the River in the distant future,' Grania said.

'A friend has put together an animated video recording of a future we can expect,' I said. 'It is an imaginary tour of Brisbane City, in a motorised gondola, in a group with the State Premier, 250 years in the future.

'The tour commences with a visit to the breach in the embankment, which had occurred when a storm surge four years previously had overtopped the levee surrounding the city. Emergency workers had tried, but failed, to sandbag the opening and a large area of the city had flooded. The breach had been repaired, but the city remained flooded. I screened for Grania a video recording our tour.

'The video is 10 years old,' I said. 'It was made when a large sea level rise caused by climate change was expected and a bund was built along both banks of the river to keep the swollen river in its channel. Recently, a revised forecast has lowered sea level rise and an update of the video would have less flooding.

Here we are gliding along inside the riverside embankment, through flooded city streets in a Gondola powered by electric batteries. Workers have driven in steel piles, to close the breach with a retaining wall. The river flows between two levees, above the city.

'The city centre has been flooded ever since the breach occurred during a spring tide.

'Construction of overhead walkways and new waterside restaurants has allowed city life to resume.

'The middle floors of most buildings are still occupied, as walk-ups. The upper floors are without electricity for lifts. We are gliding down Marta Street to Brahiminy Place. Now we're returning up Oodgeroo Street to Albert Holt Bridge.'

'The Premier, who the people know as Transcending One because of her spirituality, stands at the bow rail, with a forest of masts behind her. Sea transport has reverted to sail, because fossil fuel use is banned. In the harbour, ships are moored side by side.

'Here between Albert Holt Bridge and Crossing Point is the tidal harbour, crowded with sailing vessels. Ships leave daily for all points of the compass. The ships are catamarans with sails made from flexible sheets of solar cells, allowing them to use the wind to tack upriver, without lowering their masts. Six bridges have been dismantled and the concrete has been used to build a wall under the riverside freeway, to exclude the tidal waters from the city centre.

'The harbour has passenger and cargo sections. You can hear the sailors' shouts, watch cargoes being unloaded and smell the produce from foreign parts, such as fruit, coffee, cotton and coca leaves. Local ships bring, from paddies in the north, staples such as rice, graize and preans.

'Gantry cranes swing containers over the embankment onto waiting barges.

Our party, with T.One, goes aboard a riverboat.

'We are going downriver with the outgoing tide, through a winding canyon of levee banks, like a bobsleigh down its luge.'

We glimpse the city over high embankments, widening out to coastal sea walls. Then panoramic shots of island jetties, focussed on welcoming parties, wading out from beaches to meet us.

'I am on a campaign visiting islands of the bay at the river mouth,' T.One spoke to the camera. 'They are all that remains of the string of sand islands that have been washed away by ocean waves.'

Receding jetties with waving groups of island people. My camera lingers on the pleased faces of the locals as they greet T.One.

'I have had a busy and successful day visiting the Moreton Bay Islands,' she said. 'Now we will return to Brisbane with the tide.'

A camera shot across the city from over the levees, with tributaries pooling into lakes behind the embankments. My camera pans across the empty river estuary.

'Down here near the mouth of the River, flooding has submerged the airport, oil refineries and fertiliser plants. Without petroleum and natural gas they are obsolete. The jetties are used for fish farming. Defunct aircraft are used for restaurants, bars and theatres.'

'Beside the embankment a wind turbine is turning slowly. It is one of fifty that pump out water from behind the levee banks. It will be years before the water is pumped dry from the whole flood plain of the river. Even without further flooding, storm water has to be pumped out into the sea.'

'We hope you have enjoyed this insight into the Brisbane River,' I said as our party disembarked.

The video finished.

'Thank you, Chance,' Grania said. 'I liked the city video tour very much. I didn't realise transport by sailing ship could revive. Because sea level rise is now expected to be lower, things won't be quite as desperate, will they?'

'No, but the levee programme is a scam,' I said. 'The city is flooded with investors and workers are building bunds that are no longer necessary.

'The levee programme may have been overdone, but in China, the great Yangtze River had dykes built along its banks and tributaries', in the 1950s. Some dykes burst in the 1998 flood disaster and have been removed. The dykes help control annual flooding of the Yangtze River, 20 times longer than the Brisbane River, with 25 times more fall from the source to the sea. On a smaller scale, levees could protect Brisbane from river flooding. Flooding propensity depends on river catchment and rainfall, not river length.'

'Will changing to sailing ships make much difference to climate change?' Grania asked.

'What climate change?' I said. 'The climate has always changed and will continue to change. Dasein is ahead of itself futurally.

'IT DOESN'T TAKE X-RAY VISION TO SEE THEY ARE UP TO NO GOOD,' my Superman said, impatiently.

I high fived Grania. 'TRUTH, JUSTICE AND A BETTER TOMORROW.'

She repeated the mantra.

'My prediction of a sailing port 250 years in the future is for a different prediction of Brisbane River flooding. A sailing port is a logical extrapolation of constraints to counter climate change on fossil fuel combustion by ships and aircraft. The extent of city flooding from sea level rise is now expected to be less than the scenario assumed in the gondola video. The flooding has been exaggerated.

PART 6

AQUAPHILIA

CHAPTER 50 RISKS PEOPLE TOLERATE

'Not everyone living in a flood-prone home is fearful of dying,' I said.

'You're kidding,' said Grania. 'People don't want to think about dying. Young people especially won't want to know.'

'That is silly,' I said. 'Heidegger's 'Being There' acknowledged death as our own-most potentiality. It revealed a side of existence usually glossed over, too embarrassing to be discussed. Confronting my own death disclosed to me my own-most authenticity, in a transient mortal way. Until I know my mortality, I need to live authentically with urgency. The time to live authentically is now. I can't put it off. I have to live out my deepest possibilities.

'I suppose being in impassioned freedom-towards-death is attractive, even heroic,' said Grania.

'Flooding occurs in Brisbane irregularly with different severities, similar to seismic forces causing quakes in earthquake zones,' I said.

'Perhaps living in a flood-prone apartment is like living in an earthquake zone,' said Grania. 'Your life hangs by a thread.'

'Quakes are variable and unpredictable like floods,' I said. '20 earthquakes of magnitude greater than Richter 4.9 impacted Los Angeles County between 1769 and 2014, with a maximum of 120 deaths and $20 billion property damage. About 30 earthquakes occurred every day in Southern California. Most have a magnitude of less than 2.0 and are seldom felt. Many quakes are attributed to the San Andreas fault. Mitigation, if possible, would be expensive. People who live there accept the risk.'

'Does raising awareness of quakes and floods benefit people?' Grania asked.

'Waiting on the Brisbane River floodplain for possible flooding can be stressful. Chronic danger can disable people, affecting them compared with people who are not so exposed. Stress can affect physical and mental health.'

'People get used to living in a nanny state, with responsibility for likely risks taken care of by authorities, as they do for road accidents, axe murders, electrocutions, radioactive fall-out, chemical plant explosions, abductions, falling from a height, food poisoning and terrorism. People expect to be kept safe and they let tomorrow take care of itself.'

'How do individuals reconcile themselves to risks they can't escape from?' said Grania.

'People say 'I don't think about it. If it happens, too bad.'

'Does everyone want to be in the same boat?' asked Grania.

'They say there is safety in numbers. It is why birds flock,' I said.

'They prefer to be in a large group when they are threatened,' Grania said.

'I am one of many who are vulnerable to flooding,' I said. 'Everyone is at risk of something.'

'Not exactly,' said Grania. 'As an actuary, it helps me to imagine my risk with a statistical model. Each flood is independent of others, past and future. Further floods can fit a 'normal' model of random binary complex causation. The data appears random, with abnormal events occurring less frequently, but there could be other models, such as Poisson's distribution, which would predict a high frequency of intervals without floods, or with small floods, with a tail of infrequent large floods. Major floods have seemed to fit Poisson better than the Normal, meaning that the intervals between high floods would be further out on the tail, with low frequency.'

'I like that approach,' I said. 'People imagine causation by external agency, such as intercession by a God. Or flooding could follow a pattern they have identified. To redeem their risk they could make a sacrifice to a divine power, as if their non-observance is being reprimanded.

'I am agnostic and do not assign my safety to a higher power,' I said.

'How would you rationalise your situation?' she asked me.

'I would accept a large loss because it had been compensated for by the enjoyment I have had during many flood-free years,' I said. 'My enjoyment is existential and at many different times, whereas loss in a flood would be a sudden wrench. I want to face that loss as a necessary sacrifice, braving it without cringing.

'Our hardships from flooding of the Brisbane River are caste in the same moulds as bushfires, igneous activity and diseases. They are unpredictable. Having been partly successful with two dams, Brisbaners will probably forget about flooding until the next disaster. I am disappointed how flooding is accepted as if nothing can be done about it. I have ideas for relieving flooding.'

'One person can't do much when most don't care. Perhaps your dreaming will only make you unhappy,' Grania said.

'When I was young I could live with danger but now I sometimes feel horribly exposed,' I said. 'My amygdala pumps adrenalin and causes me to freeze, fight or take flight. Risks such as Covid and river flooding, cause me consternation because remedial actions may not be sufficient to protect me. Danger is unfamiliar and alarming. Chronic anxiety can induce in me post-traumatic stress disorder. It is terrifying, not at all like dreaming.'

'When a home has been built up over a lifetime and benefitted members of a family, flood damage draws down on that credit,' Grania said. 'A generous view could be that flood damage has already been paid for. However, losses due to flood damage are likely to rankle. I don't think I will be able to give up on wanting flooding prevented.

'I will try to accept that my good fortune to date could have to be repaid in a future flood.'

'When insurance is not available, ownership of a flood-prone home is taking a gamble,' I said. 'The circumstances that could make it attractive could differ for each individual.'

After a flood, people usually continue living there if they can. The effect of any disaster can be to decimate personal wealth. People may not be able to afford to leave. People should be compensated, as they would be for accidental losses from fire, storm or tempest.

CHAPTER 51 DARING

Nietzsche would have regarded living beside a flood-prone river as a dare, an artistic expression of ego, as will-to-power. His *ubermensch* was an overman, an artist, who chose to look down, as a dare-devil, upon the fundamental instincts of power, of nature, of religion and morality. His act of flood-prone living would be an art, with a sensation of surplus energy, on a mission to save people, rather than to gain personal power.

His overman was my hero: Superman, living in a dream:

'DREAMS LIFT US UP AND TRANSFORM US. AND ON MY SOUL I SWEAR UNTIL MY DREAM OF A WORLD WHERE DIGNITY, HONOR, AND JUSTICE BECOMES THE REALITY WE ALL SHARE, I'LL NEVER STOP FIGHTING. EVER.'

Superman inspired me not too see things as they are, but with their usefulness fuller, simpler, stronger. There was a kind of youthfulness, of vernality, a sort of perpetual elation, in my life when I followed these precepts.

'Would you move here again?' Grania asked me. She was naturally cautious and I knew she thought I had made a mistake buying Unit 2.

'Yes, I would,' I said. 'I have liked living here very much. But I would have liked it more if I had known water could flood into my garage. I would have preferred to be like an airline passenger, with flight attendants' directions in case of emergency.

'Foreknowledge does not mitigate hardship.' Grania said. 'Flood dangers are acute, like droughts, bushfires and cyclones. Graziers can suffer a series of droughts but continue because the hard times seem more than offset by good times. The balance is more than monetary: lives, health and minds can be lost or damaged by chronic difficulty.'

'Chronic hardship can add up to as much as acute pain,' I said. 'Living further from my workplace, with further to commute, day after day, year after year, would deduct more from pleasant family living than having to restore a flooded home close to work. It is a dare requiring good luck to come out ahead.

'But the act of daring could stimulate the senses, emotions, creativity, living, talking and writing, of a river person. My physical vigour could overflow and burst forth into blooming life, with artistic works, social accomplishments and extraordinary performances.

Two dams have been built on the Brisbane River and safety from flooding has not much increased. Relinquishing control so that we might take on risky ventures comes to feel foolish, or even impossible. Simply leaving our homes can become a challenge. Dependence on technology can be pathological, a false investment. Technology too easily convinces us that safety is an obtainable condition, giving a false sense of security. We have to think again, that real safety may be too expensive.

Nietzsche saw middle- and upper-class Europeans worshipping safety and he assailed it. He did not go as far as Jesus, who said that one must lose one's life to truly find it, but Nietzsche thought we must be willing to do so.

'For—believe me—the secret for harvesting from existence the greatest fruitfulness and the greatest enjoyment is—to live dangerously! Build your cities on the slopes of Vesuvius! Send your ships into uncharted seas! Live at war with your peers and yourselves! Be robbers and conquerors as long as you cannot be rulers and possessors, you seekers of knowledge! Soon the time will be past in which you had to be content living hidden in forests like shy deer!'

Nietzsche, The Gay Science

'I have dared to live here by the River,' I said to Grania. 'It has changed me. I have taken on Nietzsche's daring and Heidegger's existentialism.'

'I don't have Nietzsche's daring,' said Grania. 'Life has enough adventures for me, without going looking for them. My daring is already taken up by challenges to security and ethics. I wonder that you can entertain risk of flooding with such equanimity. Wouldn't a flood be just too much to bear?'

'I have no entitlement to safety,' I said. 'The adage 'nothing ventured, nothing gained' is a prescription for risk-taking, an exhortation to courage.

'There is much advice about courage and risk taking:

Courage moderates between recklessness and cowardice, fearing things worthy of fear.
Aristotle

He who is not courageous enough to take risks will accomplish nothing in life.
Muhammed Ali

If you are not willing to risk the unusual, you will have to settle for the ordinary.
Jim Rohn

'Living on a river floodplain may attract risk takers, 'I said. 'There is a story that sometime after humans evolved in Africa, the adventurous individuals, generation after generation of them, emigrated in sailboats, beating upwind against the prevailing westerlies, enabling them to cross the stormy Atlantic. Only the fittest of their descendants survived, like Vikings, with determination honed to fierceness.

'Their descendants became the rugged individualists and risk takers who settled along the American seaboard and pushed west,' I said. 'The others, who took the easy option. sailed downwind from Africa, developing human and group skills, living in risk adverse collectives under communism. It is a whimsical story, but explains how ancestral peoples can differ in their propensities for risk.'

'You admire Nietzsche's daring, don't you?' said Grania.

'I do.'

'People who want risk, dream and gamble.'

'Not always. Gambling is a game, having more than one play,' I said. 'Emigrating is not a game. Few people emigrate more than once. The risks don't bear repeating.'

'Few people choose to reside by more than one flood-prone river,' Grania said. 'One is enough.'

'I have emigrated twice and lived by two flood-prone rivers,' I said. 'I have also risked my all with river dams, that they will control the risk of river flooding.'

'Heidegger regarded technological change as potentially dangerous,' Grania said. 'It is sensible to compromise with risk. In Homer's story: the Iliad, Achilles was a warrior who could choose to live a short, risky, but glorious life and be remembered for all eternity. Or alternatively, he could live a long, peaceful life, but soon be forgotten. Achilles chose risk with glory. It is not a recipe for careful living, but many dwellers on river floodplains adopt it, including me. I dare to live here.'

'Technological glory-hunters have a lot to answer for,' I said. 'Dam builders take risks and public funds go to projects that capture imaginations. Their saving grace is that the performance of the dam cannot be tested in an experiment controlled by an identical situation or by turning back the clock for a rerun. We have to live with the failures.'

'Like Achilles, you have technological ambitions,' Grania said. 'Can you live with failure?'

'I live in hope,' I said. 'After setbacks like floods, we simply roll up our sleeves and restore liveability. Humans have adapted to living beside rivers that flood and it is not ideal, but they put up with it. Some have been hurt, a few badly. Learned helplessness is unhealthy, a surrender. Romantics live in hope. Learned optimism is good for you.'

'You're a closet romantic,' said Grania. 'You don't leave your fate to chance winds, but count on supernatural influence to be kind to you. It is dualism. Many intelligent people, aware of scientific explanations, face life's uncertainties not with incredulity, but with fatalism. For you, preventing flooding is like a dream, like countering climate change.'

'My friend Rachel's mantra is 'Trust in God'. Her commitment to a higher power is sheeted home by prayer, good works and sacrifice.'

'Her approach is openly romantic,' said Grania. 'Her mind deals with risk separately from her body.'

'I am not a dualist,' I said. 'I don't need a separate mind to understand flooding beyond its science. Since Aristotle, people have assigned events like flooding to supernatural causes. But it is more logical that the weather systems determining flooding are chaotic.'

'Are you saying the problem with Heidegger's monism is that something beyond comprehension might be concealed from you?' Grania asked. 'Does he expect something supernatural?'

'No,' I said. 'Heidegger was raised a Catholic and became an atheist. But many people have lingering faiths. He didn't deny God. Nietzsche had done that generations earlier. He wanted a more divine god, with more potential. I have no objection to people's prayers, so long as they respect that my response to protecting people from flooding is practical.'

'The faith lingering in you makes you a dualist,' Grania said. Supposing humans evolved from wild animals. Do wild animals decide with their minds and bodies separately? Are they dualists?'

'It's not likely,' I said. 'When female and male Emperor Penguins undertake their annual reproduction ordeal, males and females play different parts. The male, who takes responsibility for incubating the egg, is parted from the female when she goes away to get food. They don't need to think about what to do. They know their different roles instinctively. Their behaviour is monist, with minds and bodies concerted, like mine is in coping with existential flooding.'

'Is it because penguins are irreligious that the minds and bodies of penguin couples act as one?' asked Grania.

'I don't want to speculate about dualism in penguins,' I said. 'Battling flooding with you, I have appreciated your assistance, support, comfort, alternative viewpoint and diversion. You helped me because the need was there, not because we had pre-assigned roles. For daring to live by a river, having a partner is an advantage.'

'Is that your way of admitting you like having me around?' she asked.

'I suppose it is,' I said.

'Be careful not to spoil it.,' she said. 'I don't want to hear that penguin couples are not really in love.'

'Of course not,' I said. 'Their living is an impassioned togetherness-towards-death.'

'That's worse,' she said. 'Is that how authentic we are?'

'Oh yes,' I said. 'It feels good and comes naturally. It seems like love.'

'It is love,' she said. 'Except I'm not sure of the limits of good nature. Can it be distinguished from laziness?'

'What do you mean by that,' I said indignantly.

'Just testing,' she said laughing. 'Sometimes when one of a couple dies, the other does too.'

'Our monism is incontestable,' I said. 'We work together well, with understanding that is intimate. We won't survive independently.'

'I have never thought I would,' she said.

CHAPTER 52 ESCAPE PLAN

I am ready for water to flood into my apartment, with a probability of an event in any year of 1.2%. I plan to escape with my most precious possessions and my life. I will evacuate, with my son, grandson and Grania, to some place of refuge.

I would retain sufficient possessions to sustain a simple lifestyle, while evacuated, without it being Spartan and unpleasant. I have a suitcase ready to put in my car, with precious papers and a file of personal documents. When water reaches Orleigh Street outside, I will drive my car out from the garage into Morry Street. I will park 10 metres higher up than the flood peak in 1893, which would have reached the third floor, had it been built at that time.

While the flood is filling my garage in the basement, I will take the items I value most up into my apartment and raise them as high off the floor as I can. When the water level reaches the ceiling in the garage and is about to come into my living area, I will save what I can before everything is submerged.

I will take photos to submit as evidence of 'before' in an insurance claim and list valuable items before they are submerged. I will have to act quickly. By thinking through my actions with the goal of minimising damage, I will hone my response to automaticity and efficiency, aware that dithering could lose my property.

I have a personal responsibility to Michael to prepare him to take emergency action. His apartment is higher up in the building, with a lower risk of flooding, but the evacuation route from there is the same as mine and we would leave at the same stage of flooding.

I want my family to be safe in a flood. I have owned my apartment for 25 years and know the building well. Atrium is a sound building and has never had flooding above the garage.

Nothing I can do will prepare for collapse of the dams in the event of extreme cyclonic rainfall with catastrophic loss of life. Failure of the Wivenhoe Dam was reckoned by McMahon as 'a probability of one in a million, or something like that'(10). It's very unlikely and difficult to prepare for.

The uncertainty of this estimate does not reassure me of either its accuracy or insignificance. The Dasein of the Brisbane River has a threat of dam failure lurking. River flooding is more likely and an existential threat most likely to occur in the wet season, with warning of only a day or two. Catastrophic failure of the dams may never occur. It's not much of a reassurance, but all I have.

Although my escape plan has attempted to respond to likely flooding, it does not have provision for the kind of catastrophic flooding associated with dam wall failure. I am daring to leave what will happen to fate.

CHAPTER 53 WATER VOLES

The early governors of Brisbane exhorted settlers to build their homes off the river floodplain. Their admonitions were largely ignored. Modern dependence on electrical appliances and electronic technologies has made prevention of flooding of homes even more imperative today, because water conducts electricity. Like the pea that the princess wouldn't tolerate under her mattress, flooding is incompatible with civilised residential living.

Public authorities do not accept responsibility for flooding of homes caused by unusual wet weather conditions. People have to accept unlimited responsibility. Public authorities give warnings and take people to safety. A problem is that extreme events can occur in places never affected before, with unprecedented disastrous consequences.

Development of the city has accepted that certain localities that have never flooded before could flood, because every flood is different, depending on where the rain falls. Places that have been flooded before may never flood again because the dams have been built. Risk of flooding has opportunities for investors. Some individuals have more affinity for flooding than others, accepting or not understanding the risk. Some humans are risk takers and others have inherited, from ancestors, a preference for living near water. I will call their preference for water *aqua-philia*.

We can speculate how mammals adapted to irregular flooding. Water voles are an early non-marsupial mammal, an ancestor of humans. They evolved in areas that flooded and I deduce that some humans who live by rivers could be direct descendants.

Juramaia was a hairy vole about the size of a mouse, with fossil evidence that 160 million years ago, eutherian mammals diverged into marsupials, such as kangaroos, or monotremes such as the platypus, or into placental mammals like voles. Voles were the earliest mammal descendent, suckling their young, like most large animals and their descendants, including humans.

Water voles are small rodents and relatives of lemmings and hamsters. They gnaw like rats, mice, squirrels and porcupines, with strong constantly growing incisors. Their diet is vegetarian, with a few small animals and insects they catch. Unlike bilbies and other marsupials, who carry their young in pouches, young voles reside in a nest. In Britain, water voles live in burrows in river and stream banks, often with a nibbled 'lawn' of grass around the entrance.

Humans could have inherited some characteristics of water voles. Analysis of the fossil skeleton of Juramaia indicates our ancestor was an agile creature with a powerful ability to climb. Perhaps it managed to survive during the age of the dinosaurs by climbing and hiding in trees. Today water voles are found in most of Europe, Russia, West Asia, and Kazakhstan. They excavate burrows within the banks of rivers, streams. ditches, ponds, marshes, reed beds and areas of wet moorland. A preference for living in floodable places may have been passed on to their descendants, including humans.

My boyhood home, on our farm, was near a stream bank riddled with water vole tunnels along a section of 50 metres. I came across these shy and largely nocturnal animals in the farm's grain storage barns, where they went to supplement their diet.

The curious aspect for me was that after a flood had subsided, they returned home and carried on as before. Although they could survive away from flooding, their preference was for waterside living.

Whereas humans decamp or evacuate when their living places are partly flooded, water voles tolerate flooding, remaining in partly immersed burrows. During heavy rain, a vole remains within its burrow, moving to a dry refuge and does not go far afield. It dives in with a 'plop' and is less skilful in swimming than in diving. They are mistaken for rats, with the opprobrium applied to those scavengers and carriers of human diseases. But water voles can live independently of humans. They have many enemies: hawks, snakes, foxes and cats. The youngsters mature quickly, breeding within a year of birth. They live for about a year and can have several litters of 2-7 young, born into nests of grasses and reeds.

Purdue University research has shown that the vole harbours a number of puzzling genetic traits that challenge current scientific understanding. Voles are evolving 60-100 times faster than the average vertebrate in terms of creating different species. The number of chromosomes in voles ranges from 17-64. DeWoody (23) said that this is unusual, since species within a single genus often have only a single chromosome number.

Humans' affinity for water has often been remarked. Our hairless bodies have been said to have evolved like dolphins in an aquatic habitat or shallow sea. Water is an important resource for human agriculture, animal husbandry, fishing, transport and industry. Human urban populations commonly flourish near water, using it for many purposes including washing, recreation, transport, defence and disposal of corpses. But water may also have an atavistic, spiritual and aesthetic significance for some humans, possibly inherited from water voles.

Deep in my brain I am a water vole. I am drawn by forces I do not understand to make my home on a river flood plain. Like water voles, humans' feeding and building transforms the waterside environment as beavers do, creating conditions for themselves and other species to thrive.

I know I belong here, floods and all. I am not sure if my life has been improved by living beside rivers. Perhaps if I had denied my atavistic yearning for water I would have been better off. There have been difficulties of living where I do, but it feels like home and that has strengthened me.

CHAPTER 54 BEING THERE

Sarah and her children came on a six month sabbatical from her university in Canada and stayed with Michael at Atrium. We now had the family home I had wanted to achieve when I bought Unit 4. It was good to be with family at last. I cooked a celebration dinner and they all came down to my place. I felt very fortunate to have my children and grandchildren with me.

I sat on my balcony, with my daughter and son, watching evening walkers in the park and traffic on the river. The children were inside watching a movie, a treat they weren't usually allowed.

The broad reach of the river shivered in the cool evening breeze. In places, the ripples were flattened by an invisible hand, like a patchwork quilt. In my apartment, I was prepared for a range of futures, including water flooding in and over everything, destroying my books and furniture. There is nothing I would be able to do to prevent it. I am prepared to live out my mortality here, soothing my anxiety by living in the moment.

'How do you feel, Dad, living in a place which was almost reached by a flood?' asked Sarah.

'Risk is the price I pay to live at my ideal location,' I said. 'Risk can be psychologically stressful, but it doesn't have to be. Habituation helps - I have learned to ignore heavy rainfall. When airplanes fly overhead, danger doesn't register with me anymore. The probability of an airplane crash is low, as is the likelihood of a flood rising up to my living room. There is an outside chance of a flood that would damage my home, but I don't think about that. I am as prepared as I can be and worrying is pointless. I accept the weather in all its variations. When it is pouring, I tell myself that living here is not for the faint-hearted and divide by two the alarmism on the news and weather reports.'

'It's not worry free, is it?' Sarah said.

'True, but my solace is I have taken ownership of my life in authentic existence,' I said. 'Dasein accepts being flooded, not as a physical event but as existential experience with meaning and intent.'

'How would Heidegger expect you to respond to flooding?'

'Heidegger wanted us to live authentically, reclaiming ourselves from everyday ways of being we have fallen into. His is a cool and calm analysis. Kierkegaard showed how to seek reality and truth through passionate faith. Nietzsche wanted us to down-rate importance of the material world, surpass Christian morality and transcend rationality. Stoics' would reduce negative emotions in their response and resign to honing our virtues of courage, wisdom, discipline and justice. These other philosophies are less objective than phenomenology. Heidegger's authenticity is more appealing, because it is a rational approach. His response to flooding is to look for any potential. He would expect me to exhort the community and its authorities to prevent flooding any way they can.'

'I'm glad you have worked it out,' said Sarah. Few things ever bothered her. She tended to ignore anything unpleasant. 'You are sensible not worrying about flooding,' she said.

'Not everyone accepts an ontical priority of 'Being There' as a state of mind for living here,' I said. 'Denial of flood-proneness, inauthentic talk with inquirers and even dishonesty can affect an owner's evaluation of existence here and his asking price for his property.'

'Many people want to live beside a river and the attraction may be only deterred a little by flood-proneness. Henley on Thames, above London has prestigious residences beside the river, known to flood, where millionaires live happily despite the gloom and doom preached by climate change clergy.

'How has your phenomenological analysis affected your evaluation?'

'I have been able to stand back and consider what the river means to me and what I must do to stay here. I must be ready for possible flooding and will campaign for the City Council to prevent obstruction of flood water, by dredging of sediments and by preventing construction of bridge pillar islands.'

'Did you consider any alternatives for the river?'

'I have proposed crossing under it with a new underground railway, reducing congestion near the city centre. Building of further dams awaits evaluation of effectiveness of two existing dams.'

'When you want to sell, will you disclose the results of your ruminations to a potential buyer, even if they could be put off by it?' Sarah asked.

'No. My price would attract people of daring, who would do their own research.'

'What about a buyer who is naïve about riverside living and would pay a high price?' Sarah asked.

'Inquirers would receive necessary information. It is up to them to check it.'

'Like you didn't do when you bought?' said Sarah.

'I did have the opportunity. So will they. Although it is quite likely that I will give this apartment to you and Michael.'

'Wonderful,' she said. 'Maybe I could come back from Canada and live here!'

CHAPTER 55 WHAT HAS POTENTIAL?

Phenomenology omits from Dasein unprospective presences, with low potential. Its discrimination omits the young, old, weak, ill, disabled, disaffected, politically divergent, or racially few. It is morally wrong because disadvantaged people are entitled to democratic rights. Excluding them is reprehensible, discriminatory, even redolent of eugenics. True phenomenology does not exclude, from moral certitude, the interests of disadvantaged people.

The Cartesian criterion of value is the observer's ego and knowledge. Analyses could serve narrow interests, or reject disadvantaged people's interests, without obligation to explain. Descartes' maxim cogito ergo sum (I think therefore I am) has been the foundation of human knowledge by science, widely selected since the Enlightenment but does it still hold? Post-structuralism wanted selection acknowledged and bias explained. Heidegger's bias in selecting for potential is more transparent than science was earlier.

In my first job, I planned by the scientific method, extraction of minerals and loading them onto trains, without considering effects on local people or the needs of the workforce. Now I investigated the lived experience of Brisbane river flooding, its effects on people and potential for improvement.

Phenomenology can be used for good, or evil, or sometimes for both. If phenomenology's focus is solely on that part of Dasein with potential, the analyst's duty, to consider humane needs, is deficient.

The reality that phenomenology recognises is like a machine-sewn seam, with threads of science and utility, holding reality together, from below and above. If the thread of utility is pulled away, scientific reality is undone and the join unzips releasing fantasy. For science to be useful, it needs phenomenology to imagine potential. If the thread of science is removed from the seam, it unzips from the other side and the utility of the joint is lost.

Analysts can wear Heideggerian 'sunglasses' and look for potential in political, economic and social contexts. The bias of selecting subjects for their potential would reject some people, who could turn resentful. Those deemed to be without potential might not be able to seek reinstatement. Selection of potential in winners is normal in sports and other competitions, but in education the accolades are usually more muted and retrospective. Racial, genealogical and eugenic prejudices may prevail, unless the analyst is vigilant.

My potential as a teacher had faded.
'I am going to quit going to philosophy discussions at the university,' I said to Grania.
'Why?'
'My age is distracting students,' I said.
'What do you think could happen?'
'They will stop coming to tutorials,' I said. 'Already attendance is declining. It is their class and they could resent me being there.'
'Is that fair?'
'Not really. But I suppose they find my input reactionary and contradictory to the potential they imagine. They are uncomfortable with historical contexts I provide.'

The River is a mental construct as well as a physical entity. Phenomenology can identify not only potential for improvement but can find shortfalls in provision to be remedied. Being flooded could have the lived experience of dislocation, trauma and even death. Being flooded must be compared with other hardships, for rational allocation of aid to victims and re-evaluation of capital works.

Victims of flooding can be compared for public assistance to victims of cancer, Covid and bushfires. Recognition of potential could be complicated by disparities of location. The Dasein of a project to mitigate disaster can have public funding with ethical consequences determining political outcomes.

Phenomenology's gaze is screened, like polaroid sunglasses, cutting out the 'glare', from useless things, like being flooded. The Being it acknowledges has ready-to-hand value for the proponent or observer, whose Dasein is a lived experience, not as in Science' method, a stylised interaction between an egotistical subject and an unthinking object. Phenomenology screens out egos and their fantasies.

I have had to rely on intuition more than I wanted to, because observation and statistical analysis of flooding was inaccessible to me. Fallenness of the river, as an authentic conduit for flood water, was evident in proliferation of bridge pillar islands obstructing the river channel. Forward projection was dominated by the thrownness predicted for more flooding due to climate change. Moodedness of flood mitigation, in emotional commentary after the 2022 flood, revealed residents of flood-prone properties were sometimes in hopeless despair. The dams had disappointed them and benefit of damming was perceived by some as ambiguous, merely delaying or exacerbating floods, rather than attenuating them. Expression of this Dasein was not of much interest to most of the city's population, who had not been flood affected. Interest in further restriction of building on the flood plain lacked advocacy and organisation.'

CHAPTER 56 SENSE OF AN ENDING

My physical and psychological journey in search of the ontological beings of two rivers is complete. I have exposed problems overlooked by traditional scientific analysis, by phenomenological analysis. My ontological investigation of the Brisbane River has sought to understand how the river fits into our broader understanding of the world and our place within it. This has involved questions of epistemology and metaphysics, as well as exploring some physical, economic, social, political, psychological and ethical implications of our involvement with the river and the natural world.

I have rejected observer-object description of the Logan River and turned to elucidating with phenomenology the existential being of the Brisbane River. I aimed to find ultimate causes of the flooding experienced. I wouldn't have known, by observing the river as an object, that it was being held back by obstructions to free discharge of floodwater. Phenomenology identified potential for obstruction, which I then imagined with evidence.

'What have you found out from your investigation?' Grania asked me.

'My analysis by phenomenology has shown that the Brisbane River in flood has ready-to-hand processes and behaviours that allow gravity to move water efficiently, from rain fallen on catchment high ground, to the Pacific Ocean. Human ability to ease the passage of this water during floods has been insufficiently recognised by authorities who have worsened flooding by not preventing clearing of the land. They have allowed erosion of farmland; permitted residences to be built on the flood plain; accumulated sediment in the river channel without dredging it; and constructed bridge pillar islands which have obstructed flood water discharge from the river system. I am not saying that natural drainage cannot be improved by technology, but that technologies should respect natural flow.'

'It is a list of problems needing attention,' Grania said.

'My conclusion is that flooding is being exacerbated by erosion on farms, movement of sediment down the river, approval of building residences on the river flood plain, blocking of flood flow by buildings, intrusion of embankment construction into the floodway, obstruction of the river channel by sediment deposition in the river channel since dredging was terminated and by ineffective operation of dams.'

'My findings are like a cash flow analysis with benefit of few revenue items and losses from many uncontrolled outgoings. Our overall position is worsening. All that is being done to mitigate flooding is enlargement of dam storage capacities and coordination of stream gauging stations. My list mostly consists of ongoing deficiencies. When these have been verified, action plans and technologies for each type of shortfall I have identified need to be developed and implemented.

'Who will act on these problems?'

'They need to be taken up by responsible authorities. The list of factors increasing Brisbane River flooding should be remediated with urgency, as the responsibility of a Government appointee, such as a Minister for Flood Prevention.

'It could be expensive,' said Grania. 'Would there be sufficient political support?'

'Setting aside my preconceptions as an engineer, I have discovered that management of river flooding has been corrupted by greed,' I said. 'Designs of bridges and buildings constructed on the flood plain have been flawed. A forum of architects and engineers is needed to kick-start attention to reducing flood levels.

'I have exposed needs to dredge above Hamilton reach and prevention of construction of bridge pillar islands. Courage is needed to confront river authorities with these and other problems, probably requiring a high-level appointee to take responsibility. In the 2022 flood, 23,400 properties were impacted, with 23 fatalities and many more critically affected.

'There is a tendency to use the statistics as an abstract indicator of flood severity. Every person flooded matters. Every death is a tragedy.'

'There is work to be done explaining the benefits to ordinary people,' said Grania. 'When people realise what needs to be done, they will want the problems resolved.'

My anti-memoir would soon be finished. What would I do then? The writing of it had been a constant in my life. Would there be any benefit from publishing the book? Publication of my story would hopefully create technical interest. The main benefit from writing it would be a therapeutic effect that had healed my fear of the River's flooding. But that benefit would cease when the writing therapy ended, unless I had a substitute. If I took the River for granted, it would invite retribution for the obeisance I was neglecting.

Heidegger wanted our deaths to be near us psychologically all our lives, as a necessary condition of continued living, with our deepest possibilities for authentic living, not as a goal but as the true meaning of existence. I wanted my writing to record my fulfilment. I would extend my independence, without seeking new opportunities, nor refusing offers of help, nor accepting gratuitous kindness. I wanted respect.

I was neither stoical nor wilful. My attempt to establish a safe family home had been thwarted by deception, that in other contexts would have been unethical, in real estate dealing. My discomposure earlier, when after losing independence I contemplated moving away, had been resolved by planning to remain in my apartment as long as possible, even if it was flooded, hoping that a place to evacuate to would appear. I could stay to the end in a flood, even drowning in it. My lifetime had gradually uncovered and made visible to me light reflected from my inner self, like the hidden face of a new moon, beginning with a waxing crescent of childish consciousness, revealing blossoming of the whole sphere of my inner life, until a full moon was illuminated at my mid-life. Since then, a concealing shadow had stolen across the waning orb, until there would be only an inscrutable sliver in old age, before the orb of living was obscured by death and the coming of another New Moon.

I accept risks of flood danger as a part of Riverside living. By taking death into my life, acknowledging it and facing it squarely, I have freed myself from the anxiety of death and the pettiness of life. I am free to become myself and transcend into selfhood.

Grania's specialisation in drought relief had helped me analyse government assistance to flood victims. She had joined forces with me, inserting her findings from her research into my thesis where it made a strong contribution. It was appreciated by me and she looked forward to continuing to input into my work.

'What's next?' I asked her.

'We could get jobs with consultants investigating our concerns,' Grania said.

'The universities could start research programmes,' I said.

'I would like a job investigating and teaching drought mitigation,' she said.

'I hope that my reflections on my life beside the Brisbane River and before that by the nearby Logan River have revealed flood mitigation strategies that will be taken up by authorities. The consequences of risking home, health and possessions, to live beside a river, will connect with others who have also made a similar Faustian bargain for existential gain.

'Perhaps your superman could become a scourge of riverplain developers,' Grania said, 'and of farmers who erode soil.'

'You could become the bane of irrigators or a champion of water rights,' I said to her. 'Or a dam buster.'

'You could be a buttress buster,' she said.

'A butte rester?' I asked, laughing. 'Not likely. Sitting around is over. Now it is time to stand up and be counted!'

TABLE 1: LIFETIME HEART BEAT EQUIVALENCE OF ANIMAL SPECIES

SPECIES	HEART RATE Beats per minute (A)	LIFETIME Years (B)	LIFETIME Heart beats (A X B)/ 365/24/60
Hummingbird	1000	4	4000
Human	60	80	4800
Elephant	70	70	4900
Bowhead Whale	15	200	3000

Source: Google

TABLE 2: BRIDGE OBSTRUCTION OF BRISBANE RIVER

#	NAME OF BRIDGE	PILLAR ISLANDS No.
1.	Sir Leo Hilscher (2 bridges)	16
2.	Story	2
3.	Captain Cook	2
4.	Goodwill	6
5.	Kangaroo Point Green Bridge	3
6.	Neville Bonner	1
7.	Victoria	2
8.	Kurilpa	0
9.	William Jolly	2
10.	Merivale	4
11.	Go Between	2
12.	Eleanor Schonell	2
13.	Jack Pesch	2
14.	Albert	2
15.	Indooroopilly Railway	1
16.	Walter Taylor Indooroopilly	2
17.	Centenary	4

APPENDIX

EMERGENCY PREPARATION CHECKLIST
- Explain to children
- Locate clean-up help: Corporate Body
- Access mobile phone early warning alerts (www.ewn.com.au)
- Decide where to evacuate to
- Take photos of objects 'Before' and conditions for insurance
- Remove chemicals
- Find where to charge phone and lanterns with lightning cables + 240V plug USB socket.
- Ready Emergency First Aid Kit
- Take important documents, USBs, printed copies, car rego, bank account nos & PINS
- Computer passwords
- Remove rug & carry upstairs
- Secure outdoor furniture
- Tether bins
- Fill car with fuel
- Fill kettles, jugs with freshwater
- Buy supplies bread, milk
- Store computers, photos, keepsakes in Unit 4
- Tape fridge doors shut
- Tape cupboard doors and drawers together
- Tape plugs in sinks and bath
- Turn off power
- Leave windows ajar to equalise pressure
- Tell neighbours that I am evacuating and give contact
- Help elderly, disabled, children

With thanks: Floodfish Emergency Booklet

BIBLIOGRAPHY AND REFERENCES

1. Cook, Margaret 'A River with a City Problem,' UQP, 2019.
2. Persig, R. Zen and the Art of Motorcycle Maintenance, Vintage, 1974.
3. Brisbane River Catchment Flood Study Overview https://cabinet.qld.gov.au/documents/2017/Apr/FloodStudies/Attachments/Overview.pdf
4. Heidegger, M. Being and Time, 1927
5. Anderson, Nate. Emergency, Break Glass: What Nietzsche Can Teach Us About Joyful Living in a Tech-Saturated World, 2022
6. Knox, M. Brisbane Underground Railway Proposal, martinknox.com, 050219
7. Creating liveable cities in Australia: A scorecard and priority recommendations for Brisbane, RMIT Centre for Urban Research. http://cur.org.au/cms/wp-content/uploads/2018/12/brisbane-city-score-cards.pdf
8. Knox, M. Animal Farm 2, Novel Ideas, 2021, martinknox.com
9. Brisbane City Counci, https://bcc.gov.org, Floodwise Property Report, 2022
10. Typhoon Nina–Banqiao dam failure https://www.britannica.com/event/Typhoon-Nina-Banqiao-dam-failure
11. Ken, Shaw Designed to Fail, April 4, 2011 http://www.floodcommission.qld.gov.au/__data/assets/file/0003/8463/Shaw_Ken.pdf

12. What are the long-term implications for Brisbane and other flooded areas after 2022 disaster? https://7news.com.au/news/brisbane/what-are-the-long-term-implications-for-brisbane-and-other-flooded-areas-after-2022-disaster-c-5917236
13. Brisbane Times, 'Political skulduggery': the inside story of how Wivenhoe became a substandard dam, 2017 https://www.brisbanetimes.com.au/national/queensland/political-skulduggery-the-inside-story-of-how-wivenhoe-became-a-substandard-dam-20170404-gvdcdy.html
14. Knox, M The Grass is Always Browner, Zeus, 2011, Chapter 4.
15. Intergovernmental Panel on Climate Change (IPCC) Fifth Assessment Report, 2014.
16. Knox, M Time Is Gold, Novel Ideas, 2020
17. Biswas, S K, Effect of bridge pier on waterways constriction: a case study using 2-D mathematical modelling, 2010 http://www.iabse-bd.org/old/20.pdf
18. Kahneman, D Thinking Fast and Thinking Slow, Penguin, 2011
19. Pinker, S. The Better Angels of our Nature' Penguin, 2012.
20. Significant Earthquakes Impacting Los Angeles County, https://www.laalmanac.com/disaster/di02.php
21. Known Floods In The Brisbane & Bremer River Basin http://www.bom.gov.au/qld/flood/fld_history/brisbane_history.shtml
22. An overview of Brisbane River Floods, 27 January 2011 https://www.slq.qld.gov.au/blog/overview-brisbane-river-floods
23. Dewoody, A. J. Rodent's bizarre traits deepen mystery of genetics, evolution, Purdue University News, Sept 14, 2006 https://www.purdue.edu/uns/html4ever/2006/060914DeWoodyVole.html
24 Ballantyne, S Selling Queensland down the river, The Spectator Australia newsletter, 12 March 2022.
25. West, G. Scale, Penguin, 2017.

26. Stancliffe, R. Achieving Sustainable Healthcare, BMJ, 2014
27. Sangster, N. Bisnath, J., Maharajh, A Investigation of the Watercourses and measures to alleviate flooding in the Penal/Debe Region, Conference Paper June 2020, Trinidad
28. How We Measure Sea Level Rise https://www.science.org.au/curious/earth-environment/how-we-measure-global-sea-level-changes-
29. Ballantyne, S. A lesson for Lismore, Spectator Australia, 4 November 2022
30. Knox, M. Turkeys Not Bees, Novel Ideas, 2020
31. Knox, M. Presumed Dead, Zeus, 2014
32. Knox, M. Short of Love, Novel Ideas, Zeus, 2019
33. Csikszentmihalyi, M. The Psychology of Optimal Experience, Harper & Row, 1990
34. Debord, G. The Society of the Spectacle, 1967
35. Windschuttle, The Fabrication of Aboriginal History, 2002
36. Lawson, T. A British Genocide in Tasmania, History Today, 7 July 2014
37. Holt, A Forcibly Removed. Magabala Books, 2001
38. Pascoe, B Dark Emu, Magabala Books, 2014
39. Lipke, I Nargun.
40. Denham, P The River, A History of Brisbane, Museum of Brisbane, 2012
41. Morton, Steve Australian Deserts, Ecology and Landscapes, CSIRO Publishing, 2022
42. Moore, T, Brisbane River at an Ecological Tipping Point, Brisbane Times, Nov 2018.
43. Winchester, S. The River at the Centre of the World, 1996
44. Marohasy, J.(ED.) Climate Change, The Facts 2017. Institute of Public Affairs.

www.ingramcontent.com/pod-product-compliance
Lightning Source LLC
Chambersburg PA
CBHW050305010526
44107CB00055B/2107